Contents

UNIVERSITY OF
WOLVERHAMPTON
DUDLEY CAMPUS LIBRARY

KT-228-599

UNIVERSITY OF
WOLVERHAMPTON
KNOWLEDGE ▪ INNOVATION ▪ ENTERPRISE

Harrison Learning Centre
City Campus
University of Wolverhampton
St Peter's Square
Wolverhampton
WV1 1RH
Telephone: 0845 408 1631
Online renewals: www.wlv.ac.uk/lib/myaccount

Telephone Renewals: 01902 321333 or 0845 408 1631
Online Renewals: www.wlv.ac.uk/lib/myaccount
Please return this item on or before the last date shown above.
Fines will be charged if items are returned late.
See tariff of fines displayed at the Counter.

UNIVERSITY OF WOLVERHAMPTON
LIBRARY

Acc No. 852321   CLASS
CONTROL
DATE 14 NOV 1994   SITE DY   CON

WITHDRAWN

C

Me
do

Ed
Ro

For

ROUTLEDGE

London and New York

WP 0852321 5

First published in 1992 by Routledge

First published in paperback in 1994
by Routledge
11 New Fetter Lane, London EC4P 4EE

Simultaneously published in the USA and Canada
by Routledge
29 West 35th Street, New York, NY 10001

This collection © 1992, 1994 Routledge; individual chapters © 1992, 1994
individual contributors

Typeset in 10 on 12 point Times by
Falcon Typographic Art Ltd, Fife, Scotland
Printed in Great Britain by
TJ Press (Padstow) Ltd, Padstow, Cornwall

All rights reserved. No part of this book may be reprinted or
reproduced or utilized in any form or by any electronic,
mechanical, or other means, now known or hereafter
invented, including photocopying and recording, or in any
information storage or retrieval system, without permission
in writing from the publishers.

British Library Cataloguing in Publication Data
Consuming technologies: media and information
   in domestic spaces.
   I. Silverstone, Roger II. Hirsch, Eric
   306.46

Library of Congress Cataloging in Publication Data
Consuming technologies: media and information in domestic spaces
   edited by Roger Silverstone and Eric Hirsch.
   p. cm.
   Includes bibliographical references and index.
   1. Technology – Social aspects. I. Silverstone, Roger.
   II. Hirsch, Eric
   T14.5.C663 1992
   303.48'3-dc20   91-43743

ISBN 0–415–11712–7

Contributors

Ien Ang is Senior Lecturer in Communication Studies at Murdoch University, Perth, Australia.

Alan Cawson is Professor of Politics at the University of Sussex.

Colin Campbell is Senior Lecturer in the Department of Sociology, University of York.

Cynthia Cockburn is Research Fellow in the Department of Social Sciences, City University, London.

Jonathan Gershuny is Director of the ESRC Research Centre on Micro-Social Change, University of Essex.

Peggy Gray was previously a member of the Mass Communication Research Centre at the University of Leicester and is currently a freelance researcher.

Paul Hartmann was previously a member of the Mass Communication Research Centre at the University of Leicester and is currently a freelance researcher.

Leslie Haddon is Senior Research Fellow at the School of Cultural and Community Studies, University of Sussex.

Eric Hirsch is Lecturer in Social Anthropology at Brunel University.

Sonia Livingstone is Lecturer in the Department of Social Psychology, London School of Economics and Political Science.

Ian Miles is Associate Director of PREST, University of Manchester.

Daniel Miller is Reader in Anthropology at University College London.

David Morley is Reader in the Department of Communications at Goldsmith's College, University of London.

Graham Murdock is Reader in Sociology at Loughborough University.

Tim Putnam is Reader in the History of Material Culture at Middlesex University.

Roger Silverstone is Professor of Media Studies at the School of Cultural and Community Studies, University of Sussex.

Marilyn Strathern is Professor of Social Anthropology at the University of Cambridge.

Diane Zimmerman Umble is Assistant Professor in the Department of Communication and Theatre at Millersville University, Pennsylvania.

Jane Wheelock is Reader in Social Policy at the University of Newcastle.

Foreword: The mirror of technology

Marilyn Strathern

This book nicely ends with some of its subjects playing back one of its themes. The subjects here are a London family wary of television and excited by the possibility of a video camera (Hirsch). The theme is the extent to which the various communication and information devices we bracket as technologies have different effects. For they are made meaningful in different ways.

SOCIABILITY

An example particularly striking for the late twentieth-century reader is that of the Amish telephone (Umble). Members of that American sect-community are wary of what most people would regard not only as an innocent technological device but a mundane one, and as essential as the stoves they do have. However, it is not just that the telephone represents the incursion of an outside world they would prefer to keep at bay. To them, the telephone alters the nature of social interaction. On the one hand, it is seen to lure people into gossip; on the other, it substitutes long-distance communication for the face-to-face contact on which the Amish community pride themselves. In fact, it is that very double possibility of more contact (of one kind) and less contact (of another) which is seized on elsewhere. Even where it is thoroughly accepted, the telephone offers different possibilities to different people (Livingstone). In the same household, husbands and wives may be divided in their perceptions of it as a lifeline to the outside world or as an incursion into privacy. Patterns of 'computer' use between members of the same family are not predictable either (Wheelock). Indeed, meanings may be contested (Murdock, Hartmann and Gray). The circumstances and conditions of family lives in any case impose their own constraints. Through the empirical studies offered here, we begin to see how apparently uniform technological devices are pressed into specific cultural service.

Public meanings may be evident in contexts of a recognizably 'cultural' kind, as in the boundaries the Amish draw between themselves and the world, or the manner in which Trinidadians (Miller) convert American-made soap opera into marks of local identity – the local 'culture' turns these global items into manifestations of the 'local' culture. But, as we have already seen, these essays are not simply concerned with different communities. Individual experience would seem to work as a similar kind of conversion. Silverstone, Hirsch and Morley refer to personal economies of meaning; Livingstone examines the personal constructs through which people process their 'experience' of, and 'make sense' of, the television, telephone and so forth. Each individual person is in this sense a culture of one. Each becomes a repertoire of facilities for the processing of meanings through already established patterns of interpretation and evaluation – not such a fanciful idea in a world that the producers of television programmes are about to discover (Ang), that every individual is a market of one.

Scale, however, is irrelevant to the fact that these essays pay attention to a cultural context that is at once specific and ubiquitous: the home. The home contextualizes the 'behaviour' of technological devices as objects that inhabit houses, occupy a space within domestic space, are part of the dynamic of daily life and family relations (Silverstone, Hirsch and Morley). The form their enculturation takes here is 'domestication'. Information and communication devices in the home belong to the wider class of domestic technologies. They cannot fail to be brought within the habits and values of the family-households that use them; nor can they fail to have an impact on the people already living where they (so to speak) are brought to live.

If one is justified in talking of the different cultural implications of these technological devices, it is because their effect is on values and habits already made. However transformative and innovative they are, they work on what is already there, what already gives shape to people's lives. Similarly, while they have an effect on the interaction of household members, domestic technologies are not themselves the reasons for the relationships. They may, of course, become crucial to the daily routines on which the relationships come to be based – they may enhance sociability – as witness the microwave that makes it easier for householders to work (Cockburn), the computer game that stimulates a network of boys to transact with one another through a whole subculture of computer talk (Haddon). But they are as much pressed into the enactment of already existing social relationships as they stimulate the creation of new ones. They are thus 'domesticated' to social as well as cultural ends.

One recurrent theme of this book is the extent to which the technologies described here acquire social significance. This is so in the double sense that the Amish have long known. If these devices exaggerate or reflect or create power relations between family members (Murdock), then they may as much enhance as detract from a general sense of social interaction, as both Haddon and Wheelock describe. Several authors take issue with prevailing stereotypes. Far from increasing the isolation of persons from one another, communication technologies can enhance sociability, and may indeed have this as their focus. They do not just feed into the conduct of social relations, then, but seemingly give people a sense that there is more or wider interaction (more sociability) than there used to be.

But an outside observer might prefer the final Amish view: what is at issue is not so much an increase as a transformation of social interaction. While most people would no doubt classify the telephone as a means for enhancing communication, these sect members saw it as converting one mode of communication (face-to-face interpersonal contact) into something else (the risks of exposure to possibly unwelcome strangers). Indeed, there is no automatic value to be put on particular modes of sociability. If one regards streets as dangerous and aimless places, the idea that boys are at home with their friends poring over computer games (Wheelock) seems a comfortable enlargement of social life. But if one looks for the urban community in the vitality of its street life, to closet children away from casual encounters seems an impoverishing privatization of play. Certainly, kitting bedrooms out with television, telephone, cassette player, seems to replicate the privatization effect within the household (Livingstone); the function of the room is transformed from meeting a common need for family members at particular times of the day to supplying the individual with the supports for a separate existence all day long.

Given the location of these devices within homes, it is largely the social life of the family that is discussed in these chapters. Together, they constitute a context for challenging the old technological determinism that sees people as passive recipients of products. They show instead how these devices are domesticated into the society of family life and shaped by the complexities of family interactions: only by investigating the uses to which they are put will one gain some insight into how the devices behave.

BEHAVIOUR

The last point is beautifully exemplified in the efforts of the makers of television programmes to predict the behaviour of viewers (Ang). In order to produce the programme rating to influence the advertisers to fund the programmes, they have to demonstrate that programmes are being seen. The impossibility of monitoring this apparently simple activity must lead to the reluctant acknowledgement that, even if you can see someone watching a screen, you do not know what that person is seeing. All you are doing, in fact, is in turn watching that person: you cannot 'see' him or her see anything, because that is a process of perception and cognition that goes on, invisibly, inside his or her head. Unpredictability lives! One is invited to relish the 'discovery' that people are more free than the technologies suggest – that they resist colonization – and turn these devices to their own uses. Far from being dominated, they deploy them to creative ends, and to ends of their own making: the active consumer.

Now it is a theoretical intention of this book that these empirical studies should also serve as a commentary on current debate about consumption. What was for a while a term for a passive process has been reclaimed as a term for an active one: the manner in which people convert things to ends of their own (very close to an original meaning of 'domestication'). Indeed, there seems as much anxiety among social scientists to show how active the agents of consumption can be as the Simons display (Hirsch). That London family is reconciled to the VCR once they have demonstrated to themselves that it will reflect back to them not their passiveness but their activeness in all the creative things the family members do. They want the machine to mirror themselves as active agents and subjects. 'It was not the technology as such which was the problem, but the capacity to construct an active relationship with it.'

Is this the latest of a line of middle-class projects, one wonders: middle-class because this is the class that makes a project out of life, that makes experience out of interactions? The acceptable face of technology?

I raise the question as one of anthropological interest. While in one sense these technologies are no different from any other array of commodities or things or experiences that are pressed into cultural and social service, several of these papers are also at pains to emphasize the particular routines they embody. They have material effects on the use of space, perceptions of time and so forth; however active the mind that socializes with the keyboard, the body is tied to a chair. One might ask, therefore, what kind of persons people are making of themselves out of these things.

First, there is the sense of looking into the global. It is the Trinidadian version of *non*-Trinidadian forms that produces a specific identity. The local is created in the consumption of global discourse – and I wonder whether one cannot extend Miller's contrast more widely. Thus, while the threshold between inside and outside the home would suggest a public –private divide, it is not so much a public world that boys are locked into with their computer games (Wheelock) but a world that is at once local (special to computer games fans) and global (speaking a universal language). Indeed, all these technologies bring global forms 'home'. There is a world consensus, not just on what will drive refrigerators (Cockburn) but on what VCRs should be like, the type-form mentioned by Putnam. The recent burgeoning of styles in telephone handsets in this country fools no one: we have Americanized the sound they make. But then no one has so far thought that telephone bleeps could also be used to signify heritage. Perhaps one day we shall be able to buy handsets with 'historic' tones, but if so, it would only be to advertise to the rest of the world that we too (as the brown signs that nowadays pinion every town with a historic building in it tell us) have a heritage. Brown goods indeed.

Second, the global can remain socially unspecific. It is of cosmic proportions – 'out there' rather than 'in here' – yet need have no more social
attributes than simply being the receiver and sender of communications.
One is thus left to local stratagems to negotiate powers and liberties. Hence
the politics to which Silverstone, Hirsch and Morley (and see Murdock,
Hartmann and Gray) refer is a domesticated politics. The freedoms may
feel new, but the tyrannies are as likely to be all too familiar.

Third, among the most interesting material in these chapters is evidence
for the sense of enablement that domestic/communication technologies
afford. They appear to amplify people's experiences, options, choices.
But at the same time they also amplify people's experiences, options and
choices *in relation to themselves*. These media for communication compel
people to communicate with them.

Television again. The burgeoning of cable TV and the VCR that has,
as Ang describes, thrown ratings off course, made American advertisers
wary, has come about through the reproduction of programme control.
Programming was once largely in the hands of the transmitters: it is now
embodied in the transmission devices themselves and is thus in the hands
of the transmission receivers, who can zap and zip at will. Now this looks
like the subversion of programme control; but what is a programme? A
programme is laid out for consumption, providing a menu of choices as a
range from which the consumer can select. But what was thus initially done
for the viewer is now done so to speak by the viewer *for* the programme.
Once the programmer provided the range, the viewer the selection; now the
viewer can recreate the range, it is the programmer who appears to offer a
selection. Far from subverting programme control, the viewer is made to
or chooses to reproduce it in his or her own person, an active substitute.

Although several contributors refer to the construction of the person as
the (individual) consumer, perhaps we should bypass the constructionist
metaphor. What is intriguing is the way in which the person is seen to
work, for this becomes the same way as – after Cockburn's performative
– technology 'works'.

INTERACTION

The inventions discussed here are in the main electronically based; all
require activation, but what is activated are their already programmed
functions. Such technologies are also circuited; they entail a routing of
messages through their components. Communication technologies are, of
course, doubly circuited, for they are circuits to create circuits (Silverstone,
Hirsch and Morley). In short, they work when they are active. A circuit
exists only when it is switched on; but all a person can switch on is the
circuit. And this existential condition has a significant implication. The
devices exist *as technology* by virtue of being activated. So technology is

never completely controlled or subdued (domesticated) because a condition of its existence is its active relationship with the users of it. And this ongoing relationship means that the users can never completely consume it. Rather, the technology is persistently there, summoning response. The (middle-class) consumer's own existential problem becomes that of demonstrating a counter-activity, whether of a positive or negative kind.

'Technology' is not to be consumed so easily, then. Rather, there is a glassiness even to the surface of domestic technologies. And the consumer in turn, I suggest, is as much mirror as duct. In the person of the consumer perhaps technology 'sees' a mirror of itself, at once individual and society. Or at least such a view seems to inhabit our descriptions of the processes at issue.

A circuit that communicates between its parts: this could well describe one of the principal twentieth-century definitions of modern society, constituted in individual persons who communicate with one another through the language and culture that flows between them. But society, like the person, exists only when it is switched on, when the communication is activated. Thus society must be made evident in sociability even as persons must evince a perpetual and individual subjectivity, constantly recreating themselves as subjects rather than objects. This description of modern society is also a modernist one. As far as technology is concerned, it follows that persons – and their social relations – are never completely controlled or subdued (technologized), because a condition of their existence is their active relationship with its devices. In short, it is those very autonomous, self-circuiting, social realities of the person as an active individual agent that makes consumers most mirror the technology with which they 'interact'.

To which one may add a postscript: such a modernist description is *also* after the event. An intriguing aspect of this triangulation is the equation between individual and society. Here we see what has been consumed. Technology does not mediate the individual person's relationships with society; it has come to mirror the individual person's *consumption* of society. Social relations with others are absorbed into the person's 'experience' of them. For all that sociability is enhanced, it is pressed into the service of individual desire (Campbell) – a means rather than an end – and while the most elaborate social transactions may lie behind the game tripping over itself on the computer screen, the screen does not reveal them. Given the constraining ways in which people have represented relationships to themselves in the recent past – including family imagery and the hierarchies of age and gender on which several of these essays comment – possibly such depictions of relationless persons will allow people to get on with their social lives with a new sense of freedom. Or possibly it will only be the social scientist who will continue to identify anything 'social' in the interaction of persons, anything that gives it a dimension distinct from other kinds of interactions people have with the world.

The microwave oven may open up new relational possibilities, but the relationships – like the microwave – appear simply enabling of (in this case) the consumption of food. Indeed, the very idea of interaction has already been taken over by those who would reproduce it as a technologized feature of the compact disc system or 'smart house' (Miles, Cawson and Haddon). Building-in 'interaction' is not quite the self-advertising process it seems. One may expect a kind of reverse of the programme-effect seen in television. The device becomes the active substitute.

Campbell points to the inner-directedness of renewed desire. In these essays, the individual agent as author is reborn, but less as the author of what is consumed than as the author of *how* things will be consumed. These domestic consumers are all Trinidadians; they are not the primary producers. What they bring to the technologies are their experiences, and that is what they seem to take away again. The consumer is a processor, the turner of things into social and cultural values, but most active in the self-referential authorship of its own processes of consumption. Freshness and innovation are absorbed by the novel when what this process of consumption reproduces above all is experience itself. The saving grace of the studies that follow lies in their demonstration that no one lives by consumption alone.

Acknowledgements

This book has its starting point in a workshop organized at the Centre for Research into Innovation Culture and Technology at Brunel University, under the auspices of the Economic and Social Research Council's Programme on Information and Communication Technologies (PICT). Subsequently, a small number of additional papers were commissioned. We are grateful to all of those who participated in the workshop and to those who later commented on various drafts. The editors are particularly grateful to Marilyn Strathern and Jay Gershuny for framing the collection so graciously, and to Donna Baston for her endlessly supportive secretarial and administrative skills.

Roger Silverstone
Eric Hirsch

Introduction[1]

Roger Silverstone and Eric Hirsch

> A main characteristic of our society is a willed coexistence of very new technology and very old social forms.
>
> (Raymond Williams)

CONSUMING TECHNOLOGIES

Our aim in this book is to open up for analysis some crucial, but barely examined, areas of social, cultural and economic life. At its core is a concern with the complex set of relationships that mark and define the place and significance of the domestic in the modern world – a place and significance enhanced, mediated, contained, even constrained, by our ever-increasing range of information and communication technologies and the systems and services that they offer the household. The issues raised are, we believe, of wide relevance. Both public and academic debate have for many years been preoccupied with the domestic in its relationship with what is often perceived as the steadily increasing commodification and privatization of everyday life. These debates have also been preoccupied with the impact of technological change on established social structures and cultural values. Yet many of the discussions on these issues have not been informed by substantive empirical work. And some of the core questions for an understanding of the nature of modern industrial society – on the nature of consumption, on the appropriation of communication and information technologies and their mediated meanings, on the contradictory significance of the domestic sphere – have been remarkably under-studied. We offer, through the pages of this book, an attempt to address some of these questions and to redress the balance between assertion and informed argument.

Our domestic life is, of course, suffused by technology, and information and communication technologies are becoming a central component of family and household culture. Our social relations, both inside the home and outside it, are sustained by the publicly generated and privately consumed meanings that they transmit. The title we have chosen for this volume is purposely ambiguous. The conjunction of 'consuming' and 'technologies' suggests two potentially contradictory images. On the one hand there is the image of these technologies in general, and information and communication technologies in particular, being consumed increasingly in the domestic context of our everyday lives. On the other hand there is the image of these technologies consuming us, the users, of transforming us to the potential inherent in them. We are, indeed, great consumers of technology. At the same time we are often quite anxious about technologies' capacity to consume us. There is a delicate line to be drawn between voluntarism and determinism in all of these discussions, and, through the essays which follow, we attempt to draw it. Through these essays we want to suggest that the significance of information and communication technologies in modern society requires us to see them as social and symbolic as well as material objects, and as crucially embedded in the structures and dynamics of contemporary consumer culture.

The contributions to this volume cut across a range of established literatures in a number of different fields, a range of literatures which have remained both curiously isolated from each other and limited in their willingness to acknowledge this essential intertwining of the social, the technological and the cultural. For example, up to now family studies have generally taken very little account of technological and media relations. Social studies of technology have opened up the question of technology's status as a cultural form, but have not yet approached, other than in broad terms, the issue of its construction in consumption. They have also been undertaken in apparent ignorance of media studies' long-standing concern with similar issues. Studies of consumption have barely begun to examine the social and social-psychological dynamics of the appropriation and use of objects in general and information and communication technologies in particular. And the study of the television audience has only just begun to confront its embedding in the complex relations of everyday life.

There is, within the study of the domestic consumption of technology, a substantial potential for seeing the relations and determinations relevant to our consumption of information and communication technologies (and of course also to the information and communications which they transmit) as emanating from several different sources. We are aiming for a particular dialogue, a dialogue between perspectives defined from within different disciplines but focused on the particular conjunction of the psychological, the social, the economic and political which we think is required for a mature understanding of the relations between technology, consumption and the domestic sphere. These various contributions are far from integrated, but in coming at a set of core issues from a number of different directions, they do, we hope, provide a framework and a basis for further research and debate.

The issues that are raised in the various contributions, and the questions asked as well as tentatively answered, go to the heart of much that is particular about our everyday lives in modern society. These issues concern the highly gendered character of our relations to technology, and in particular both in the way in which technologies can be seen to become gendered in the dynamic processes of production and consumption, and also in the way in which technologies are involved in the definition of, or changes within, our individual identities and social relations. They also concern the effects of media and information technology on the changing balance between globalizing and local cultures; and they concern our capacity to exercise control over the cultural and highly mediated products of an increasingly globalizing society. But the nature of 'local' culture is also at issue, as is the nature of domestic culture. Attention is focused on the changing character of our own domesticity, both inside and outside the home, and on the changing character of the social groups – principally the family – that still define much of its character. Finally, there is the whole range of issues that have to do with consumption itself, the heart and lungs of modern industrial society. Here we can acknowledge both the status of media and information technologies as quintessentially novel objects, and therefore as the embodiment of our desires for the new, as well as their status as transmitters of all the images and information that fuel those desires.

TECHNOLOGY, CONSUMPTION AND THE DOMESTIC

As Cynthia Cockburn points out at the beginning of her contribution, we no longer need to rehearse the arguments against technology as determining social relations. Technology is produced in environments and contexts, as a result of the actions and decisions, interests and visions, of men and women at work in organizations and institutions of complex and shifting politics and economics. These organizations and institutions often provide the framework for alliances and networks of actors to engage in the potent work of the research and development, production and distribution of technologies. Technologies emerge, we now increasingly clearly see, as a result of these complexes of actions and objects, politics and cultures. And technologies (both hardware and software) incorporate, in their design and in their engineering, something of that complexity as well as carrying both the marks of their social production and their capacity to reproduce the social and political values of the society that created them.

But the work of production and reproduction does not end with the disappearance of a new technology into the home, any more than it ends with the introduction of a new technology into a society that previously had no experience of it. It continues in consumption. There is a 'politics of technology' but it is not a totalitarian politics. It has to be understood in its full range, as a mixture of strategy and tactics, subject to the passage of time, and vulnerable to the capacity of local and domestic cultures to spoil or redefine the political and cultural inscriptions which we can now begin to decipher in the structures of the machine.

The technologies that provide the principal focus of this book are, arguably, especially intertwined in everyday life and perhaps especially inscrutable, by virtue of their status as communicators and transmitters of meaning. The images and ideas, sounds and words, information and entertainments, that define the character of the media and information technologies of the twentieth century, in turn offer another dimension of the articulation of these technologies into our daily lives. They provide a means both for the integration of the household into the consumer culture of modern society – into a national as well as an international culture – and for the assertion of an individual's, a household's or an island's own identity: a domestic as well as a local culture. They consist, as Marilyn Strathern suggests in her foreword, in an infinite play of mirrors, at once both material and symbolic. As such, media and information technologies are doubly articulated into our domesticity. However, that double articulation, as Ien Ang, Diane Umble, Daniel Miller and Eric Hirsch in their essays here variously suggest, is not without its contradictions and its resistances.

So our understanding of the place of technology, and especially information and communication technologies, in our everyday lives is in turn based on our ability to make some headway in understanding both the nature of consumption and the nature of domesticity in modern times. And, as Jonathan Gershuny implies in his postscript, the history of information and communication technology and of technology as a whole is, in these respects, of a piece.

The study of consumption has only recently begun to occupy something of a centre stage in accounts of modernity. Questions initially raised, in typically strident fashion, by the theorists of the Frankfurt School have now been taken up, developed and largely transformed by anthropologists and cultural analysts drawing on both the experiences of consumption behaviour in non-capitalist societies on the one hand and in 'postmodern' societies on the other. At issue is the complex and often contradictory nature of consumption, which is increasingly being seen as alternatively fragmenting, homogenizing, alienating, or liberating our daily social and economic relationships. At issue too are the degrees of freedom accorded to the consumer (in theory and in practice) to use the products and commodities of late capitalism to define and express his or her own identity, status and membership of a wider group. The questions raised are historical, as Colin Campbell points out; industrial, as Ian Miles, Alan Cawson and Leslie Haddon point out; and economic. But they are perhaps above all cultural. Consumption is a transformative and transcendent process of the appropriation and conversion of meaning. Eric Hirsch, Daniel

Miller, Roger Silverstone and his co-authors, and Tim Putnam, each in their various ways, address this aspect of consumption and of technology's role in its articulation. Together they provide a basis for seeing consumption in its anthropological and historical guises as not only deeply ingrained in the industrial structure of contemporary society but equally deeply ingrained in the structures of the domestic sphere: local, private, persistent.

But we can turn the coin over and see consumption as something to be studied not just from the point of view of the consumer, but as something else: as an extension and embodiment of the persisting need of modern society to sustain itself; and as structured by and through the abiding inequalities of class, status and power of that same society. The consumption of technology, as well as technology's role in consumption, as Graham Murdock suggests, have to be understood within this framework.

Finally, there is the issue of 'the domestic'. The domestic is variously approximated to the household, to the family and to the private. In each of its guises it has its own history, and in each of its guises it has been variously celebrated and condemned, written off and reinstated, as a central component of, if not every society, then certainly ours. The domestic with which we are now faced, however, must be seen as the product of a particular set of historical conditions which emerged with industrial societies. Notwithstanding the continuing debates that have surrounded both the status of the individual and of the institutions of kinship, at least in British society, the particular character of our domesticity is, arguably, quite modern. And in modern industrial societies the character of the domestic has been defined through its necessary and constant interrelationship with the public sphere. What is clear, of course, is that this relationship has itself been the subject of constant variation, depending on changes in the political and economic circumstances of the times.

Recent work on the household and the family in Western societies points both to a gradual increase in the diversity of household types and the decreasing statistical significance of the nuclear family household in these societies. At the same time, and perhaps in part as a consequence of these structural changes, the ideological commitment to the nuclear family shows no signs of abating. And here, for example, much of the evidence shows a continuing commitment to family-style living arrangements. Writers in this collection make no judgement about the future of the family or the future of technology within it. Nor are they exclusively concerned with the family as such. But they are concerned, again variously, to engage with some of the key dimensions of the articulation of technology and domesticity, in which the latter is problematized not just historically but, as in Sonia Livingstone's and Jane Wheelock's essays, in terms of the dynamics of its internal composition and its structuring through gender and generation. This problematization extends also to its boundaries, where it is clear, as Leslie Haddon argues, that information and communication technologies number among many facilitators of the extension of the household into peer- or work-group culture and neighbourhood. The domestic, therefore, has to be understood in its relationship with the public sphere. And information and communication technologies, be they institutionalized in broadcasting, as for example in the case of television, or in close proximity to the worlds of work or school, as in the case of the computer, have to be seen as being constitutive of the domestic as well as themselves being domesticated.

The domestic is, however, constituted in its difference, and that difference is, potentially, distinctive and multifaceted. Both Roger Silverstone and his co-authors and Eric Hirsch describe it through the framework of a 'moral economy', a term which has resonance also in Jane Wheelock's account. But, as Tim Putnam suggests, and Cynthia Cockburn, Daniel Miller and Eric Hirsch himself illustrate, one must be careful about reifying such a notion. Families, households, the domestic *tout court*, are nothing if not multifaceted. At their heart lies an indeterminacy. In the sphere of consumption not all families, even those equivalently placed, consume equally or with the same consequences.

THE BOOK: ARGUMENTS AND CASES

The purpose of this book is to set an agenda. This is the particular task of the essays in the first part, 'Conceptual and thematic issues'. Here the five authors offer, in a focused rather than a comprehensive way, a number of routes into the character of, and the relationship between, domesticity, consumption and technology.

Roger Silverstone, Eric Hirsch and David Morley's essay, based on empirical work, offers a model of the household as a 'moral economy', a social, cultural and economic unit actively engaged in the consumption of objects and meanings. Information and communication technologies are, they suggest, centrally involved in the articulation of this moral economy. They are crucial to the household's more or less successful achievement of its own identity, integrity and security; and they are crucial too for the household's ongoing engagement with the commodities and symbols of the public sphere. Some of the themes identified by Silverstone and his co-authors are taken up and developed in subsequent papers, especially by Eric Hirsch and Sonia Livingstone, while Jane Wheelock provides a parallel model of the household as a social economy, and Tim Putnam argues for a view of the consuming household less tied by the strings of status differentiation and display.

Cynthia Cockburn focuses on the issue of technology and gender, reviewing and offering a critique of recent sociological theories of technology, for their inadequate treatment of what she argues is this central component of technology and technical change.[2] Her focus of attention is the microwave oven: not an information or communication technology as such of course (though it is dependent technically on the microchip), but a technology that raises many of the issues central also for an understanding of domestic information and communication technologies. In examining the production of the microwave oven she traces the highly gendered dynamics of power and identity which are inscribed both in the institutional structures surrounding the production of technology, and also within the design of the technology itself. In an argument which connects with that of Ian Miles, Alan Cawson and Leslie Haddon in the next part, she identifies the close links between the cultures of production and consumption, both in their determinacy (which Cockburn stresses) and their indeterminacy.

The final essay in this part of the book is by Colin Campbell. Developing arguments recently explored in his *The Romantic Ethic and the Spirit of Modern Consumerism*, he focuses on modern society's consuming desire for the new. This desire needs itself to be explained, and Campbell does so through a discussion of different kinds of 'newness', the central significance of novelty, and its origins both in the nature of individual desire and in the particular role and character of the 'bohemian' in modern society. Campbell also traces how this desire for the novel is inscribed into the dynamics of consumption through an eternal cycle of day-dreaming, longing, desire for the new, consumption, disillusionment and renewed desire; a cycle well understood in the world of advertising and expressed in the constancies of fashion and innovation in consumer goods, including technologies.

The search for the new is also the focus of Ian Miles, Alan Cawson and Leslie Haddon's contribution, which marks the beginning of the second part of the book, in which we bring together a group of essays focusing on information and communication technologies in the home. Miles and his co-authors ask the question: What role does knowledge of consumption play in the generation of new products? And they approach the consumption of information and communication technologies, particularly new, 'novel', technologies from the point of view of producers' attempts to define the market for them. Knowledge of the consumer, however inadequate, informs and inflects the design and marketing process of new technologies, but it also reveals, the authors suggest, a profound indeterminacy at the heart of the relationship between the production and consumption of new technology.

The following essays in this part each take on a different aspect of this complex interrelationship between information and communication technologies and the domestic environment, revealing that neither technology nor domesticity are to be taken for granted. An understanding of technology's place within the household depends crucially on two things. It depends on the need to understand the household in all its structured complexity, as a social unit in its own terms, vulnerable to the exigencies of family relations and the dynamics of gender and generation; and it depends on the need to understand the household as an element of the wider environment into which it spills and within which it is vulnerable, in one way or another, to various attempts at control and inspection.

Leslie Haddon examines the significance of the home computer from both an historical and a sociological point of view. He takes his starting point from early, mostly psychological, work on the home computer and more recent work on information technologies in the home. As well as drawing on his own empirical research on the home computer, he argues for an understanding of the influence of the home computer which extends beyond the home, as a focus of subcultural activity and as significantly but complexly gendered. While Haddon suggests that an understanding of the domestic environment in which the home computer is used is essential from the point of view of understanding the particularities of its cultural biography, it is vital to recognize that many of the distinctive character-istics of its use in the home are a product of, and extend into, the wider environment of work and leisure.

This theme is developed by Jane Wheelock. She presents data and argument from a recently completed study of the household use of home computers undertaken in Wearside, and offers a model of the household as a 'complementary economy'. Her argument, implicitly, takes issue with those models of the domestic economy which assume a utilitarian rationality in essence no different from that supposed to articulate behaviour in the formal economy. Her concern is with gender and age differences and the different ways in which computers are mobilized within the household for education, training or leisure. The computer, in her account, is clearly the focus of many conflicting ambitions and desires, and she suggests that the way in which it is appropriated into the household is a function of the particular characteristics of the system of distribution operating within it. The computer is seen, often, as both an object of consumption and as a means of production (and reproduction), but in both guises it is subject to the complex relations of gender and age identity forged both inside and outside the home.

This equation of gender, social relations within the family, and the place and significance of information and communication technology within the home is also pursued by Sonia Livingstone. She bases her argument on research conducted as part of a wider study (see chapters 1 and 13) in which she conducted a detailed analysis of personal attitudes towards technologies within the home. Livingstone argues that, although informa-tion and communication technologies are strongly gendered, and gendered in ways defined for them in the public sphere, an understanding of the variations within the gendered patterns of perception and use requires close attention to family dynamics. Whereas Leslie Haddon has problematized the definition of the domestic principally in terms of its boundedness,

Livingstone now offers an account of its complexity, and shows how a focus on information and communication technology can reveal something of that complexity as well as, very often, contributing to it.

There follows an essay by Ien Ang which transposes some of the terms but keeps the structure of the overall argument of the book intact. Her concern is with the pressing problems faced by the television industry in measuring the activity of 'watching television'. This is clearly not simply a technical matter. At stake are questions of audience measurement, as well as what constitutes 'watching television'. But what is above all at stake is the indeterminacy at the heart of the domestic in the consumption both of the technologies and the meanings they transmit. Television is the supreme example of what Silverstone and his co-authors refer to as a doubly articulated technology: it is an object of consumption and it facilitates consumption in its circulation of public meanings. The dilemma which Ang addresses is one posed by this doubly articulated status, for driving the industry's preoccupation with accurate measurement is the need to deliver television's audiences to its advertisers.

The final essay in this part also involves a transposition. In a chapter also based on original data, Graham Murdock argues for an understanding of home computer use not just in terms of its domestication within a specific set of social or familial relations, but also – and crucially – in terms of the material constraints that affect its appropriation. The meanings that are attached to information and communication technologies and the uses to which the technologies are put, indeed even their very availability, are the product of historical, biographical and, in the broadest sense, political and economic circumstance. The domestic too has to be understood in terms of the limits set by these material factors.

In the final part of the book, 'Appropriations', these conjunctures of public and private, local and global, determinant and indeterminant, are explored through a series of quite different, but exemplary, case studies. Three of the authors deal with a specific example of the way in which different cultures, domestic, local, national, come to terms – their terms – with the products of a global culture, a formal economy. And the fourth, Tim Putnam, draws some more general conclusions relevant to the consideration of consumption in general through the perspective of a model of appropriation.

Daniel Miller focuses his account on the island of Trinidad. His concern is with the significance of an American soap opera, 'The Young and the Restless', in the construction of Trinidadian identity. Actually identity should be plural, for Miller argues for a conception of the soap opera's status in Trinidad as a result of recognizing two separate manifestations of local culture – he calls them the the transient and the transcendent. And he also sees the relationship between global and local forms, the soap opera on the one hand and the bacchanal on the other, and their incorporation into the domestic, as one of a constant toing and froing; a cultural dialectic which consistently redefines and reaffirms the authenticity of the local hybrids. The soap opera, Miller argues, has become a key instrument for forging a highly specific aspect of Trinidadian culture.

Whereas the Trinidadians have dealt with this otherwise alienating product of modern society by creatively transforming it into their own image, the Amish, the subject of Diane Zimmerman Umble's essay, have dealt with another potentially alienating manifestation of twentieth-century technology in a much more cautious and resisting way. The telephone was early seen by the Amish community (or more strictly by its leaders) as threatening the moral order of their society. Their solution, eventually, was not to ban it, but to transform its use by denying it access to the private spaces of the home (where it could be used, among other things for unlicensed and unmanaged – female – gossip). The telephone instead was confined to public booths and, at least initially, to the receipt of incoming calls only. Umble argues that the case of the Amish illustrates the possibilities for transformation of even the most ostensibly recalcitrant technologies, a transformation which constantly serves the needs of a local community to reaffirm its identity and status.

In making a more general argument about the nature of consumption, and seeing it in terms principally of appropriation, Tim Putnam returns to the domestic as such. His argument is one that provides an important corrective to those who see modern consumption practices as simply the product of a given set of taste cultures, which are themselves seen as merely an expression of class position. On the contrary, he suggests that consumption is an expression of competence. And that competence, expressed in the exhibits brought into the 'Household Choices' exhibition at the Victoria and Albert Museum, in diary records in the Mass Observation Archive, and in recent studies of the life and times of the three-piece suite, is in turn expressive of the capacity of historically situated individuals to create their own meanings within the context of their own life projects.

The last essay in the collection brings the project of the book full circle. Eric Hirsch traces, as a result of ethnographic work with families in the south-east of England, the fine grain of the relationships that families and family members have with their technologies. Hirsch too criticizes Bourdieu through this analysis, stressing the contrary temporalities – those of a short-term morality associated most explicitly with individualism in the market place, and of a long-term morality associated with the reproduction of collective and domestic forms – which Bourdieu significantly underplays in his account of consumption. The appropriation of things in general and information and communication technologies in particular makes explicit the potentially contradictory relations between these distinct moralities valorized within the family. He develops the theme announced by Raymond Williams in the epigraph to this introduction: the need to understand something of the paradox of novelty and tradition at the heart of the place of technology in the modern society.

NOTES

1 Our aim in this introduction is to provide a brief review of the contexts from which the book emerges. Accordingly we have not provided a set of references. These are contained in the papers that follow.
2 We have specifically included Cynthia Cockburn's chapter on gender and technology, despite the fact that her empirical work is based around the microwave oven and not around ICTs. This is because she raises, in an important way, the crucial issues surroundings gender and technology which have been picked up and developed both in this collection (especially Livingstone) and elsewhere with regard to ICT.

Part I

Conceptual and thematic issues

Chapter 1

Information and communication technologies and the moral economy of the household[1]

Roger Silverstone, Eric Hirsch and David Morley

In this chapter we sketch out the framework of a model aimed towards understanding the nature of the relationship between private households and public worlds and the role of communication and information technologies in that relationship.[2]

'No general model of how people use objects can ignore household practices and relations' suggests James Carrier in a recent (1990: 3) paper. The reverse is also true. No general model of household practices and relations can ignore how people use objects. But when those objects are communication and information technologies: televisions, telephones, videos and computers, the problems of modelling become extremely complex.

Why? Why do communication and information technologies pose especial problems? One simple answer is, of course, that these technologies are not just objects: they are media. And it is their status as media which distinguishes them relatively, if not absolutely, from other objects such as plants or pictures, and other technologies such as refrigerators or hair dryers or hammers. That difference is relative and not absolute because information and communication technologies are also objects (Csikszentmihalyi and Rochberg-Halton 1981), bought for their aesthetics as well as their function, and valued (or not) in the same way as other possessions are. They are also technologies, and like other technologies they have had and will continue to have, an impact on the social and economic order of the household (Cowan 1989). But communication and information technologies have a functional significance, as media; they provide, actively, interactively or passively, links between households, and individual members of households, with the world beyond their front door, and they do this (or fail to do this) in complex and often contradictory ways. Information and communication technologies are, as we have argued in previous papers, doubly articulated into public and private cultures.

In other papers (especially Silverstone *et al.* 1989; Silverstone 1990b) we have discussed the significance of information and communication technologies in the home from a number of different perspectives, including the following: the significance of family system and structure and the particular culture and patterns of behaviour within the family/household as a basis for understanding the appropriation of technologies into the domestic sphere; the problem of the 'embedding' of the family/household in the wider environment of work and leisure; the relationship between the public and the private and of the role of information and communication technologies and services in creating a basis for the construction of personal and national identity; the media's involvement in the construction of domestic time and space; ways of approaching technology as culture in such a way as to open its meaning and its uses to construction and negotiation within the household; the issue of the gendering of technology, not as intrinsic to technologies, but as an aspect of its construction through gender relations within households and their marketing; finally, the problem of consumption as a way of identifying the overarching mechanisms through which both objects and meanings, technologies and texts, are appropriated by individuals and households, and in that appropriation define a position (or series of positions) for themselves both in public and in their private spheres.

What we have not yet done is to provide an integrative frame for the consideration of household practices and relations and the consumption and use of information and communication technologies, as objects and as media. This is the task of the present chapter.

THE MORAL ECONOMY OF THE HOUSEHOLD

In pursuit of this notion of the household as a moral economy we draw on a literature, principally in anthropology (Appadurai 1986; Cheal 1988; Parry and Bloch 1989) and, albeit on a broader canvas, in historical research (Thompson 1971), in which households are conceived as part of a transactional system of economic and social relations within the formal or more objective economy and society of the public sphere. Within this framework households are seen as being actively engaged with the products and meanings of this formal, commodity- and individual-based economy. This engagement involves the appropriation of these commodities into domestic culture – they are domesticated – and through that appropriation they are incorporated and redefined in different terms, in accordance with the household's own values and interests.

Jonathan Parry and Maurice Bloch (1989) are concerned, in their discussions, with the meanings of money. These meanings are, they argue, subject to transformation as they cross the boundaries between the public world of individual- and commodity-based transactions and the private world of domestic reproduction, where a different set of values associated with the longer-term interests of the social or cosmic order is dominant. The meanings of money are negotiable in the same way that others have argued that the meanings of media and information are negotiable: vulnerable to the active or reactive work of individuals and households as they transform and translate the public and alienating offerings of the formal economy into accessible and acceptable terms.

Indeed we can see these processes at work at both a macro-social and a micro-social level. Whole cultures (if one can talk about such things) faced with a monetary economy (Parry and Bloch 1989), an imposed set of religious beliefs (Bastide 1978) or new media (Ferguson 1990) negotiate with the meanings of the new impositions, and with varying degrees of success forge a specific symbolic reality which stands behind the objective economy of visible transactions either in the exchange of commodities, religious conversion or in the 'globalization' of the new world information order. And equally these processes take place in the practices of everyday life (de Certeau 1984): crucially so within the domestic sphere, where the public meanings inscribed by and through commodities, beliefs and media and information consumption are similarly open to negotiation, a negotiation defined by and articulated through what we want in this chapter to call the 'moral economy of the household'.[3]

One way of both exploring and revealing the particular quality of this moral economy is through what Igor Kopytoff (1986) calls the biography of the thing (or object). Things have biographies in the same way as individuals do and their lives are not just a matter of change and transformation but through those changes and transformations they reveal the changing qualities of the shaping environments through which they pass:

> The biography of a car in Africa would reveal a wealth of cultural data: the way it was acquired, how and from whom the money was assembled to pay for it, the relationship of the seller to the buyer, the uses to which the car is regularly put, the identity of its most frequent passengers and of those who borrow it, the frequency of borrowing, the garages to which it is taken and the owner's relation to the mechanics, the movement of the car from hand to hand and over the years, and in the end, when the car collapses, the final disposition of its remains. All of these details would reveal an entirely different biography from that of a middle-class American, or Navajo, or French peasant car.
>
> (Kopytoff 1986: 67)

In the context of contemporary society, and in the framework defined by our present study of both domestic life and the place of communication and information technologies within it, this notion has much to recommend it. For information and communication technologies define both some of the main routes along which the biographies of ideas and meanings, information and pleasures, are constructed, but also they themselves, as objects and as things, have their own biographies as they too become domesticated into the distinct cultures of families and households.

Indeed, although it is not possible to develop this here, it must be said that objects in general and information and communication technologies in particular have not one biography but many. These various overlapping and interconnecting biographies are those of the individual object (my computer), the product (the Olivetti M24), the generic technology (computers). Through these various biographical lines, the life of an object can be traced in all its glorious certainty and uncertainty, from invention to production to marketing to use and disuse, and the uniqueness of that life can be used as a tracer of the social and cultural contexts of its continuous creation and recreation. And, from the point of view of their status as media (and therefore their double articulation), the computer software, the television programmes and the telephone conversations also have biographies as they too pass through a succession of phases and stages in their life cycles and as they reveal, in their passage, the containing cultures and environments which help define their particular meanings.[4]

The moral economy of the household is therefore both an economy of meanings and a meaningful economy; and in both of its two dimensions it stands in a potentially or actually transformative relationship to the public, objective economy of the exchange of goods and meanings. The household is a moral *economy* because it is both an economic unit, which is involved, through the productive and consumptive activities of its members, in the public economy, and at the same time it is a complex economic unit in its own terms (Pahl 1990). The household is a *moral* economy because the economic activities of its members within the household and in the wider world of work, leisure and shopping are defined and informed by a set of cognitions, evaluations and aesthetics, which are themselves defined and informed by the histories, biographies and politics of the household and its members. These are expressed in the specific and various cosmologies and rituals that define, or fail to define, the household's integrity as a social and cultural unit. Within the moral economy of the household the principles of personal valuation and the bases of exchange and reciprocity will be, with varying degrees of intensity, distinguished and distinguishable from those that operate in the market and the public sphere. Different households in contemporary society will share elements of their moral economies according to their positions within the social structure, of course, but equally each household will reveal a particular and unique culture which provides the basis for the security and identity of the household or family as a whole, as well as that of its individual members (see chapter 13).[5]

Objects and meanings, technologies and media, which cross the diffuse and shifting boundary between the public sphere where they are produced and distributed, and the private sphere where they are appropriated into a personal economy of meaning (Miller 1987), mark the site of the crucial work of social reproduction which takes place within the household's moral economy. Information and communication technologies are, of course, crucially implicated in this work of social reproduction, not just as commodities and appropriated objects, but as mediators of the social knowledges and cultural pleasures which facilitate the activities of consumption as well as being consumables in their own right.

To understand the household as a moral economy, therefore, is to understand the household as part of a transactional system, dynamically involved in the public world of the production and exchange of commodities and meanings. But that involvement is not simply a passive one. At stake is the capacity of the household or the family to create and sustain its autonomy and identity (and for individual members to do the same) as an economic, social and cultural unit. In the continuous work of reproduction – and via the mesh of class position, ethnicity, geography and the rest – the household engages in a process of value creation in its various daily practices: practices that are firmly grounded in, but also constitutive of, its position in space and time and which provide the bases for the achievement of what Anthony Giddens defines as 'ontological security' – a sense of confidence or trust in the world as it appears to be (Giddens 1989: 278).[6] At stake too – and this is particularly true in an advanced capitalist society – is the family/household's ability to display, both to itself and to others, through the objectification of those practices, its competence and its status as a participant in a complex public economy (Douglas and Isherwood 1980; Bourdieu 1984; Miller 1987). Different families will draw on different cultural resources, based on religious beliefs, personal biography, or the culture of a network of family and friends, and as a result construct a (more or less permeable, more or less defended) bounded environment – the home. Their success or failure is also, of course, a matter of political and economic resources.

The moral economy of the household is therefore grounded in the creation of the *home*,[7] which may or may not be a family home but which will certainly be gendered, and which itself is multiply structured, both spatially and temporally (Giddens 1984: 119). And while mediated and non-mediated meanings, commodities and objects are formed and transformed as they pass across the boundary that separates the private from the public spheres, it is the quality of the achievement of 'home-ness' – that which turns space into place, that which supports the temporal routines of daily life – which expresses the project which Giddens sees as particular, and particularly problematic, in modern society (cf. Giddens 1984: 119; 1990). Objects and meanings, in their objectification and incorporation within the spaces and practices of domestic life, define a particular semantic universe for the household in relation to that offered in the public world of commodities and ephemeral and instrumental relationships. But they do so through an evaluative – a moral – project, which in turn results in the creation of a spatially and temporally bounded sense of security and trust, a sense of security and trust without which domestic (indeed any) life would become impossible.

Information and communication technologies make the project of creating ontological security particularly problematic, for media disengage the location of action and meaning from experience, and at the same time (and through the same displaced spaces) claim action and meaning for the modern world system of capitalist social and economic (and moral) relations.[8] Indeed, the media pose a whole set of control problems for the household, problems of regulation and of boundary maintenance. These are expressed generally in the regular cycle of moral panics around new media or new media content, but on an everyday level, in individual households, they are expressed through decisions to include and exclude media content and to regulate within the household who watches what and who listens to and plays with and uses what. Similarly, and in relation to media other than television or the video, for example in relation to the telephone, access to incoming and well as outgoing calls is both constitutive of individual identity (the adolescent constructs her or his identity and social network through it; the mother of the family takes responsibility for the maintenance of the conjugal kin or friendship network through it) and the subject of regulation (the costs of calling, but also anxieties about unwelcome calls).

The computer, too, in its problematic status as games machine, as educator, or as work-facilitator, potentially and actually extends and transforms the boundaries around the home (both homework and the games exchange culture, as well as possible links with school in reality – and the magical potential ascribed to the technology in fantasy) and can threaten to shift or undermine what is taken for granted in the routines of domestic life. In fact, of course, this challenge is often thoroughly dealt with by the technology's incorporation into the moral economy of the household: it is the computer which is, as often as not, transformed by this incorporation, much more than the routines of the household. But it is worth pointing out that it is in having to face and to manage these various media-instigated (and other) challenges that the moral economy of the household is thrown into relief and visibility, for the members of the household as well as for those, like us, who observe and interpret.

ELEMENTS OF THE TRANSACTIONAL SYSTEM IN WHICH THE MORAL ECONOMY OF THE HOUSEHOLD IS EXPRESSED

We would like to distinguish four non-discrete elements or phases in the dynamics of the household's moral economy as it is constituted in the transactional system of commodity and media relations:

- appropriation
- objectification
- incorporation
- conversion.

Information and communication technologies are, as we have already suggested, involved in all aspects of these processes. But they are so involved in a particularly intensive and compelling way. This is by virtue of their 'double articulation'[9] in economy and culture, and by virtue of their status as both objects and media. Both the television and the television programme are objects to be consumed, and to be consumed in ways dependent on the particular cultures of the household (Leal 1990). However, television's double articulation into domestic culture extends beyond its status simply as object and medium, for in its status as medium and through the provision of services, information and entertainment (each of which is respectively a commodity) television provides the basis for an 'education', a competence, in all aspects of contemporary culture (Haralovich 1988). Television is, of course, usually the 'leading object' (Lefebvre 1971) in this double articulation, but to a lesser, though still to a significant, extent this argument holds for all information and communication technologies. The VCR, the computer and the telephone, each in their different ways provides (or fails to provide) a route for the consumption and articulation of publicly generated messages and exchanges that feed back into the household, and, of course, for privately generated messages and exchanges to be circulated in return.

We will briefly sketch out what we mean by each of these four elements of the transactional system.

Appropriation

An object – a technology, a message – is appropriated at the point at which it is sold, at the point at which it leaves the world of the commodity and the generalized system of equivalence and exchange, and is taken possession of by an individual or household and *owned*. It is through their appropriation that artefacts become authentic (commodities become objects) and achieve significance. As Daniel Miller suggests:

> The authenticity of artefacts as culture derives, not from their relationship to some historical style of manufacturing process . . . but rather from their active participation in a process of social self-creation in which they are directly constitutive of our understanding of ourselves and others. The key criteria for judging the utility of contemporary objects is the degree to which they may or may not be appropriated from the forces which created them, which are mainly, of necessity, alienating.
>
> (Miller 1987: 215)

From this perspective appropriation stands for the whole process of consumption as well as for that moment at which an object crosses the threshold between the formal and the moral economies.[10]

While Miller is concentrating here on the significance of appropriation for the status of the commodity-objects, it ought also to be said that acts of appropriation – the transactions involved in the passage of artefacts from commodity to object – are, or can be, central to an individual's or a household's efforts at self-creation: defining and distinguishing themselves from, and allying themselves to, each other.

There are two points to be made. First is that this work of appropriation is not confined only to material objects but crucially also applies to the appropriation of media content, to the selection of programmes to watch, computer software to buy, telecom services to subscribe to; though 'ownership' of these things is of a different order from the ownership of objects. However, the meanings ascribed to both objects and mediated texts and services within the household are not those necessarily ascribed to them in the public sphere.[11] Their entry into the moral economy of the household through their appropriation provides a basis for understanding that economy and the dynamics of its particularity.

This leads to a second point. As Miller (1988) himself argues, in a study of council house tenants' kitchens, there are different strategies available to a household in its appropriation of the alienated commodity (in his case the alienation of public housing tenancy). One is passive: the alienation is interiorized and no effort is made to alter the decoration of the kitchen. The second is an attempt 'to use aesthetic construction to impose a facade which as far as possible drew attention away from the fixtures and towards items directly chosen by, or associated with, the tenants'. And the third is when 'the alien forms themselves were expelled or thoroughly transformed' by a concerted effort at remodelling.[12]

Objectification

If appropriation reveals itself in possession and ownership, objectification reveals itself in display and in turn reveals the classificatory principles that inform a household's sense of its self and its place in the world (see Csikszentmihalyi and Rochberg-Halton 1981). These classificatory principles will draw on perceptions of, and claims for, status and will express and in turn define differences of gender and age as these categories are constructed within each household culture.

Objectification is expressed in usage (see below) but also in the physical dispositions of objects in the spatial environment of the home (or in extensions of the home).[13] It is also expressed in the construction of that environment as such. Clearly it is possible to see how physical artefacts, in their arrangement and display, as well as in their construction and in the creation of the environment for their display, provide an objectification of the values, the aesthetic and the cognitive universe, of those who feel comfortable or identify with them. An understanding of the dynamics of objectification in the household will also throw into strong relief the pattern of spatial differentiation (private, shared, contested; adult, child; male, female, etc.) that provides the basis for the geography of the home. Once again information and communication technologies are as much a part of this process of objectification as other objects.

As Ondina Fachel Leal suggests in her study of television in Brazilian homes:

> The plastic rose in the 'golden' vase, the photographs, the religious image, the laboratory flask, and most of all the television set and the spaces they occupy in the domestic order are meanings that comprise a cultural rationale. That is, a symbolic system, including an ethos of modernity, that is itself a part of a larger symbolic universe that has as its principal significance the city and industry.
>
> (1990: 25)

Once again there are a number of points to be made. The first is that television need not be the only technology to be treated in this way. All technologies have the potential to be appropriated into an aesthetic environment (and all environments have, in some sense, an aesthetic). And many are purchased as much for their appearance and their compatibility with the dominant aesthetic rationality of the home as for their functional significance.

The second is that the appropriation and display of individual artefacts, technologies included, does not take place, nor can it be understood, in isolation. In this example the television, the vase, the painting, the plastic rose all signify, but they signify together as an expression of the systematic quality of a domestic aesthetic which in turn reveals, with varying degrees of coherence (and contradiction), the evaluative and cognitive universe of the household.

The third is to say that objects appear, and are displayed, in an already constructed (and always reconstructable) meaningful spatial environment. In Leal's study a rearrangement of a room involved moving the television to where it could be seen from outside. The arrangement and decoration of rooms, from kitchens (Miller 1988) to lavatories (Bernstein 1971: 184) to living rooms (Putnam and Newton 1990), is a central component of the process of objectification which, constrained by material circumstance as well as by preference and interest, provides a basis for approaching the ways in which the physical arrangement and structure of the household defines and contains the inner workings of the moral economy.

But what of the non-material object? In what sense can we approach the non-material or semi-material artefacts (the television programmes, computer software, videos or the stuff of telephone conversations) as being objectified in the same or similar ways to material artefacts? There are a number of ways of so doing. The first is to see them quite properly as commodities for consumption in the same way as material artefacts. The second is to recognize, as we have already done, that they are subject to similar kinds of appropriation as material objects are, that their meaning is not fixed in production. The third is to see that they can be articulated into the moral economy of the household, not so much through their physical display (though photographs of soap-opera or rock-music stars, for example, provide a mechanism for their material objectification) as by their incorporation into the temporal structure or fabric of the household. And finally it is to acknowledge that the content of the media is objectified in the talk of the household, for example in the ways in which accounts of television programmes, or of characters in soap operas, or events in the news, provide a basis for identification and self-representation (see Hobson 1982; Radway 1984; Ang 1985).

Incorporation

Through the idea of incorporation we want to focus attention on the ways in which objects, especially technologies, are used.[14] Technologies are functional. They may be bought with other features in mind and indeed serve other cultural purposes in appropriation. They may indeed become functional in ways somewhat removed from the intentions of designers or marketers. They may have many functions. Functions may change or disappear altogether (many home computers bought for educational purposes have become games machines or have been relegated to tops of wardrobes or backs of cupboards). To become functional a technology has to find a place within the moral economy of the household, specifically in terms of its incorporation into the routines of daily life. That incorporation may release time for other things (Gershuny 1982); it may facilitate 'control' of time, for example in the time-shift capabilities of the video or the microwave oven: it may simply enable some times to be 'better spent', for example the use of the radio as a companion for the tea-break, or as part of the routine of getting up in the morning.

   Whereas a concern with objectification principally identifies the spatial aspects of the moral economy, incorporation focuses on the temporalities. Once again, it is in research on television that this is most clear, for in a number of different ways broadcast television provides a framework both for the household's involvement in the sequencing of public time (the televising of national rituals, for example: Chaney 1986; Scannell 1988), and for the sustaining of domestic routines through the broadcast schedules (Paterson 1980; Modleski 1984).[15]

Incorporation into the moral economy of the household also of course brings to the fore questions of both age and gender, as well as questions of the visibility or invisibility of technologies within that moral economy. Technologies are incorporated into the household as articulations of gender (Gray 1987) and age differentiation, as well as reinforcements or assertions of status. Where a technology is located and when and how it is used (and of course by whom) become crucial elements in the moral economy of the household as a whole. Teenagers will create 'a wall of sound' in their bedrooms with their stereos. Battles will be fought and won over control of the remote switch for the television (Morley 1986). Ownership and use of the computer will follow and reinforce a family's gendered culture of technology.

The incorporation of artefacts, technologies and texts into the moral economy of the household, together with their objectification, provides, therefore, a basis for the constant work of differentiation and identification within and between households. This work of differentiation and identification, of the construction and assertion of identity, is, in turn, sustained through display and use. Spatial and temporal boundaries are created and defended within and around the household. The politics of the family and the neighbourhood, the conflicts over ownership and control of (*inter alia*) information and communication technologies and the status of family or household members are all expressions of, as well as elements within, the continuous work of social reproduction that provides the basis for the coherence of the household's moral economy.

Conversion

Whereas objectification and incorporation are, principally, aspects of the internal structure of the household, conversion, like appropriation, defines the relationship between the household and the outside world – the boundary across which artefacts and meanings, texts and technologies, pass as the household defines and claims for itself and its members a status in neighbourhood, work and peer groups in the 'wider society'.

The metaphor is a monetary one. Meanings are like currencies. Some are convertible; others – private, personal meanings, for example – are not. A household's moral economy provides the basis for the negotiation and transformation of the meaning of potentially alienating commodities but, without the display and without the acceptance of those meanings outside the home, that work of mediation remains private: inaccessible and irrelevant in the public realm. The work of appropriation must be matched by this equivalent work of conversion if the first is to have any significance outside the home (see Douglas and Isherwood 1980; Bourdieu 1984).

Once again we turn to research on television for illustration of what we mean. Television is the source of much of the talk and gossip of everyday life (Hobson 1982). The content of its programmes, the twists of narrative, the morality of characters, the anxieties around news, provide in many places and for most of us, with greater or lesser degrees of intensity, much of the currency of everyday discourse. Computer software has the same status for certain groups. Telephone conversations are as important as face-to-face communication as a means of transmission. Discussions about a recent or future purchase, a purchase prompted by television advertising perhaps or by the particular culture of neighbourhood or class, are similarly ubiquitous. So once again we can point to the ways in which information and communication technologies are doubly articulated: facilitating conversion (and conversation) as well as being the objects of conversion (and conversation).

Yet the appropriation of an object is of no public consequence unless it is displayed symbolically as well as materially, for through that display a household's (or a household member's) criteria of judgement and taste, as well as the strength of his or her material resources, will be asserted and confirmed (Veblen 1925). Some households, of course, will resist (or not acknowledge) this aspect of the transactional system, and sometimes, as in the case of the satellite dish, enforced display might prove to be a mixed blessing (Brunsdon 1991). But equally, the conversion of the experience of the appropriation of meanings derived from television, for example, is an indication of membership and competence in a public culture, to whose construction it actively contributes.

This aspect of the expression of the moral economy of the household is particularly significant for teenagers, who will use their consumption of recorded music, or their collection of computer games, literally as a ticket into peer-group culture. The exchange of games and records, and talk about games and records, provides a mechanism for the individual to become a member of a peer-group culture, but also, of course, constitutes that culture in fundamental ways. The boundary of the moral economy of the household is extended and blended into the public economy through these exchanges. But equally, within the household the private rooms of both male and female teenagers provide the locus for converting activities, as friends with similar interests are drawn into the cultural 'mint'.

CONCLUSIONS AND IMPLICATIONS

The intention behind this approach to the dynamics of technologically mediated consumption (and the consumption of technology) is not difficult to suggest. It is to provide a framework for an understanding of the complex interrelationships of cultures and technologies as they emerge in the practices of institutions and individuals, and through the unequal but never totally determining or determined relations of public and private spheres. Within this model, technologies are both shaped and shaping; the balance between the two is both a matter for further theoretical but of course, also, empirical enquiry.

It should be said that the doubly articulated biographies of information and communication technologies are not exhausted at the point at which objects or meanings cross the various material and symbolic thresholds of the domestic sphere. Pursuing those biographies also provides, in another register, the basis of an historical and an anthropological account of social and technological change on the one hand, and of both large- and small-scale cultural variations on the other.

From the point of view of the producers, the regulators, the advertisers and the consumers of these complex technologies and technological processes it can be suggested that a model such as this (together with the empirical data emerging to support it) opens up the possibility of attending to some of the realities of the significance of information and communication technologies in and for everyday life; and to the realities of how they are transformed, or in many cases rejected, at the point of consumption and, just as significantly, thereafter.

And for those who worry about the family and its future in a technologically mediated world, perhaps we can say that here too an understanding of process, variation and constraint is of the essence. Families and households work with these technologies as much as they work with every other aspect of their daily lives, with greater or lesser degrees of success, control, competence and composure, depending on the resources they have to sustain their own moral economy.

NOTES

1 This chapter arises from a project funded by the ESRC within its Programme on Information and Communication Technologies. The research was conducted by a group at Brunel University which included Eric Hirsch, David Morley, Sonia Livingstone and Andrea Dahlberg.

2 The chapter stems from research designed to explore the relationship between households and communication and information technologies. The research comprises an ethnographically oriented study of twenty families in the south-east of England. Each family consists of both parents and school-age children. Each family owns at least three of the following 'core' ICTs: the television, telephone, computer and VCR.

   Two other chapters in this volume arise from this research: chapters 7 and 13.

3 In chapter 6, Jane Wheelock offers a version of the household as a 'social economy', and, although this draws much more closely on the economics literature, the conceptualization of the household in terms of a different kind of rationality – different, that is, from the rationality dominating the world of public affairs and the formal economy – is broadly the one being offered here.

4 We are grateful for comments on this aspect of our argument to colleagues at the PICT Network Conference, Wakefield, March 1991. Miles, Cawson and Haddon (chapter 4) provide supporting evidence of the cultural biography

of technologies, especially in the context of production. Cynthia Cockburn (chapter 2) also illustrates this theme with her discussion of the gendered biography of the microwave oven.

5 This paragraph, and one or two of those that follow, is adapted from Silverstone 1991.

6

Ontological security is founded psychologically upon the formation of trust relationships, focusing initially upon the parental figures, especially the mother. Erikson says trust in the developing infant is based upon toleration of absence – acceptance that the mother still exists, and cares for the child, even when she is not physically in his or her presence. Trust, to use my terminology, even on a psychological level, is intrinsically a medium of time-space distanciation.

(Giddens 1989: 278)

7 The term 'homeless' or 'with no fixed abode' is not, in our society, simply a descriptive one. It is, of course, powerfully evaluative. Being without a home comes to mean being without morality.

8

What tends to disappear is the meaning of places for people. Each place, each city, will receive its social meaning from its location in the hierarchy of a network whose control and rhythm will escape from each place and, even more, from the people in each place. . . . The new space of a world capitalist system . . . is a space of variable geometry formed by locations hierarchically ordered in a continuously changing network of flows. . . . Space is dissolved into flows. . . . Life is transformed into abstraction, cities into shadows.

(Castells 1983: 31 (quoted in Gregory 1989: 203))

9 By 'double articulation' we mean to refer to the ways in which information and communication technologies, uniquely, are the means (the media) whereby public and private meanings are mutually negotiated; as well as being the products themselves, through consumption, of such negotiations of meaning.

10 We are grateful to Leslie Haddon for pointing this out.

11 cf. Miller 1987:

All objects are the direct product of commercial concerns and industrial processes. Taken together they appear to imply that in certain circumstances segments of the population are able to appropriate such industrial objects and utilise them in the creation of their own image. In other cases, people are forced to live in and through the images held of them by a different and dominant section of the population.

(Miller 1987: 175)

12 This logically inclusive tripartite classification bears, not surprisingly, a remarkable resemblance to the account of the various strategies deployable in working-class politics discussed by Frank Parkin (1973; cf. Morley 1980). In both cases, of course, they stand only as ideal types – powerful and focused – but much too simple to encapsulate the subtle, and differently determined and inflected, strategies of appropriation actually mobilized in various households.

13

What science has to establish is the objectivity of the object which is established in the relationship between an object defined by the possibilities and impossibilities it offers, which are only revealed in the world of social uses (including, in the case of a technical object, the use or function for which it was designed) and the dispositions of an agent or class of agents, that is, the schemes of perception, appreciation and action which constitute its objective utility in a practical usage.

(Bourdieu 1984: 100)

14 Quite clearly there is no unambiguous dividing line between incorporation and objectification as we are using the terms, though there is a difference between use and display which we wish to identify and which, of course, has a special relevance for technology.
15 Equally, of course, the emergence of the VCR and, to a lesser extent, cable and satellite television, has had the reverse effect, providing an opportunity for viewers to liberate themselves from the tyranny of the schedule and opening up the temporal structure of the household as a result.

REFERENCES

Ang, Ien (1985) *Dallas: Soap Opera and the Melodramatic Imagination*, London: Methuen.
Appadurai, Arjun (ed.) (1986) *The Social Life of Things: Commodities in Cultural Perspective*, Cambridge: Cambridge University Press.
Bastide, Roger (1978) *The African Religions of Brazil: Towards a Sociology of the Interpretation of Civilisations* Baltimore: Johns Hopkins University Press.
Bernstein, Basil (1971) *Class, Codes and Control*, vol. 1, London: Routledge & Kegan Paul.
Bourdieu, Pierre (1984) *Distinction: A Social Critique of the Judgement of Taste*, London: Routledge & Kegan Paul.
Brunsdon, Charlotte (1991) 'Satellite dishes and the landscapes of taste', *New Formations* 15: 23–42.
Carrier, James (1990) 'Reconciling commodities and personal relations in industrial society', *Theory and Society* 19: 1–16.
Certeau, Michel de (1984) *The Practice of Everyday Life*, translated by Steven Randall, Berkeley: University of California Press.
Chaney, David (1986) 'A symbolic mirror of ourselves: civic ritual in mass society', *Media, Culture and Society* 5 (2): 119–36.
Cheal, David (1988) *The Gift Economy*, London and New York: Routledge.
Cowan, Ruth Schwartz (1989) *More Work for Mother: The Ironies of Household Technology from the Open Hearth to the Microwave*, London: Free Association Books.
Csikszentmihalyi, Mihaly and Rochberg-Halton, Eugene (1981) *The Meaning of Things: Domestic Symbols and the Self*, Cambridge: Cambridge University Press.
Douglas, Mary (1976) *Natural Symbols*, Harmondsworth: Penguin.
Douglas, Mary and Isherwood, Baron (1980) *The World of Goods: Towards an Anthropology of Consumption*, Harmondsworth: Penguin.
Ferguson, Marjorie (1990) 'Electronic media and the redefining of time and space', in Marjorie Ferguson (ed.) *Public Communication: The New Imperatives: Future Directions for Research*, London: Sage, 152–72.
Gershuny, Jonathan (1982) 'Household tasks and the use of time', in S. Wallman et al. *Living in South London*, Aldershot: Gower, 149–81.
Giddens, Anthony (1984) *The Constitution of Society*, Cambridge: Polity Press.
——(1989) 'A reply to my critics', in David Held and John B. Thompson (eds)

Social Theory of Modern Societies: Anthony Giddens and his Critics, Cambridge: Cambridge University Press, 249–301.

——(1990) *The Consequences of Modernity*, Cambridge: Polity Press.

Gray, A. (1987) 'Behind closed doors: women and Video', in H. Baer and G. Dyer (eds) *Boxed-in: Women on and in TV*, London: Routledge, 38–54.

Gregory, Derek (1989) 'Presences and absences: time–space relations and structuration theory', in David Held and John B. Thompson (eds) *Social Theory of Modern Societies: Anthony Giddens and his Critics*, Cambridge: Cambridge University Press, 185–214.

Haralovich, Mary Beth (1988) 'Suburban family sitcoms and consumer product design', in Philip Drummond and Richard Paterson (eds) *Television and its Audience*, London: British Film Institute, 38–60.

Hobson, Dorothy (1982) *Crossroads: The Drama of a Soap Opera*, London: Methuen.

Kopytoff, Igor (1986) 'The cultural biography of things: commoditization as a process', in Arjun Appadurai (ed.) *The Social Life of Things: Commodities in a Cultural Perspective*, Cambridge: Cambridge University Press, 64–91.

Leal, Ondina Fachel (1990) 'Popular taste and erudite repertoire: the place and space of television in Brazil', *Cultural Studies* 4 (1): 19–29.

Lefebvre, Henri (1971) *Everyday Life in the Modern World*, London: Allen Lane.

Miller, Daniel (1987) *Material Culture and Mass Consumption*, Oxford: Blackwell.

——(1988) 'Appropriating the state on the council estate', *Man* 23: 353–72.

Modleski, Tania (1984) *Loving with a Vengeance: Mass Produced Fantasies for Women*, London: Methuen.

Morley, David (1980) *The 'Nationwide Audience'*, London: British Film Institute.

——(1986) *Family Television: Cultural Power and Domestic Leisure*, London: Methuen.

Pahl, Jan (1990) 'Household spending: personal spending and the control of money in marriage', *Sociology* 24 (1): 119–38.

Parkin, Frank (1973) *Class Inequality and the Political Order*, London: Paladin.

Parry, J and Bloch, M. (eds) (1989) *Money and the Morality of Exchange*, Cambridge: Cambridge University Press.

Paterson, Richard (1980) 'Planning the family: the art of the schedule', *Screen Education* 35: 79–85.

Putnam, Tim and Newton, Charles (eds) (1990) *Household Choices*, London: Futures.

Radway, Janice (1984) *Reading the Romance: Feminism and the Representation of Women in Popular Culture*, Chapel Hill: University of Northern Carolina Press.

Sahlins, Marshall (1976) *Culture and Practical Reason*, Chicago: University of Chicago Press.

Scannell, Paddy (1988) 'Radio Times: the temporal arrangements of broadcasting in the modern world', in Philip Drummond and Richard Paterson (eds) *Television and its Audience*, London: British Film Institute, 15–31.

Silverstone, Roger (1990a) 'De la sociologia de la television a la sociologia de la pantalla: bases para una reflexion global', *Telos: Cuadernas de Communicacion, Technoligia y Sociedad* 22: 82–7.

——(1990b) 'Television and everyday life: towards an anthropology of the television audience', in Marjorie Ferguson (ed.) *Public Communication: The New Imperatives*, London: Sage, 173–89.

——(1991) 'From audiences to consumers: the household and the consumption of information and communication technologies', *European Journal of Communication* 6: 135–54.

Silverstone, Roger, Morley, David, Dahlberg, Andrea and Livingstone, Sonia (1989) 'Families, technologies and consumption: the household and information and communication technologies', CRICT discussion paper, Brunel University.

Thompson, E. P. (1971) 'The moral economy of the English crowd in the eighteenth century', *Past and Present* 50: 76–136.

Veblen, Thorstein (1925) *The Theory of the Leisure Class: An Economic Study of Institutions*, London: George Allen & Unwin.

Chapter 2

The circuit of technology
Gender, identity and power

Cynthia Cockburn

The sociological understanding of technology has made great strides in the past two decades. One sign of this is the fact that today there is no need to begin an article about technology with a disclaimer of 'technological determinism'. It is taken as given that technology is not a prime mover, that it is socially shaped, a suitable case for treatment by social science. Another claim, however, cogently argued over the same period, has not yet become an accepted proposition in mainstream theories of technology. This is feminists' claim that the social relations of technology are gendered relations, that technology enters into gender identity, and (more difficult for many to accept) that technology itself cannot be fully understood without reference to gender.

Despite agreement that technology is social, there remain unanswered questions that are especially insistent when one is exploring technology from a women's viewpoint, or more particularly when one is making a feminist analysis. What do we mean by social when we speak of technology? What do we mean by technology when we speak of gender? What is the connection between technology and power? What kind of power are we talking about? In this chapter I will explore, in the process of developing the logic of a particular current research project, the relations of gender and technology and the space between some mainstream theories and feminist theories of technology.

At the outset a brief review of some of the representations of technology-as-social that have found expression in the last decade may be helpful. It is possible to distinguish simpler and more complex visualizations of the link between the notion of 'technology' and that of 'the social'. A relatively simple view is that which has become known as the 'social shaping' approach. Donald MacKenzie and Judy Wajcman and the authors they assembled in *The Social Shaping of Technology* (1985) firmly dismissed the case for technological determinism. They illustrated the social shaping of technology by economic interests, 'the choices arising from a need to reduce costs and increase revenues', and showed these to differ in different social contexts. 'The way a society is organized, and its overall circumstances, affect its typical pattern of costs, and thus the nature of technological change within it' (MacKenzie and Wajcman 1985: 17). They also illustrated the shaping of technological choices by the state, particularly through military purchasing policy (and see Noble 1977 on the emergence of modern technology and the rise of corporate capitalism).

A somewhat more complex rendering of the relationship of the concepts 'technology' and 'society' was that of Trevor Pinch and Wieber Bijker who, in a path-breaking study of bicycle design published in 1984, attempted a unification of ideas arising in the study of science and those current in the sociology of technology. They 'set out the constitutive questions that such a unified social constructivist approach must address analytically and empirically' (Pinch and Bijker 1984: 399). They began by adopting from the sociology of science the 'empirical programme of relativism' (EPOR), an approach to understanding the content of the natural sciences in terms of social construction. EPOR emphasized the fact that scientific findings are open to more than one interpretation ('interpretative flexibility'), that it is social mechanisms that limit this flexibility, and that 'closure' mechanisms are related to the wider social-cultural milieu.

Applying EPOR to an empirical study, Pinch and Bijker evolve an approach they call SCOT ('social construction of technology'). They demonstrate that the development of the bicycle was a process of alternating variation and selection of designs, that closure and stabilization of a model occurred not in accordance with some essential technological logic but through effective rhetoric on the part of some 'relevant social group' (making claims that stick), or by redefinition of the problem.

Also intent on this convergence of the sociologies of science and technology was Bruno Latour: indeed, he adopted the term 'technoscience' to emphasize this closeness. In Latour's work, and that of Michel Callon and John Law, his colleagues at the Ecole des Mines in Paris, we see the construction of facts (science) and machines (technology) represented as a *collective* process. The collectivity is a network of actors, each playing a part in the unfolding of events.

> By themselves, a statement, a piece of machinery, a process are lost. By looking only at them and at their internal properties, you cannot decide if they are true or false, efficient or wasteful, costly or cheap, strong or frail. These characteristics are only gained through incorporation into other statements, processes and pieces of machinery.
>
> (Latour 1987: 29)

Rather, 'the fate of facts and machines is in later users' hands; their qualities are thus a consequence, not a cause, of collective action'. Thus, 'we are never confronted with science, technology and society, but with a gamut of weaker and stronger *associations*; thus understanding *what* facts and machines are is the same task as understanding *who* the people are' (Latour

1987: 259). Nature, 'the facts', are not a sufficient explanation for the closure of controversies in science or technology.

Curiously, this understanding of technological change is both more and less 'social' than those it challenges. We see that 'black boxes' (closed controversies, settled artefacts) only occur when *people* ally to close them and others forbear (temporarily no doubt) to reopen them. On the other hand, the risk of voluntarism in the simpler social approaches is averted. Material, non-human actors are recovered and firmly identified in the process. As John Law summarizes the difference between 'social constructivism' and the actor–network concept, 'social constructivism works on the assumption that the social lies *behind* and directs the growth and stabilization of artifacts. Specifically, it assumes that the detection of relatively stable directing *social interests* offers a satisfying explanation for the growth of technology.' By contrast, he suggests that other kinds of factors also enter into both the shaping of artefacts and the social structure that results. 'The stability and form of artifacts should be seen as a function of the interaction of heterogeneous elements as these are shaped and assimilated into a network' (Law 1987: 113). In a study of Portuguese imperial expansion he shows that the actors include not only the monarch, boat-builders, explorers and natives of distant lands but also boat-building materials, winds, currents and reefs.

One further useful concept introduced by the 'actor–network' school should be mentioned here, that of 'translation'. It had been conventional to represent the invention of a new technology as followed by a process of 'diffusion' and practical innovation in production or everyday life. Latour makes the point that a project continually changes shape and content as alliances are stitched together to achieve it. To build a 'black box', whether this is a theory or a machine, it is necessary to enrol others so that they believe it, take it up, spread it. The control of the builder is therefore seldom absolute. The new allies shape the idea or the artefact to their own will – they do not so much transmit as *translate* it (Latour 1987: 108).

WOMEN, TECHNOLOGY AND THE USES OF THEORY

A difference between the sexes in relation to 'technology' was a lived reality throughout the industrializing years of the nineteenth century in Britain, as it had been for centuries, perhaps millennia, before. Men were the technologists and technicians of the industrial revolution, women were the factory hands that operated the new machines. Nor was this only the preference of employers. In earlier work I have shown for instance that some machines were indeed held by employers to be suitable for operation by women and others not; and also how men in the printing industry resented and resisted women seeking to learn their skills and use their tools (Cockburn 1983). There are many such examples. In the twentieth century the struggle of women to be admitted to the engineering union was not won until 1942, despite two world wars in which women were used to fill the engineering jobs of men drafted to the military. The advent of microchip technology does not, as some believed it might, break the technical sexual division of labour and give women the knowledge and know-how to design, produce and control, as well as merely supply parts to or press buttons on, electronic equipment (Cockburn 1985).

In the new-wave feminism of the 1970s the distance of women from 'men's' technologies was identified as an aspect of women's disadvantage. Among the liberatory projects of the contemporary women's movement have been attempts to help women overcome the barriers to gaining technical knowledge and know-how. Women have organized training workshops in which women, taught by women, can get a grounding in carpentry, masonry, electronic engineering and other skills that in the economy at large are almost exclusively 'masculine'.

The feminist technology project has not ended here, however. Many women pointed out that the masculine trades and technologies were pre-eminent in society only because men themselves were dominant. New-wave feminism therefore also comprised a project to recover and recognize women's traditional technologies. Midwives, for instance, became a focus for a feminist counter-movement against the dominance of a masculine medical profession.

Third, new-wave feminism included a clear critique of the exploitative and destructive uses of technology. It was expressed, for instance, in women's activism against nuclear weapons, in women's environmental projects and in solidarity work for women disadvantaged in processes of development in third world countries.[1]

These several approaches to understanding technology-as-social have been highly relevant to women working for an analysis of technology that would help sustain these liberatory projects; and feminist social science has contributed to them.

Donald MacKenzie and Judy Wajcman, for instance, had clarified that 'technology' should be seen not only as a piece of hardware but also as a process of work and a kind of knowledge. Such a definition fitted well with women's redefinition as 'technological' of many of the things that women traditionally know and do. Cooking, whether with a wooden spoon or an electric liquidizer, is technological. Who can weigh one expert knowledge against another, and who can say when knowledge becomes or ceases to be 'technical' (cf. McNeil 1987)?

In a classic 'social shaping' essay Langdon Winner had demonstrated that artefacts have politics.

The things we call 'technologies' are ways of building order in our world. Many technical devices and systems important in everyday life contain possibilities for many different ways of ordering human activity. Consciously or not, deliberately or inadvertently, societies choose structures for technologies that influence how people are going to work, communicate, travel, consume, and so forth over a very long time. In the processes by which structuring decisions are made, different people are differently situated and possess unequal degrees of power as well as unequal levels of awareness.

Winner was not speaking of women, but he was talking the same language as feminists. Women were saying, for instance, that nothing could be clearer than the different impact on women and men of the invention and dissemination of high-rise housing or the ovulation-inhibiting contraceptive pill (Stanworth 1987).

It was, of course, apparent that women as a sex were distant from the laboratories, drawing offices and board rooms from which decisions about new technologies were emerging. The social shaping literature fitted well with women's beliefs that this might prove a source as well as a sign of women's disadvantage. Work such as that of David Noble on numerically controlled tools (1984), of William Lazonick (1979) on the self-acting mule, of David Albury and Joseph Schwartz (1982) on the miner's safety lamp, showed variously that class, military, national or other interests might shape the design of tools and artefacts. Women were showing that male interests too were a factor influencing technological outcomes. Linotype composing machinery invented in the late nineteenth century was shaped according to a compromise between manufacturers, printing employers and the interests of a body of male printers organized in a craft union (Cockburn 1983). Often the choice of new technologies reflects calculations by (usually male) employers as to the most profitable exploitation of female labour, whose position in the labour market is systemically weakened by male-dominant social relations (Glucksmann 1990). Finally, if social contexts mould technological choices, what of family? Feminists were showing how gender relations in the Western household and its characteristic sexual division of labour powerfully shape the way domestic technologies are taken up and used (Cowan 1983; Bose et al. 1984).

WOMEN AS ACTORS IN TECHNOLOGY NETWORKS

It was within a feminist theoretical context that a research project was initiated in 1988 by the European Centre for Coordination of Research and Documentation in the Social Sciences (The Vienna Centre). The Centre brought together women from eleven countries in the hope of stimulating some similar and simultaneous research, in countries with contrasting political economies, on the relationship of technological change to changes occurring in relations between the sexes. In this framework, several such empirical investigations are now under way. From Britain we are contributing to the Vienna Centre project a case study of the design and development, production, marketing and use of the microwave oven.[2]

We approached the empirical work feeling that the actor–network approach would be a productive way into a theme of this kind. And so, up to a point, it has proved. We find, for instance, the anticipated links between the development and use of the magnetron for military and industrial purposes and the application of microwaves to cooking. We can trace a history of the mobilization of support for the launching of the microwave oven as a consumer durable in the white goods range. We can see that what microwave cooking becomes depends crucially on the association with the process of millions of women (and men) in as many households. When a new generation of microwave ovens, with the addition of grill, rotisserie and convection heating facilities, adopts the attributes of old conventional ovens, we see that enough women wishing to roast their chickens to crisp, brown perfection the way their mothers did can constitute a collective actor with the power to influence technological development.

We can see actors playing clear alliance-building roles: the manufacturer's home economist (female) who invents the recipes that bind manufacturer, artefact and housewife together; the advertiser who projects an image of the artefact and its associated cooking process that can be 'translated' into a sales pitch by a manufacturer's team of demonstrators and the sales staff of the distributive stores. We can see the possible forging of a collectivity of interest between the manufacturers and distributors of microwave ovens, on the one side, and, on the other, an emergent industry, the manufacturers of cook-chill foods.

Finally, we can see that the actors in this network are truly heterogeneous. Take the British manufacturing operation. Some of the actors are human. There is a corps of Japanese managers, complete with Japanese traditions of management, newly arrived on the Celtic fringe of Britain to set up a manufacturing facility for microwave ovens and other products. There is the local Labour mayor who has the connections to deliver a no-strike one-union agreement in exchange for several hundred new technology jobs. There are the young women made redundant by the closure of sewing factories, with work discipline and plentiful skills that may be exploited at low cost. Their existence is not without influence on the design of the assembly process: it bears on which jobs are automated and which are not.

There are non-human, material actors in the network. There is the geographical location, the distance of the site from European markets, that is a factor in calculating production costs and retail prices. There is the conductivity and weight of certain materials deployed in manufacture;

the energy of microwaves that some actors declare damaging to human health, others claim are harmless. At one moment of crisis, when demand for microwave ovens collapses, production must be cut back and jobs are threatened, it is because a new actor has emerged onto the scene: the listeria bacterium that infects cook-chill foods and frightens off the nation's home makers, who decide microwaves are risky and go back to their old habits.

The drama of the evolution and, from moment to moment, the closure, the 'black boxing', of any one model of the microwave oven can readily be told in these terms. We have come to feel, however, that the actor–network approach falls short in three ways from being a fully adequate tool for a feminist analysis.

The first problem is the easiest to remedy. It is the invisibility of women. The actor–network approach focuses mainly on the design and development phases of an artefact's life. The actors, being mainly design and development engineers, entrepreneurs and financiers, are just that: not actresses. To take the microwave case, no women are visible among the top management of the Japanese multinational, nor are they present in the engineering phases of the microwave development. Ironically, women's invisibility has been increased by the shift we have made from technological impact studies to social shaping studies. For a hard fact remains that, in matters of technological change, women are more impacted upon than impacting.

Women can, however, be introduced as actors by the expedient of ensuring that the net of the 'network' is cast wide enough, that it includes the lowest-paid workers producing the artefact, the individuals who use or refuse it. This is why our Vienna Centre research projects selected as a focus domestic technologies, artefacts that are applied in the home. It is also the reason for our decision not to halt the research at the point of design closure, when the prototype becomes an unproblematic 'black box' and enters production as this year's model of washing machine, vacuum cleaner or food processor. Instead we are following the trajectory and tracing the relations of the artefacts from design along the spiral of development, manufacture, marketing, sales, purchase, use, service and repair – not forgetting the feedback to design as one model supersedes another.

Besides, we are supposing that two sets of probabilities are inscribed in the artefact's design: first, the social relations of its use, but also, second, the social relations of its production. For, as some of us are finding, the manufacturer-designer of the artefact is sometimes frankly uninterested in who will buy it and what their needs are. (He will rely on an advertising campaign to create a market.) His main concern is how cheaply the artefact can be mass-produced. In the wide 'network' enlisted in birth-to-death biography of our artefacts we can be sure to find women in many phases of their many lives. They will be visible as manual workers, as marketing consultants, as home economists, trainee engineers, unpaid domestics, as shoppers, wives, mothers, daughters.

Though women as a sex can be scripted in, however, their presence does not guarantee a gendered analysis. And the language and concepts provided by the actor–network discourse seem not quite adequate for generating one. The other two shortcomings in the approach can, I believe, be encapsulated as follows. First, there is a lack of concern with subjectivity, which leads to a neglect of the way technology (particularly as knowledge and process) enters into our *gender identity*. Second, there is an incomplete representation of the historical dimensions of *power*, so that we cannot explain what we see with our eyes every day: that men as a sex dominate women as a sex, a relation in which technology is implicated. Indeed, it is only by tackling these two issues that we can explain the first – women's relative absence from the processes of design and development of technology. I will expand a little on these points.

GENDER IDENTITY AND THE RELATIONS OF TECHNOLOGY

Gender is a term increasingly used to convey a differentiation, by cultural processes involving appearance and behaviour, action, thought and language, of two ideal social categories, the masculine and the feminine, and their normative mapping onto male and female bodies respectively. By extension, gender is used to symbolize other differences (of size or importance for instance) and other phenomena (such as colours) are enlisted as symbols of gender. Think of the iteration between hierarchical dualities such as pink/blue, weak/strong, body/mind, woman/man. There is observed to be a strong tendency within gender processes to complementarity: what is masculine is not feminine, and vice versa. Together masculine and feminine are conceived as making a whole human being – the couple or dyad.

Just as there has been a shift in the last decade away from technological determinism, so there has been a shift from biological determinism. It has been a significant conceptual breakthrough to acknowledge that gender is not predestined by biological sex difference. What we perceive as 'facts of nature' – 'man', 'woman', 'sexuality' – are largely cultural constructs. If gender differentiation has a source in human social history, the best claim to it may well be a deeply rooted cognitive practice of generating dichotomies through which to order our world – up/down, day/night, white/black, good/bad – dichotomies that are simultaneously hierarchies (Goodison 1990). Like Latour's scientific 'fact' or technological 'black box', gender is more of a doing than a being. Gender is a social achievement. Technology too.

Yet, in the social processes that comprise gender, as in the social processes of technological development, are caught up material actors.

Much as climate and geomorphology, electrons and magnets, may play a part in the networks that enable a certain technological outcome, so physique (hormones, average height, menstruation and ovulation) enter into the social representation and the relational play that is gender. Gender identity is what people do, think and say about material and immaterial things *in relation to* other people conceived of as sexed. It is necessarily relational (Connell 1987: 79).

Technology too, as we have seen, is increasingly understood as relational. As deployed in production, in everyday life, in the household, technological artefacts *entail* relations. They embody some (those that went into their making). They prefigure others (those implied in their use, abuse or neglect). But they also enter into and may change relations they encounter. There is yet nothing gendered about this perception, but gendering is inevitably present.

Take the microwave oven. It embodies its relations of design and production. These relations are, among class and other things, a matter of ethnicity and gender. The relationship between head office designers in Japan and local engineers in Britain (a relationship not without its tensions) has shaped certain variations in the model we buy. The assumptions made by an entirely male design team about the households in which their artefact is to find a role will be based on a masculine experience of domesticity (mediated of course by class and race positioning). The punishing relations of the assembly line, where women (in the main) spend their days in a relentless 35-second cycle of lifting, inserting, screwing, clipping, while men (in the main) hunk heavy goods about, maintain machinery and control the production process, have contributed the microwave oven's internal structure. The negotiation between cooks (mainly women) and those for whom they cook (mainly men and children) concerning what is 'good cooking' have given a certain product its combination of microwave and convection heat sources.

The microwave brings forward from the factory into the kitchen certain relational possibilities. It opens up, for instance, a new casualness in the ease with which individual members of a household, instead of taking a meal together, eat whenever it suits them. It enables unskilled cooks to 'cook' things. It calls for a negotiation of unaccustomed safety rules between adults and children, governing the various dangers of unexpected heat, unseen radiation, inadequately sterilized food.

On the other hand, the microwave oven enters a household where certain relations are well embedded. Perhaps here the wife works, the man is unemployed. There will be a pattern of cooking practices: who cooks for whom. Perhaps the teenage daughter is anorexic (a relational illness) so that food is a highly political topic in the family. There will be compromises concerning who makes decisions about purchases and does the shopping.

The practice may differ as regards food and as regards consumer durables such as a microwave oven.

Clearly it is difficult, if not obtuse, to attempt an understanding of technology in such a context without taking account of gender identities. It is not, however, as is sometimes supposed, only when women are present that gender exists. Studies of the introduction of new technology may sometimes seem to enter a world peopled entirely by men. There are, for instance, few women actors in the world in which David Noble (1984) saw computerized, numerically controlled machine tools taking shape and getting used. Yet the relations of this technology are relations of masculinity – and what is that if not gender?

As we are identified by others, and constitute our own identities in the course of a lifetime's interactions, part of the process is invariably gendering. Ineluctably, technology enters into our gendered identities. Since their inception in the Renaissance, modern science and technology have been deployed symbolically by men, the active sex in this project, as masculine. This holds true for many periods and many technologies. Francis Bacon called his fellow sixteenth-century scientists to 'penetrate the secrets of Nature' in inaugurating with him 'the truly masculine birth of time' (Farrington 1970). The culture and imagery of the scientists responsible for the atom bomb in the Los Alamos laboratories during the Second World War were strikingly masculine (Easlea 1983). Tracy Kidder's novel, *The Soul of a New Machine*, is a late twentieth-century celebration of hi-tech machismo in a computer design project (Kidder 1981). The heroic age of mechanization had shaped and been shaped by muscular male identities. There was a hope (or was it a fear?) that the age of electronics, of informatics, would weaken the masculine identification of and with technology. Recent studies, however, have shown that IT, mediated by different symbols, has in its turn been appropriated for masculinity (Gray 1987; Haddon 1988).

The development of modern technoscience and of modern Western masculinity have been performed simultaneously, through an overlapping set of relations. What we think of as 'technology' is the doings of men (women's doings do not count); what we think of as a man is a 'hands-on' type. Similarly, contemporary Western femininity has involved the constitution of identities organized around technological incompetence. In the extreme patriarchal relations of fascist Italy, Mussolini wrote of an incompatibility between women and machines and banned women from the operation of machinery in production – until he found his war economy could not do without them (Macciocchi 1979).

From the microwave oven study we could draw an instance of the explanatory value of a perception of identity. The senior home economist in the manufacturing company was a woman. It is not incidental that her daughter was employed in her department. Her report of her work in interview showed her to identify as a woman and homemaker, as well as an employee, and to identify with the housewife-customer using her company's microwaves. She was also aware of (and angry about) the high evaluation of men's engineering skills relative to women's domestic science qualifications; that there were few women managers in the firm; and that she herself was denied management status. This gender set – identity/identification/disidentification – was significant in the position, responsibility and activity she negotiated for herself in the firm. It coloured the way she guided her team of women consultants, published recipe books, advocated features of microwave design and represented her department *vis-à-vis* the rest of the firm. She had insisted that the word 'Test' be prefixed to the sign 'Kitchen' above their door.

Technology, then, can tell us something we need to know about gender identity. Gender identity can tell us something we need to know about technology.

THE PECULIARITIES OF POWER

Among the things gender may be able to clarify for us about technology is the nature of its implication in control, exploitation and domination. For gender is not merely a relation of difference, it is one of asymmetry. Women commonly experience the masculine relations of technology as relations in which they are dominated and controlled. Some feel there is a connection between their own experience and what they observe to be the damaging relation of industrial technoscience with the natural environment. A concept of power is by no means absent from the actor–network theory of technology. But it is a representation of power as capacity, whereas in the lived world power is often experienced as domination. A representation of power as capacity, or effectiveness, does not readily accommodate what feminist theory has come to understand by 'male power' – that is, a persistent pattern in which men as a sex dominate women as a sex, exploiting and controlling women's sexuality and reproductive capacities and benefitting from their labour.

An important insight of feminism has been a concept of systemic male power, sometimes designated 'patriarchy'. An extensive literature on this theme unfolded in the 1970s and 1980s (Rubin 1975; Kuhn and Wolpe 1978; Eisenstein 1979; Sargent 1981; Walby 1990). In brief, the notion supposed the existence in all societies of some kind of normative arrangements governing reproduction/sex/gender – just as there are some kind of systemic arrangements governing production/labour/consumption. In the way that a mode of production might in one culture and at one historical moment be feudal, at another capitalist, so a sex/gender system might in theory at one moment and in one society be matriarchal, in another patriarchal, or indeed involve sex equality. A focus of feminist study was why almost all societies of which we have knowledge through anthropology and history evince a pattern (though in differing forms) of male power, female subordination.

Into the social shaping approach, which was often in a neo-Marxist framework and carried a subtext of partisan opposition to class domination, feminists were relatively easily able to insert considerations of male domination and by discussing its possible connections with class exploitation. It has proved more difficult in the case of the actor–network approach, which is characterized less by liberatory politics than by an enthusiasm for the minutiae of technical decision-making as intellectual puzzle and human drama.

For here the notion of power is not derived from class. Such structures are eschewed, not perhaps as erroneous so much as, for these purposes, irrelevant. In the actor–network account of the emergence of theories and artefacts, power expresses itself as the *influence* that can mobilize opinion for one's arguments, the constraints limiting one's *capability* to mould materials or sway opinion in accordance with one's individual or corporate will. In case studies of the generation of new technologies (the bicycle, 'bakelite', the electric car) power takes the low profile form of 'reduced discretion' among the network of actors (Law 1986b: 17).

None the less, some of these same authors have usefully amplified their concept of power in other essays. Latour, for instance, suggests that power 'is not something one can possess – indeed it must be treated as a consequence rather than a cause of action' (Latour 1986: 264). Power over something or someone is, he says, a composition made by many people and attributed to one of them. 'The amount of power exercised varies not according to the power someone has, but to the number of other people who enter into the composition' (Latour 1986: 265). It is a logical derivative of the actor–network/translation model of technoscience. In another essay he and Michel Callon sketch the process in which those entities we see as powerful acquire their scale and reach. There is no inherent difference, they say, between a small weak actor and a massive strong one. The first grows into the second by a process of associating other actors in its projects. Organization, in effect, is no different from any other kind of 'black box': it is a negotiated achievement, of dubious stability (Callon and Latour 1981).

Latour, then, is not saying that class power is not 'real', or that male domination does not 'exist'. Perhaps it is accurate to say he is agnostic about such things, saying that we can learn more about power by putting such concepts aside and looking at the mechanisms by which power can be shown to be effective. The approach is not dissimilar to that of

Michel Foucault whose cumulative essays on medicine, the prison and sexuality portray power as operating not by repressing subjectivity but by deploying and regulating it. For Foucault power has to be understood in 'an ascending analysis', starting from its 'infinitesimal mechanisms' in the individual. This individual is not (as in feminism and socialism) the subject of a liberatory project. Rather subjectivity, even the body of the subjugated, is the effect and vehicle of power. In a celebrated lecture he put it as follows:

> [P]ower, if we do not take too distant a view of it, is not that which makes the difference between those who exclusively possess and retain it, and those who do not have it and submit to it. Power must be analyzed as something which circulates. . . . power is employed and exercised through a net-like organization [cf. actor–networks]. And not only do individuals circulate between its threads; they are always in the position of simultaneously undergoing and exercising power. . . . individuals are the vehicles of power, not its points of application.
>
> (Foucault in Gordon 1980: 98)

The similarity with Latour's 'power as the consequence, not the cause, of action' will be immediately apparent.

Let us return to the microwave oven. Actor–network language is capable of expressing much of what we see. Women at least are not cast as passive victims – they too can be actors. The women who may try and fail to acquire engineering skills, or, having obtained them, to get jobs in the white goods industry; the women in the office and assembly line who may defer to men's 'natural' ability with technology; the housewife who 'prefers' to be the one to do the cooking even though that means effectively being a personal servant to her husband – we need not assume they are unwitting dupes. We can wonder whether, from their position of subordination, they strike some kind of bargain. As Foucault says, 'what makes power hold good, what makes it accepted, is simply the fact that it doesn't only weigh on us as a force that says no, but that it traverses and produces things, it induces pleasure, forms knowledge, produces discourse' (Foucault in Gordon 1980: 119). Women can recognize themselves in this.

There is, however, difficulty in responding with the actor–network approach to feminist questions that continue to call for an answer. Perhaps it is that in mainstream technology theory the key question has been how to explain change, while for feminists it seems more urgent to explain continuity. Why do gender relations survive so little changed through successive waves of technological innovation? What is the connection between organization and gender identity? Can men as a sex be said to organize their power over women? Are technology relations a medium through which they do it? What part do women play i. perpetuating this? Is there an erotic dimension linking technological and sexual control and abandon (Hacker 1989)?

In the actor–network approach to technoscience power is visible only as capacity. In life it often manifests itself as domination. In actor–networks, the performative approach, the social can have no predisposing patterns. For just as 'Nature' is not taken as pre-existing the performance of the drama of actor and network, neither is 'Society'. When in life, time and again, men are cast for the parts that forge the alliances that influence technological outcomes, nothing explains why men are chosen. The theory permits actors to bring to the struggle certain 'resources'. Presumably women, being absent or in relatively powerless relationships to technological trajectories, lack these 'resources'. Hidden within the innocent concept of resources, however, is packed something of enormous scope that it is barely competent to carry and which continually invites unpacking: the historical patterning of the social by class, race and gender. We know that such patterns or structures are not unchanging, that performance or practice can alter them. In dwelling on them we do not need to be determinist or functionalist. But we also know that in 'the social' there is a loading of the dice that produces a probability that the collective associations and translations that result in effective power in these technology networks will continue to afford one sex domination over the other – unless it is somehow interrupted through an active politics of sex/gender.

ACKNOWLEDGMENT

My thanks to Judy Wajcman, to Susan Ormrod (my co-researcher on the microwave oven study), and to other members of the Vienna Centre group, for reading and commenting on this chapter. It has benefited greatly from their advice, but remains a personal view.

NOTES

1 For a thorough review and analysis of two decades of feminist interaction with technology see Judy Wajcman's forthcoming book *Feminism Confronts Technology*.
2 The British component of this research, described here, is funded by the Economic and Social Research Council and being carried out at The City University, where the author is a research fellow in the Centre for Research in Gender, Ethnicity and Social Change.

REFERENCES

Albury, D. and Schwartz, J. (1982) *Partial Progress: The Politics of Science and Technology*, London: Pluto Press.

Baehr, H. and Dyer, G. (eds) (1987) *Boxed-in: Women on and in TV*, London: Routledge.

Bijker W., Hughes, T. P. and Pinch, T. (eds) (1987) *The Social Construction of Technological Systems*, Cambridge, Mass.: MIT Press.

Bose, C., Bereano, P. and Malloy, M. (1984) 'Household technology and the social construction of housework', *Technology and Culture* 25: 53–82.

Callon, M. (1987) 'Society in the making: the study of technology as a tool for social analysis', in W. Bijker *et al.* (eds) *The Social Construction of Technological Systems*, Cambridge, Mass.: MIT Press.

Callon, M. and Latour, B. (1981) 'Unscrewing the big Leviathan: how actors macro-structure reality and how sociologists help them do so', in K. Knorr-Cetina and A. V. Cicourel (eds) *Advances in Social Theory and Methodology*, London: Routledge & Kegan Paul, 277–303.

Cockburn, C. (1983) *Brothers: Male Dominance and Technological Change*, London: Pluto Press.

——(1985) *Machinery of Dominance: Women, Men and Technical Knowhow*, London: Pluto Press.

Connell, R. W. (1987) *Gender and Power*, Cambridge: Polity Press.

Cowan, R. Schwartz (1983) *More Work for Mother*, New York: Basic Books.

Easlea, B. (1983) *Fathering the Unthinkable: Masculinity, Science and the Nuclear Arms Race*, London: Pluto Press.

Eisenstein, Z. R. (ed.) (1979) *Capitalist Patriarchy and the Case for Socialist Feminism*, New York: Monthly Review Press.

Farrington, B. (1970) *The Philosophy of Francis Bacon*, Liverpool: Liverpool University Press.

Glucksmann, M. (1990) *Women Assemble: Women Workers and the New Industries in Interwar Britain*, London: Routledge.

Goodison, L. (1990) *Moving Heaven and Earth: Sexuality, Spirituality and Social Change*, London: The Women's Press.

Gordon, C. (ed.) (1980) *Michel Foucault: Power/Knowledge*, Brighton: Harvester Press.

Gray, A. (1987) 'Behind closed doors: women and video', in H. Baehr and G. Dyer (eds) *Boxed-in: Women on and in TV*, London: Routledge, 38–54.

Hacker, S. (1989) *Pleasure, Power and Technology: Some Tales of Gender, Engineering and the Cooperative Workplace*, Boston: Unwin Hyman.

Haddon, L. (1988) 'The roots and early history of the British home computer market: origins of the masculine micro', Ph.D. thesis, Imperial College, London University.

Hughes, T. P. (1987) 'The evolution of large technological systems', in W. Bijker *et al.* (eds) *The Social Construction of Technological Systems*, Cambridge, Mass.: MIT Press, 51–82.

Kidder, T. (1981) *The Soul of a New Machine*, Harmondsworth: Penguin.

Knorr-Cetina, K. and Cicourel, A. V. (eds) (1981) *Advances in Social Theory and Methodology*, London: Routledge & Kegan Paul.

Kuhn, A. and Wolpe, A. M. (eds) (1978) *Feminism and Materialism*, London: Routledge & Kegan Paul.

Latour, B. (1986) 'The powers of association', in J. Law (ed.) *Power, Action and Belief: A New Sociology of Knowledge?*, London: Routledge & Kegan Paul, 264–80.

——(1987) *Science in Action*, Milton Keynes: Open University Press.
Law, J. (ed.) (1986a) *Power, Action and Belief: A New Sociology of Knowledge?*, London: Routledge & Kegan Paul.
——(1986b) 'Power/knowledge and the dissolution of the sociology of knowledge', editorial introduction to J. Law (ed.) *Power, Action and Belief: A New Sociology of Knowledge?* London: Routledge & Kegan Paul, 1–19.
——(1987) 'Technology and heterogeneous engineering: the case of Portuguese expansion', in W. Bijker *et al.* (eds) *The Social Construction of Technological Systems*, Cambridge, Mass.: MIT Press, 111–34.
Lazonick, W. H. (1979) 'Industrial relations and technological change: the case of the self-acting mule', *Cambridge Journal of Economics* 3: 231–62.
Macciocchi, M. A. (1979) 'Female sexuality in Fascist ideology', *Feminist Review* 1: 67–82.
MacKenzie, D. and Wajcman, J. (eds) (1985) *The Social Shaping of Technology*, Milton Keynes: Open University Press.
McNeil, M. (ed.) (1987) *Gender and Expertise*, London: Free Association Books.
Noble, D. F. (1977) *America by Design*, New York: Knopf.
——(1984) *Forces of Production: A Social History of Industrial Automation*, New York: Knopf.
Pinch, T. and Bijker, W. (1984) 'The social construction of facts and artifacts: or how the sociology of science and technology might benefit each other', *Social Studies of Science* 14: 299–341.
Reiter, R. (ed.) (1975) *Toward an Anthropology of Women*, New York: Monthly Review Press.
Rubin, Gayle (1975) 'The traffic in women: notes on the "political economy" of sex', in R. Reiter (ed.) *Toward an Anthropology of Women*, New York: Monthly Review Press, 157–210.
Sargent, L. (ed.) (1981), *Women and Revolution: A Debate on Class and Patriarchy*, London: Pluto Press.
Stanworth, M. (1987) *Reproductive Technologies: Gender, Motherhood and Medicine*, Cambridge: Polity Press.
Wajcman, J. (1991 forthcoming) *Feminism Confronts Technology*, Cambridge: Polity Press.
Walby, S. (1990) *Theorizing Patriarchy*, Oxford: Blackwell.
Winner, L. (1985) 'Do artifacts have politics?' in D. MacKenzie and J. Wajcman (eds) *The Social Shaping of Technology*, Milton Keynes: Open University Press, 26–38.

Chapter 3

The desire for the new
Its nature and social location as presented in theories of fashion and modern consumerism[1]

Colin Campbell

INTRODUCTION

Theories of modern consumerism generally stress its dependence on the presence of a continuing desire for the new on the part of consumers, identifying this as the feature which most distinguishes it from more traditional patterns. Indeed, the central dynamic of modern consumerism is seen to be closely related to this desire, especially as it is manifested in the institution of fashion, and hence credited with accounting for the extraordinarily high levels of demand for goods and services in contemporary societies. Thus, to understand modern consumerism means to understand the nature, origin and functioning of the processes through which novelty is continuously created, introduced into society and then disseminated through all social classes.[2] It follows from this that a satisfactory theory of modern consumerism must explain (a) the mechanisms which serve to ensure the continuous supply of cultural novelty which is embodied in products and services; (b) the nature and social location of the group whose valuation of the new is so strong as to overcome the inertial forces of tradition and conservatism and hence act as a channel through which novelty can enter society; (c) the associated ethic or body of moral thought which can serve to justify such innovations; and (d) the motives of the larger population which impel them to prefer the new to the familiar and hence desire new products.

THE VEBLEN–SIMMEL MODEL

The traditional answers to these questions tend to draw upon what one may refer to as the Veblen–Simmel theory of fashion and consumption. That is to say, Simmel's observations on the 'trickle down' nature of fashions and their role in social equalization and discrimination are embedded within Veblen's broader theory of conspicuous consumption to constitute one overall theory of how novelty is first introduced and then disseminated throughout a society.

Veblen's theory of conspicuous consumption (which is both more complex and more ambiguous than is generally assumed),[3] actually makes no assumptions concerning either the new or the novel. It starts with the premise that wealth confers honour and hence that individuals are esteemed to the degree that they possess wealth. Consequently individuals strive to 'excel in pecuniary standing' and so 'gain the esteem and envy of their fellow-men', conduct which Veblen identifies as embodying 'the emulative motive' (1925: 32). Individuals are assumed to be continually engaged in the making of invidious comparisons between themselves and those 'with whom they are in the habit of classing themselves' and consequently striving to outdo their peers (ibid.: 103). In order, however, to impress others with one's wealth it must be manifestly exhibited in the form of pecuniary strength, something which requires the individual to engage in conspicuous (and wasteful) consumption. Since an individual's efforts to out-consume rivals in this way can only serve to spur them to even greater exertions, such conduct initiates an endless battle for status. Veblen assumes that there is one single and generally agreed system of social stratification in existence in society with 'the leisure class' at its head. Hence the form of the consumption embodied in these emulative endeavours will be dictated by the habits and preferences of this class as they percolate down through the subordinate strata.

Simmel's highly formalistic treatment of fashion assumes that it should be understood as the outcome of the tension generated by the opposed forces of conformity and individualization (1957: 549). Fashion, for Simmel, 'represents nothing more than one of the many forms of life by the aid of which we seek to combine in uniform spheres of activity the tendency towards social equalization with the desire for individual differentiation and change' (ibid.: 543), tendencies which he acknowledges serve both to unite individuals into groups of equals and to divide them into status hierarchies (ibid.: 544). In this respect Simmel echoes Veblen's stress on the functional significance of the purchase and display of goods (in this case mainly dress) for the confirmation of an individual's position within a status system. Unlike Veblen, however, Simmel does not suggest that status is to be perceived as fundamentally stemming from such consumption activity. Fashion for Simmel is not the source of status but merely its expression. But where Simmel does agree with Veblen and, what is more, goes on to add his own distinctive contribution, is in relation to the role of the elite 'leisure class'.

For Veblen the distinctions between strata are essentially a matter of differences in wealth, as embodied in the degree of ostentatious expense displayed in consumption habits. For Simmel, on the other hand, different fashions serve to discriminate strata with the result that members of inferior classes are assumed not to be emulating the ostentation of their superiors (as in Veblen's model) so much as imitating their taste.

This apparently small difference between the two theories actually has a significant implication as it tends to supply the Veblenesque model with its missing dynamic.

One of the many problems with the Veblen model is that there is no explanation for the changes that occur in consumption patterns. Status competition through conspicuous display does not require novel products and coexists happily with an unchanging traditional way of life.[4] In addition, it is not obvious whom those at the pinnacle of the leisure class could be said to be emulating, or, if they are not driven by emulation, what might be the nature of their consumption motives. Simmel tries to resolve these problems by stressing the fact that fashion involves both imitative and differentiating tendencies and by crediting the masses with a special propensity to engage in the former and the elite with a special inclination to the latter (ibid.: 545).[5] By formulating a 'chase and flight' model (see McCracken 1988: 94f.) and attributing different motives to the different classes in this way rather than assuming, as Veblen does, that everyone is driven by the same motives, Simmel manages to explain what it is which causes continuous changes of fashion to occur.

Whilst it is clear that the conduct of the upper classes cannot be understood as stemming from imitative tendencies (as there is no one for them to imitate) but, on the contrary, is to be explained in terms of their need to replace any given style before their immediate inferiors have successfully adopted it, this does not seem to imply that their enthusiasm for novelty need be any greater than that of those in the classes beneath them. Since the members of each stratum are presumed to have an equal desire to distance themselves from their immediate inferiors, they will presumably have an equal desire to embrace the new in order to achieve this end. At the same time, Simmel's theory does not mean that the new styles which each stratum is continually being forced to adopt must be culturally 'novel' as opposed to merely temporally 'new'. He does, however, appear to make just these assumptions, associating the desire for novelty (or 'foreignness') not just with 'civilization' in general but with the 'man of culture' in particular (Simmel 1957: 546). What is especially interesting in Simmel's argument is the suggestion that a particular category of person (identified as 'the man of culture') is intrinsically attracted by whatever is perceived as 'exceptional, bizarre, or conspicuous' independently of any need to adopt a new fashion in order to keep social imitators in their place. For it is the presence of this assumption, when combined with the presumption of a need to maintain social distance, which provides Simmel's theory with the apparent ability to explain the dynamic and ever-changing nature of modern fashions. When, therefore, these two assumptions are set within the larger framework of Veblen's claims concerning the status functions of consumption in general, we have the outline of the popular Veblen–Simmel model of modern consumption. The primary assumptions of this model are: (a) consumption is an essentially other-directed activity, in which (b) considerations of status maintenance or enhancement predominate; (c) the motives underlying consumption are imitative and emulative such that the patterns manifested by superior groups are imitated by inferior ones; and (d) the elite classes (who are intrinsically attracted to 'the new') must be continually adopting novel fashions and consuming novel goods in order to maintain their position of superiority.

Many criticisms can be levelled against this model but those of most significance in this context relate particularly to the treatment of novelty, with perhaps the most obviously contentious claim being the assertion that new fashions originate with the upper classes and then 'trickle down' the status ladder as a result of imitation and emulation by those in inferior positions. Simmel is quite unambiguous on this point, claiming that 'the latest fashion [affects] only the upper classes' (1957: 545). But many investigators have suggested that research reveals a more complex picture (e.g. Riesman and Roseborough 1965: 120). For example Paul Blumberg, writing in the late 1970s, noted that

> many standards in fashion have been set, not so much by the upper or even middle classes, as by the *déclassé*, anti-class youth, and counter-culture. Long hair, head bands, beads, pretie-dyed [*sic*] apparel, vests, miscellaneous leather and suede, carefully faded and neglected dunga-rees, and all the other paraphernalia of the counterculture costume, not only mock the materialistic status symbols of the established classes, but have successfully spread into the enemy camp, Fifth Avenue and main street, where they have caught on and been copied . . . When blue denim work shirts are selling at New York's Bloomingdales and when rock star Mick Jagger is voted one of the world's best-dressed men, there is obviously something wrong with the theory that sees fashion styles established at the top and trickling down.
>
> (1974: 493–4)

On the basis of this evidence Blumberg suggests that, as far as changes in fashion are concerned, the previous decade had seen as much 'percolating up from the bottom' as 'trickling down from the top' (ibid.: 494). Leaving aside for the moment any doubts one might have over the accuracy of describing Mick Jagger's social position as at the 'bottom' of society, there is nevertheless considerable support for the general claim that fashions are as likely to 'trickle up' and 'trickle across' as they are to 'trickle down' (McCracken 1988: 94f.); a conclusion which would seem to suggest that we should reject Simmel's claim that the upper classes have a special inclination to seek out the new.

However, this conclusion means that the Veblen–Simmel model of changes in fashion and consumption no longer seems to work. In the first place, if the upper classes cannot be credited with any special enthusiasm to embrace the novel for its own sake then it is hard to believe that they would go to the trouble of doing so merely in order to differentiate themselves from those they consider beneath them.[6] Not only are there other and easier ways of defending one's exclusivity (see, e.g., Steiner and Weiss 1951), but it has often been claimed that the mark of a true aristocrat is that one's superiority is so completely taken for granted that the imitative conduct of others is hardly even noticed. Second, we now have the difficult task of explaining why those at the top of the social hierarchy should bother to imitate the dress and behaviour of those 'beneath' them. Finally, if the elite are not the primary channel for innovative fashion and consumption practices, who is, and what is the nature of their motivation?

Of course, part of the problem here stems from the difficulty of determining who constitutes the elite or 'upper' class in a modern industrial society. For Veblen this seems largely to have been a matter of wealth; whilst for Simmel, the stress, as we have seen, was placed on the degree of 'civilization' or 'culture'. Both, however, seem to have assumed a more coherent and unitary system of stratification than is the case and hence failed to anticipate the full complexity of contemporary patterns of imitative and emulative consumption.

There are at least three important qualifications which need to be made to their assumption of one unitary and hierarchical system of emulative striving. The first, as we have seen, is that modern societies (especially in Western Europe) are characterized by a dual elite structure in which an older, land-based aristocracy is increasingly challenged by a newer, urban professional class. The second, which is closely associated with this, is that one group's claims to a superior position may be rejected by another, with the result that status striving takes a competitive but non-imitative form. Finally, the efforts of would-be upwardly-mobile individuals to imitate the style of life they imagine to characterize the elite may be so markedly unsuccessful (as in the case of those labelled *nouveaux riches*) that their superiors do not consider that an innovative response is necessary.

THE NEW, THE INNOVATIVE AND THE NOVEL

Before an alternative to the Veblen–Simmel model of the origin and dissemination of the new can be offered it is first necessary to make some conceptual distinctions which are glossed over in that account, distinctions which concern the concept of newness itself. There are in fact three different senses in which one can use the term 'new'. There is, first, the new as the fresh or newly created; second, the new as the improved or innovative; and third, the new as the unfamiliar or novel.

In using the word 'new' to mean fresh we are opposing it to 'old' where old means worn, used or merely aged. This is the sense in which we talk of a new moon, or of a new baby or of the new shoots on our rose bush.

In none of these contexts does the word 'new' imply anything novel or significantly different from what went before. The new moon is, in effect, very familiar and so are babies and shoots. The contrast here is purely temporal, referring as it does to monthly, generational or seasonal change. The basic assumption is that all things age with time, hence requiring regeneration if they are to continue: and we use the word 'new' to indicate that generation has indeed taken place.

Now we can assume that consumers in all societies are familiar with the difference between old and new products in this sense and that many of them may well have a preference for the new. In our society, for example, items which are in pristine condition often command a higher price than similar objects which, although still fitted to perform the function for which they were designed, show obvious marks of use. One possible explanation for this preference is that some people actually see use as serving to 'contaminate' products. Support for this interpretation can be found in the fact that, while some consumers are reluctant to purchase second-hand goods of any description, consumers are in general more willing to purchase goods that have been put to less 'intimate' use than those which have been closely connected with the user. Thus, those unwilling to buy second-hand clothes might buy second-hand furniture, for example, whilst those prepared to buy second-hand outer garments may be unwilling to buy second-hand underwear. This process of devaluation as a result of a perceived contamination through previous use can thus result in a product or product-category-specific form of neophilia.[7]

This variety of the desire for the new obviously plays a significant part in modern consumerism, which can be said to embody the general presumption that consumers will spend the majority of their disposable resources on 'fresh' products. Clearly before the desire for the new in this sense could have become institutionalized, both the techniques of mass production and a comparative degree of affluence would have to have become the norm. This process seems to have been well under way in England by the end of the eighteenth century, by which time it had become generally unacceptable to wear second-hand clothes (Lemire 1988).

But a preference for the new in this sense, although characteristically modern, still does not explain that exceptionally high turnover of goods which lies at the heart of modern consumerism. For although contributing to these high levels of demand it is a purchasing pattern which is still dependent on the natural processes of use to diminish an object's appeal. Demand is thus fundamentally dependent on objective processes of 'erosion' to create a sense of replacement need. Thus clothes, carpets or shoes all need to be demonstrably 'worn out' before there is an unanswerable case for their replacement. Now even though it could be claimed that modern manufacturers do tend to produce goods which will quickly become unusable whilst consumers themselves are constantly raising their definitional threshold of what 'worn out' might mean, this source of demand would by itself still be insufficient to explain the exceptionally high turnover of goods characteristic of modern consumerism.

There is a second sense of 'new', however, which relates more to efficiency and technical capacity than to newness in the purely temporal sense. Here the 'new' is the improved, the innovative or the latest in a long line of products which have been manufactured and offered for sale over the years in order to satisfy a given need. In this respect 'new, improved X' is the product which represents the present 'state of the art' in the relevant technology, that which embodies the most recent scientific or technical expertise.[8] What precisely is new in this context therefore (or claimed to be new) is the degree to which the product is able to meet a specified need. Thus a 'new' improved battery or tyre may be advertised as lasting 25 per cent longer than its predecessor, or a product may be 'improved' in the sense of giving greater volume for the same price, or by having been made lighter, less bulky or constructed of more durable materials. Here the principal dynamic which generates newness is scientific and technical advance itself, clearly a highly significant force in modern society. Once again one can say that a concern with 'improved' products is a marked feature of modern consumerism, and signals a departure from a more conservative and traditional pattern in which one does not contemplate changes in technical efficiency. Indeed, modern consumers have come to take it for granted that science and technology will combine to produce a continuous flow of inventions and improved products in this sense – this expectation being part of the Enlightenment faith in progress.

Of course, in many market situations consumers are simply not offered a choice between the old and the new improved product, the former simply being replaced as a product line by the latter. Where, however, such choices still exist, consumers do not necessarily demonstrate a preference for the new. They may indeed feel quite content with the manner in which their present products meet their needs and hence fail to be attracted by the 'extra' which the 'improved' product offers. Thus, for example, individuals may appreciate the advantages, say, of having a privacy button and an automatic redial facility on their telephone without feeling any great need to rush out and replace their existing handset, and whilst it may be true that, in some circumstances, 'necessity is the mother of invention', all too often an aggressive advertising campaign is required to persuade consumers that they 'need' what someone else has invented. Hence, although it is clearly the case that scientific and technical advance provides one important source of the continuing turnover of wants which characterizes modern consumerism, it is again to be doubted if this in itself is powerful enough to account for its phenomenal dynamism.

But there is a third sense in which the word 'new' is used which relates to neither the fresh nor the improved but to that which is 'novel' or unfamiliar.

Here the contrast is purely experiential and therefore differs significantly from the previous two uses. For while the novel may also be new in the sense of the freshly created, this does not have to be the case, as objects which are old may still be unfamiliar to the person encountering them. Similarly whilst some new improved products may also strike consumers as novel, many will so closely resemble their forerunners as to strike individuals as fundamentally familiar. This is because, although the consumer may not have encountered this precise product before, there is familiarity with the product genus and hence an understanding of the functions which it is designed to fulfil. This is especially the case with much modern technology where the crucial working parts are frequently hidden and only the consequences of innovation are apparent.

This suggests that both freshness and improvement are intrinsic qualities of products, freshness relating to how much a product has been used and improvement the degree to which it can satisfy a given need efficiently. By contrast, novelty is more likely to be a judgement which an individual makes on the basis of previous experience and is largely unrelated to any given characteristics of the product itself. Consequently judgements of novelty vary significantly with age and experience, being closely related to the marked differences in taste between generations. What are familiar objects to one generation tend to be strange to the next one.[9] Now it is this sense of the new which is centrally embodied in the modern phenomenon of fashion, an institution which serves to introduce a controlled degree of novelty into goods with high aesthetic significance, and which can be credited with providing more of the crucial dynamic for modern consumerism than either freshness or innovation. For the turnover of goods which is attributable to these forms of the new is small when compared with that arising from the requirements of fashion. This is because novelty is virtually exhausted in the act of consumption itself, disappearing rapidly with the consumer's own familiarization with the purchase, a process which both occurs faster and is more easily accomplished than either 'wearing the shine off' freshness or accomplishing the improvement of products.

One can conclude, on the basis of the above discussion, that three different kinds of neophiliac[10] may be found in contemporary society: first those who crave the fresh and untouched, and whose inclination is to inhabit only new houses, drive only new cars, wear only new clothes and replace their furniture and fittings as soon as they display the slightest signs of wear. These, following the observation on the possible significance of the fear of contamination through use, may be called the 'pristinians'. Such individuals presumably make good consumers, yet their tastes could well be highly conservative, with new purchases largely identical to those they replace, in which case their readiness to spend resources on new products is offset by a comparative indifference to changes in style. It is not obvious what social or demographic features might be distinctive of this group, but it is quite possible that the *nouveaux riches* might be especially inclined to assume that an elite lifestyle requires that possessions should not display any marks of wear. In addition, if they subscribe to the Veblenesque view that it is important to display pecuniary strength, then they will be concerned to consume not merely expensive goods but ones which have been recently acquired.

Second, there are those whose preference is for the newest product lines and innovations and who are particularly attracted to whatever embodies the latest technology. Such consumers are most probably technophiles of one sort or another and possibly members of a informal social group with a shared enthusiasm, like computer buffs or motor sports enthusiasts (see, e.g., Moorhouse 1983). Technophiles also tend to make good consumers and, whilst this is especially true of those who purchase ready-made products (who are generally eager to purchase each new line as it becomes available), it is also true of the do-it-yourself hobbyists, although the consumption emphasis here is naturally more on components than on finished products.[11] In addition, IT technophiles may find their enthusiasm to be doubly relevant to the process of acquiring the new, as the products themselves may serve as an important channel of information about recent developments, just as they themselves may serve as trailblazers for other, less technophiliac, consumers (see chapter 1). Research suggests that this category of lovers of the new is more likely to comprise young males rather than females or the elderly.[12] The obvious limitation present in this form of neophilia stems from the fact that the intensity of the consumer's desire for new products is likely to be offset by the specialized focus of the interest. In addition, the predominant concern with 'performance' is likely to be at the expense of any great interest in the stylistic attribute of goods or in fashion more generally.

Finally, there are those neophiliacs whose craving for the new takes the form of a preference for the novel, the strange or even the bizarre. These are the individuals who appear to place a high value on the stimulus which is provided by the unfamiliar whilst perceiving the known as boring. These are not necessarily the same people as the 'tastemakers' or the initiators of a fashion or in a society (Lynes 1959), as that implies both creativity and an additional inner-directed readiness to defy current norms. Rather they are the ones who are likely to be among the first to respond to a new fashion and, in addition, to change their product preferences swiftly and continuously.

It is this category of consumers who are likely to make the most vital contribution to the dynamic nature of modern consumerism because their high sensitivity to fashion creates a rapidly changing and continuous sequence of new wants. This will be most apparent in the case of dress, but a sensitivity to fashion is likely to lead to a similar high degree of want turnover in such other areas as furniture and furnishings, holidays and cultural products such as records, films and books. In addition, their enthusiasm for the novel means that they will probably respond enthusiastically to any commercial innovations in retailing which appear to offer new experiences to the consumer. It is hard to identify the social characteristics of these lovers of the 'exotic' but such a sensitivity appears to be rare among the old, whilst the traditional view is that it is more prevalent among females than males.

ORIGINS OF THE NOVEL

Recognition of the relative importance of different categories of neophiliac to the central dynamic processes of modern consumerism does not, however, amount to a theory of how novelty is actually introduced and disseminated throughout society. Whilst it is helpful to have some conception of the nature of these critical groups, it is still necessary to have a fuller understanding of their motivation as well as the way in which novel cultural items are introduced into the fashion system. These two issues can be treated, for the sake of convenience, as conceptually distinct aspects of the one overall problem. The first concerns the motives which impel individuals to desire novel products, while the second involves accounting for the general societal acceptance of novel cultural material. These two problems can be described as that of motivation at the personal level and justification at the cultural.

The purchase of fresh products rarely requires much justification; all that is normally required is a demonstration that the old product in question is worn whilst the need which it fulfilled persists. Only if the existing product is of an age or a rarity to acquire a scarcity value is it likely that such an assumption would be challenged. The principle of replacement consumption is so well established in contemporary society that, at least until recently, it rarely created any general society-wide problems of justification. This may, however, become less true if 'green consumerism' gains ground and the fashion for recycling products leads to an associated reduced readiness to define a product as in need of replacement. The introduction and use of improved or innovative products has, by contrast, long been more controversial and does sometimes meet with resistance. One can think, in this instance, of the religious and moral objections levelled against the contraceptive pill, for example, or the environmental objections made against bringing supersonic aircraft into general commercial use. New 'progressive' products can thus sometimes require cultural justification and, as suggested earlier, the most likely source for this would be that cluster of Enlightenment values which centre on 'progress' and 'development'.

The introduction of newness in the form of novelty, however, has very commonly met with fierce opposition. As Simmel observes, in traditional societies novelty tends to be feared whilst the familiar, in the form of the customary, is clung to tenaciously. But even in modern societies powerful traditional forces exist which work to oppose the acceptance of novelty. Thus, although the fashion system itself is generally accepted, it is quite common for particular styles to be regarded as embodying more novelty than the culturally conservative sections of society are prepared to accept and hence serve to provoke an outcry. This is generally because the novelty embodied in the new products and services is perceived to be a threat to established morality. An 'affront to morality' has been the charge made against new female fashions for more than a century, from the bustle to the mini-skirt, whilst new forms of entertainment from the waltz to rock 'n' roll have all been denounced as threats to public decency. Hence it is in this context, with respect to the legitimation of the novel, that some countervailing radical cultural force is most needed, one which would serve both to attack the basis of traditional authority and to justify the continuous introduction of the unfamiliar. For without this, the modern fashion system would itself become ever more timid, routinized and traditionalistic (as, indeed, it tends to be in totalitarian societies).

It is tempting to claim that the modern fashion system is so successfully institutionalized in contemporary societies that the continuous introduction of novelty is taken for granted and hence is not in need of any special cultural justification. As the examples mentioned above suggest, however, attacks on the 'outrageous' and 'immoral', not to mention 'ridiculous' character of what are perceived as the more intensely novel styles are commonplace and yet cannot be successfully repulsed from within the system. Neither the couturiers, fashion houses, the buyers, the fashion correspondents nor the retailers can be said to be in a position to advance any distinctive moral claims with which to counter these arguments. The only appeals which they can make are either to the sovereign principle of consumer choice – which has always been recognized as subordinate to the demands of morality – or the freedom of action to which the 'couturier as artist' is deemed to be entitled.

The justification of novelty in a society is naturally closely associated with movements which oppose tradition and seek to attack all taboos and restrictions on individual conduct. Although the production, distribution and sale of novel goods are thoroughly commercial operations, their continuance in the face of the moral condemnation of traditionalists is actually dependent on the activity of moralists whose concerns are likely to be entirely non-commercial. In this case the irony hinges on the fact that idealistically based demands for artistic freedom of expression turn out in practice to be inescapably linked to demands for a widespread freedom to consume without constraint.

In fact, we can return to Blumberg's earlier quotation and his observation that new fashions are often introduced by what he called *déclassé* elements for an illustration of this process. As he noted, fashions in the 1960s frequently originated with members of the counterculture, a movement which was self-consciously opposed both to the traditional values and ideals of the establishment and to a market ideology. In place of these, counterculturalists asserted the central principles of individual self-expression and self-realization, placing a special value on direct experience, individuality, creativity, authentic feeling and pleasure. In so doing they were reasserting the core values of Romanticism as these had been formulated during the second half of the eighteenth century and subsequently reaffirmed in the 1890s and 1920s.[13] By invoking romantic ideals to justify greater individual freedom they were countering the arguments of the traditionalists with equally powerful moral claims of their own. Hence their demands for personal (and especially artistic) licence, whilst advanced out of the highest possible motives, actually served to legitimate a greater freedom to produce and market previously taboo products.

This, then, would seem to be the principal means through which the introduction of novelty into society is justified and the objections of traditional moralists overcome, at least with regard to the new in its distinctly experiential or novel form, and it is a primarily romantic cultural tradition which is crucial to this process. In this sense ideas which have their origins in Romanticism serve to legitimate the introduction of novelty in the same way that ideas derived from the Enlightenment serve to legitimate the introduction of technical innovation. While in the latter case the crucial carriers of these beliefs are the scientists, technologists and associated 'scientific' professionals, in the former it is primarily those with 'artistic' pretensions.

We can in fact be rather more precise than this and conclude that it is bohemians (or the *déclassé* element as Blumberg calls them) who are the social group most crucial to this process. This is because those who pursue this unconventional and artistic way of life both espouse a romantic philosophy that sets the highest possible value on originality and creativity and also because they are continually seeking to overthrow the conventional morality upheld by the bourgeoisie. Thus in the mid-nineteenth century in Paris, the original bohemians were responsible for pioneering such outrageous innovations as red waistcoats and punch-bowls (Grana 1964), whilst their female American counterparts in the 1920s shocked the middle classes by smoking and wearing make-up (Parry 1960). These artistic and social experiments were undertaken both because of their intrinsic exotic appeal and because they were seen as symbolic rejections of bourgeois conventionality and timidity. This does not mean, of course, that bohemians sought to set the fashion for society. On the contrary: when, after a short time interval the bourgeoisie imitate their taste, they are forced to move on to embrace new forms of 'outrageous' conduct and dress. In this respect Simmel was correct in perceiving that, in so far as the innovatory group was motivated by a desire to distance itself from those they saw as the conforming majority, then the mechanisms of social imitation and differentiation would operate to push it into a policy of continually embracing the new. His mistake was to identify this group with the established social elite whilst failing to realize that its members would need to embrace a philosophy which extolled novelty. In fact, the bohemian's rejection of a bourgeois way of life is less a means of protecting social status than a way of gaining reassurance concerning a fundamentally spiritual superiority, whilst the best means of alleviating any doubts about their own 'genius' is to be subject to the condemnation of respectable society.

If Romanticism can be credited with serving the function of justifying the introduction of novelty into modern societies, with bohemians acting as the crucial innovatory group, we are still left with the problem of explaining the motives which impel ordinary, non-bohemian members of society to embrace novelty. If, once the initial shock and outrage at the conduct of the bohemians has worn off, their conduct and attire become more acceptable and the subject of widespread imitation via commercial exploitation, what is it that persuades ordinary members of society to abandon the familiar for these novel styles? As we have seen, emulation is hardly a convincing motive when the innovatory group lacks elite status, although there are, of course, reasons other than the enhancement of status for wishing to embody the ideals displayed by others. But then emulation, like imitation, is not an explanation of the specific conduct in question as almost all forms of social action, including the carrying forward of traditional conduct, proceeds on this basis. What is required is a theory which accounts for the specific features of the behaviour in question, which in this case is the desire for novelty.

A possible answer can be found by looking more closely at the motives which impel romantic bohemians to revel in the strange and exotic and recognizing that central among these is the pleasure to be gained from such experiences. For although it is clear that bohemians have a fierce idealistic commitment which underpins their way of life, this does not preclude, but rather embraces, a determined hedonism. However, when the respectable middle classes find themselves drawn to imitate and adopt bohemian innovations in behaviour and dress, it is the promise of pleasure and not the idealism which seems to attract them.

The answer to why the introduction of novelty should be so central to this process is to be found in self-illusory hedonism, a term which stands for a form of pleasure-seeking which focuses on imaginative stimuli and their necessarily covert enjoyment and which relies on emotion rather than direct sensation.[14] In other words, the stimulation which provides pleasure results from the emotional impact of imaginative scenarios conjured up by the individual, a practice which is perhaps best described as day-dreaming. In one sense it is obvious that the truly novel can only be comprehended by individuals through the use of their imagination, as their past experience cannot serve as a reliable guide. In order to desire the novel, however, such imaginative exercises must be accompanied by pleasure. This is why day-dreaming is crucial, since it tends to promote longing or a diffuse unsatisfied desire to experience 'something more' than life has provided to date. The enjoyment associated with imaginative pleasures is experienced as superior in quality (if not intensity) to that encountered in actuality, with the result that individuals become dissatisfied with everyday life and long to experience such perfected dreams in reality. Such an attitude creates a desire for novelty, since the familiar is already experienced as unsatisfactory whilst that which has not yet been experienced can be taken as embodying the realization of the longed-for dream. This kind of hedonism requires advanced psychic skills and is dependent on the development of literacy, privacy and the development of a modern conception of the self. It is also closely linked to the imaginative enjoyments offered by the modern mass media. Almost all adults in modern society day-dream several times a day whilst a high proportion of the content is narcissistic or involves idealized self-images (Singer 1966; Wagman 1967). Consequently it is to this hidden inner world that much advertising directs its message, encouraging consumers to believe that the novel products described may indeed serve to make their dreams come true. Since experience of the products is unlikely to match up to these expectations (being literally disillusioning), individuals return to their day-dreaming and thus create the necessary circumstances for the craving for novelty to be reinvigorated. Naturally enough, 'new' products then emerge to satisfy this continuing need. As can be seen, this is a cycle of day-dreaming, longing, desire for the new, consumption, disillusionment and renewed desire which is entirely inner-directed and does not depend on processes of imitation or emulation.

CONCLUSION

Social theorists have long observed that modern consumerism is dependent upon the existence of a desire for the new, especially with respect to the crucial institution of fashion. Yet their theories have generally failed to offer any satisfactory explanation of the nature of this desire or indeed of what precisely is to be understood by 'the new'. In addition, claims about the critical social group responsible for the introduction of novelty into society have been unconvincing. By distinguishing between different forms of 'newness' and showing the critical significance of novelty it is possible to show that bohemians, because of their espousal of a romantic philosophy, constitute the social group most likely to act as a channel for the new, whilst the formulation of a theory of self-illusory hedonism facilitates the development of an inner-directed theory of the desire for novelty on the part of ordinary consumers.

NOTES

1 This is a revised version of a paper presented at an ESRC/PICT Workshop on Domestic Consumption and Information Communication Technologies, Brunel University, May 1990.
2 For a critique of Veblen's theory of conspicuous consumption see Colin Campbell (1987: 49–57).
3 The origin of a new style is a different matter from its introduction into the fashion system. A variety of complex factors may determine the specific style of dress which is favoured by a given subcultural group; these are unlikely to be related, however, to the reasons why it is adopted by non-members and hence becomes a new fashion in society at large.
4 See, for example, Herskovits's (1960: 462f.) discussion of competitive yam growing among the Ponapaean in Micronesia.
5 It is not at all clear how far Simmel could be said to offer an explanation of fashion rather than a highly abstract description of the phenomenon. Not only is his terminology somewhat imprecise but he attempts to account for behaviour in terms of certain general 'impulses' or 'instincts' which combine in various proportions to produce the different outcomes. These differ for each social class and status group and even category of individual (like the dude), but Simmel does not explain how each group comes to be possessed of these distinctive impulses.
6 One of the central methodological problems raised by such a claim (and which applies to Bourdieu's theory of consumption of cultural goods as much as to the Veblen–Simmel model) is that the tendency to deduce the conscious purposes and motives of individuals from the observed consequences of their actions leads to confusion over how explicit intentions relate to the functional outcome of conduct. Thus, in the Veblen–Simmel model, for example, are we to assume that individuals desire the new because they perceive the need to maintain their social distance from putative imitators? Or are we to assume that they genuinely do desire the new and that the maintenance of social distance is a largely unintended and unrecognized outcome of their actions?
7 The very predominance of this pattern in modern society is also largely responsible for the associated countervailing tendency to prize 'antiques'. Whilst the opposite of the freshly made is the 'old' in the sense of the 'used' and 'worn', that which is 'old enough' to be identified with a world prior to modern mass production, whilst not showing excessive wear and tear, becomes valued because of its comparative rarity. In this respect there tends to be a bipolar distribution in the valuation of goods by age in modern societies, with one peak when the product is brand new, and another (once the good is no longer in production) represented by the oldest extant versions which are still in good condition.
8 See chapter 4 for a discussion of how technological innovation in the field of IT relates to the introduction of 'new' consumer products in this sense.
9 Of course, some cultural artefacts may be too novel and unfamiliar to be desired by anyone except the exceptional few. This idea lies behind the concept of the avant-garde.

10 This term is taken from Christopher Booker (1969).
11 There is, of course, no logical reason why technophiles should have a preference for the latest technology, and an enthusiasm for the artefacts of an earlier period could easily coexist with a dislike of contemporary products, in the manner, for example, in which steam-train enthusiasts frequently express such contempt for their modern diesel-powered or electric equivalents.
12 For material on gender differences in both enthusiasm for and use of IT see chapters 6 and 7.
13 For material on the counterculture see Frank Musgrove 1974, R. Mills 1973 and Kenneth Westhues 1972, whilst discussion of Romanticism and its connection with Bohemianism can be found in Campbell 1987: chapter 9.
14 For a fuller discussion of self-illusory hedonism and its relationship to modern consumerism see Campbell 1987: chapter 5.

REFERENCES

Blumberg, Paul (1974) 'The decline and fall of the status symbol: some thoughts on status in a post-industrial society', *Social Problems* 21: 480–98.
Booker, Christopher (1969) *The Neophiliacs: A Study of the Revolution in English Life in the Fifties and Sixties*, London: Fontana-Collins.
Bourdieu, Pierre (1984) *Distinction: A Social Critique of the Judgement of Taste*, London: Routledge & Kegan Paul.
Campbell, Colin (1987) *The Romantic Ethic and the Spirit of Modern Consumerism*, Oxford: Blackwell
Fallers, Lloyd A. (1954) 'Fashion: a note on the "trickle effect"', *Public Opinion Quarterly* 5 (18): 402–5.
Grana, Cesar (1964) *Bohemian versus Bourgeois: French Society and the Man of Letters in the Nineteenth Century*, New York: Basic Books.
Herskovits, Melville J. (1960) *Economic Anthropology: A Study in Comparative Economics*, New York: Knopf.
Lemire, Beverly (1988) 'Consumerism in preindustrial and early industrial England; the trade in secondhand clothes', *Journal of British Studies* 27: 480–98.
Lynes, Russell (1959) *The Tastemakers*, New York: Grosset and Dunlop.
McCracken, Grant (1988) *Culture and Consumption: New Approaches to the Symbolic Character of Consumer Goods*, Bloomington, Ind.: Indiana University Press.
Mills, R. (1973) *Young Outsiders: A Study of Alternative Communities*, London: Routledge & Kegan Paul.
Moorhouse, H.F. (1983) 'American automobiles and workers' dreams', *The Sociological Review* 31: 403–26.
Musgrove, Frank (1974) *Ecstasy and Holiness: Counterculture and the Open Society*, London: Methuen.
Parry, Albert (1960) *Garrets and Pretenders: A History of Bohemianism in America*, New York: Dover (first published in 1933).
Riesman, David and Roseborough, Howard (1965) 'Careers and consumer behaviour', in David Riesman *Abundance for What? And Other Essays*, New York: Doubleday Anchor Books, 107–30.
Simmel, Georg (1957) 'Fashion', *American Journal of Sociology* 62 (6): 541–9.
Singer, J. L. (1966) *Daydreaming*. New York: Random House.
Steiner, Robert L. and Weiss, Joseph (1951) 'Veblen revised in the light of counter-snobbery', *Journal of Aesthetics and Art Criticism* 9 (3): 263–8.

Veblen, Thorstein (1925) *The Theory of the Leisure Class: An Economic Study of Institutions*, London: George Allen & Unwin.
Wagman, Morton (1967) 'Sex differences in types of daydreams', *Journal of Personality and Social Psychology* 7 (3): 329–32.
Westhues, Kenneth (1972) *Society's Shadow: Studies in the Sociology of Counter-cultures*. Toronto: McGraw–Hill Ryerson.

Information and communication technologies in the home

Chapter 4

The shape of things to consume

Ian Miles, Alan Cawson and Leslie Haddon

JUST THE PLACE FOR A SNARK

'Just the place for a Snark!' the Bellman cried.
'Just the place for a Snark! I have said it twice
That alone should encourage the crew.
Just the place for a Snark! I have said it thrice:
What I tell you three times is true.'
    (Lewis Carroll, *The Hunting of the Snark*)

The Snark is a new consumer product; it stands to make the innovating firm who can 'capture it' a great deal of money. Consumer markets are large. Consumers are believed to be on the lookout for new household technologies: thus the home is just the sort of place in which a Snark might be found.

New consumer products are not called out of the air by consumer demands: they are the result of suppliers, in various industries, seeking to establish products that will capture a slice of household expenditures. Not all products succeed, even when the market had been well primed with media coverage and celebrity endorsements. And even those products which have been established in the market are frequently subject to continuing innovation, to make them more attractive to consumers *vis-à-vis* competitors for money – especially competition from products with similar functions. Suppliers are not able simply to will their products to be successes. There is feedback of a sort, from the consumer markets to suppliers, bluntly felt in the form of purchase decisions, but other channels can also be explored. Market research of various kinds can be used to assess current levels of satisfaction or discontent with products, and to test reactions to relatively minor changes in products. When rather more substantial innovations are involved, however, the scope of feedback from these sources is reduced: after all, sales of an unreleased product cannot be ascertained, and the reactions of potential consumers are unlikely to be based on intimate knowledge of the product. How do suppliers and innovators cope with the absence of conventional feedback mechanisms in such circumstances? What role does knowledge of consumption play in the generation of new products? This chapter describes some results of an investigation of the ways in which perceptions of consumption are generated and utilized in the creation of such innovations based on new Information Technology (IT).

Information Technology makes it possible to handle much greater quantities of data, much more rapidly, with cheaper, smaller and more robust equipment than previously. These points are well known, having received considerable coverage in popular books, magazines and TV programmes, and having been built upon extensively in science fiction books and films. Trends in the core technologies are also widely discussed, and extrapolations of performance into the future are frequently cited, in trade and professional publications (especially in electronics-based industries, but in many others too – for instance the construction and office press). Engineers, and a wider community of designers, managers and technical staff in many industries are familiar with these accounts of the underpinnings of the 'IT Revolution'. We have commonly encountered innovators who would think nothing of basing their projections of future projects on assumptions about such technological trajectories. Thus they take it for granted that chips many times more powerful than those commercially available today will be commonplace in a matter of a few years. Indeed, they would regard it as foolish not to, since their competitors are liable to be on the look-out for ways to exploit these new capabilities.

Change in the capabilities of core technologies is seen as allowing for new applications opportunities. Things that are currently ruled out for mass markets because of their high costs may become cheaper (for example, fax machines have plummeted in cost since the mid-1980s, so that people are now speculating about fax machines being purchased for the home by more than just the obvious target group of professional workers). Things that cannot yet be achieved can be assumed to be within grasp (for example, the compression and decompression of full-screen, full-motion video data, so that substantial amounts of TV-quality digital video can be put onto and retrieved from Compact Discs (CDs)). Consumer product innovations are being imagined and worked on in the light of such assumptions. These may range from minor improvements in familiar applications (e.g. somewhat smaller devices) through to major transformations of products (e.g. new combinations of devices, substantially new functions associated with devices), and to radically new products (with little in common with established products).

The question arises as to how innovators develop their notions of new consumer products. How do these organizations understand the consumption processes which their products are aimed at? How, if at all, does this knowledge enter into the shaping of the innovations? What sort of knowledge, from what sources, is being drawn upon?

Our study examined three specific sets of new products: new *multimedia* products, with the emphasis on compact disc-based systems (Interactive Compact Disc (CD-I), Interactive Digital Video (DVI), Commodore Dynamic Total Vision (CDTV), etc.); *home automation systems* ('smart houses', 'intelligent homes', 'domotique', etc., where proprietary systems, sold under a large number of brand names, so far offer only part of the functionality that is envisaged); and new *messaging systems* (fax, electronic mail, and interpersonal communications through systems like Prestel, etc.) This chapter also draws upon previous and ongoing interest in home computers, High Definition Television (HDTV), and videotex-based tele-services. These are cases where there are efforts to develop and introduce new products, based on IT, that are substantially different from existing domestic goods and services, that offer new capabilities and whose use implies new patterns of consumer activity – i.e. they are radical consumer innovations. Of these cases, HDTV, while technologically very innovative, might be seen as the least radical in terms of introducing a completely new item of equipment and involving new activities. Rather, it may substitute for the existing TV, with a bigger image of photographic quality. But the industrial lobby for HDTV suggests that it will be a radically different experience for consumers, bringing cinema-type impact into the living room; and used for many purposes alien to current TVs.

Innovators believe that there will be, in the near future, some sort of consumer multimedia, home automation, and electronic messaging systems, some sort of enhanced TV, as market successes. The time-scale is uncertain, the specific suppliers to win out may be drawn from a larger number of (international) competitors, and the particular features that will characterize the product remain contentious. The home is 'just the place for a Snark': the problem is to find it. Of course there are the sceptics who suggest that Snarks don't exist . . . and others who warn that innovators can be landed with expensive failures while others are succeeding in the same areas.

TAKE IT HOME BY ALL MEANS

'If your Snark be a Snark, that is right:
Take it home by all means – you may serve it with greens,
And it's handy for striking a light.
. . .
. . . beware of the day,
If your Snark be a Boojum! For then
You will softly and silently vanish away,
And never be met with again.'
(Lewis Carroll, *The Hunting of the Snark*)

Forecasts of improving performance of the core technologies used in IT products are often expressed in terms of widely used parameters – for instance, measures of information-processing capacity such as MIPS (millions of instructions per second), of the 'feature density' of chips, of the channel capacity of communications media, the megabytes of data that can be stored in memory devices, and so on. Trend graphs and accounts of technological trajectories are presented in quantitative terms using such parameters. But application opportunities are as much a matter of the functions to which devices are put, and the system of artefacts and social practices within which these functions are located, as a feature of the core technologies.

Trends in applications characteristics may be expressed via sectorial concepts, based on more or less economic classifications of activities – within the consumer product field these may include such broad categories as education, entertainment, home-based work, etc. For instance, Mulder (1991) argues that marketing studies agree that ISDN (Integrated Services Digital Network) services will first be used by large multisite firms, then by smaller and single-site companies, by home-based workers, and finally by consumers. The hopes of creating new applications of IT in consumer activities are manifested in ugly terms to suggest that hybrid products can somehow span familiar activities: thus 'edutainment', 'infomercials', and the like.

Another terminological strategy builds upon existing product labels. Thus innovations may be identified as 'extensions to' the television, the telephone, the kitchen appliance, and the like. Elaborate visions of how the device is liable to evolve are circulated among suppliers and sometimes to consumers. There may be a variety of reasons behind this. In 1990, for example, the Japanese firm Sharp was running advertisements in colour magazines featuring a colour flat-screen liquid crystal TV, not yet available for purchase but establishing the firm as a technological leader. On the other hand, Rediffusion's (1987) warning that 'in three years, TV as we know it will cease to exist' is using HDTV to persuade consumers to avoid buying 'obsolete' products and rent from Rediffusion instead. Other firms claim that their current offerings actually do represent the future of TV. Here the consumer is being encouraged to pursue the Snark – and warned that there may be Boojums about.

Other terms describing IT development are often imported from the computer domain. 'Miniaturization' describes not only the core technology of microelectronics, and the reduction in size of many products which apply IT. The move in computer environments to 'personal computing', with the term 'PC' coming to displace 'microcomputer' in most business discussions, signifies a shift in attention from physical size towards the image of the computer becoming accessible to the end-user. Accordingly, smaller and more portable computers are labelled 'laptop', 'notebook' and 'handheld', 'palmtop', or 'pocket' computers, reflecting the expected mode of use.

In the consumer field, 'personal' is mainly used to describe individual or portable products with goods often discriminated from their professional equivalents by the term 'home' as in 'home computer', 'home office' and, speculatively, 'home fax'. 'Micro-' labels are common in consumer products, not merely signifying diminishing size, but also in part signifying the incorporation of microelectronic components, in part cashing in on the breathless excitement of the 'microelectronics revolution'. (Home computers, widely known as 'micros' in the 1980s, are still referred to in this way by some enthusiasts; for those owning BBC micros a magazine called *The Micro User* continues to be published. But the office terminology, PC, for personal computer, has now become commonplace to describe the more work-oriented home machines.) Following other terminological trends in office and industrial applications, the adding of functions such as memories, and the ability to respond differentially to distinct inputs, is described as making devices or systems 'intelligent' or 'smart'. (A US promotional video for builders and suppliers illustrates the habitual and offensive antonym imported from the IT industry: 'if you're not building a smart house, you're building a dumb house.')

Other popular terms suggest complex design concepts: 'user-friendliness'; 'networks', 'multimedia' and 'hypermedia'; and perhaps most significantly, 'interactivity', called into play in 'interactive video', 'interactive TV', 'interactive compact discs', etc.

There is a process of innovation and diffusion not only of technological products, but also of concepts about these products. Considerable terminological transfer accompanies the technology transfer process from industrial to consumer markets. Such products as interactive video, electronic messaging, and 'smart buildings' are more familiar in industrial than in residential applications (with the possible exception of Minitel in France), which act as 'models' for domestic use of IT. The R&D laboratory may itself become an experimental site as researchers use themselves and their colleagues as 'models' of consumers.

Awareness of application potentials is often, in part, constructed from accounts of trajectories of technological change, and patterns of usage, in a range of industrial and professional applications. These non-consumer markets are often looked to as if they provide visions of the future of consumption. These sources of information are combined with other types of evidence to produce various types of imagery concerning applications potential and associated prospects for the evolution of consumption. Several of these types of imagery are circulated very widely in a 'continuous chatter' about the prospects for new products.

Developments in core technologies transform the perceived scope for product development. Awareness of technically viable products is constituted from knowledge of trends in this core, in the immediate class of applications under consideration, and in various application areas that are seen as being in certain respects analogous. This awareness is typically constructed in circumstances of intense social interchange.

FORKS AND HOPE

> They sought it with thimbles, they sought it with care;
> They pursued it with forks and hope;
> They threatened its life with a railway-share;
> They chased it with smiles and soap.
> (Lewis Carroll, *The Hunting of the Snark*)

Radically new products confront innovators with the problem of imaginatively constructing a market which does not yet exist. There are open questions as to what sort of people are going to use the new products, in what circumstances, and in what ways. There are considerable uncertainties about exactly where the 'Snark' may be located. In principle the uncertainties extend from very early stages in the innovation process – when people are talking about products that are decades away, that only exist on paper or as the roughest mock-ups (typically made of balsa wood) – right up to the actual launch to mass markets. Even in these later stages the nature of the product itself is liable to be rather unstable. The innovation literature asserts not merely that early versions of new products are rough-and-ready ones that are awaiting refinement, but that there is a 'design paradigm' that has to be established (see especially Teece 1986). The uncertainties surrounding radical innovations concern how people might use the potential product, and they involve questions concerning the nature and design of the products themselves. Scenarios of future product use are also scenarios of the product specification itself. Often we find that the 'scenarios' discussed by innovators are merely alternative product configurations, with some suggestions as to their timetabling and functionality, rather than the future histories beloved of social forecasters.

In the case of established products, the task of conceptualizing consumption is a conventional one – which is not to say that it is an easy one. Social scientists may well be critical of the validity of the evidence and expertise that are drawn upon (e.g. the offended tones of Tomlinson 1990), but familiar types of market research into consumer behaviour and attitudes, and imagery from everyday life and the media, can be inspected and interpreted. A 'commonsense' of received and standard theorizations of social structure and economic activity forms the typical undergirding of accounts of consumption.

The more familiar forms of market research tend to be reserved for the latter stages of new product development. As product details become more clearly specified and 'frozen', and as product launch dates approach, we are more likely to find trials taking place of new products. Such trials may involve demographically targeted groups of consumers, often among 'samples of convenience' who are close to hand such as the firm's own employees, or local residents. Full-scale trials appear to be more common for large technical systems such as the British, French and German videotex systems – where such trials do not seem to have informed the decision to go ahead with the product launch, which was made on more 'political' than market grounds. Only in the French instance were lessons from the trials incorporated into product redesign (Schneider *et al.* 1991). Such trials are, depending upon organizational and political context, a mixture of market research and technology assessment. Japanese firms pursue a rather different approach to trialling and assessment of market potentials, at least within Japan – or so we have been told by European managers and Japan-watchers – releasing early versions of new products at high prices into domestic markets. A large group of enthusiasts in new technology – what in the UK are sometimes called 'zappers' – provides market feedback on the potential demand for such a product, and the characteristics that should be designed into it.

It is widely believed by suppliers that conventional market research can be of little use as a source of insight concerning radically new products. But decisions still need to be made, that may end up committing substantial funds to product development and/or choosing between alternative products to devote efforts to. Determining the features of possible consumer markets, at early stages of product development, is thus a 'political' task. Not only does one's own company need to be persuaded of the viability of the proposed product: it is frequently necessary to build a wide 'constituency' behind the product (cf. Molina's (1989a: 1989b) discussion of sociotechnical constituencies, which has features in common with 'actor–network theory' and similar approaches to the sociology of technology; not to mention the mobilization of the crew by the Bellman in *The Hunting of the Snark*).

The members of such a constituency can include:
- Groups within one's own organization: senior management, company finance, company marketing departments. External sources of information on possible market developments and on the strategies of competing firms in the product space are often used to gain internal support.
- External sources of finance, be they government agencies, investors or organizations with whom joint ventures are envisaged. In the case of CD-I, HDTV and home automation, financial support from governmental and intergovernmental bodies (e.g. the European commission's ESPRIT programme) has been significant.
- Suppliers of complementary products: for instance, software suppliers for computers, programme-makers for audiovisual equipment, manufacturers of peripherals for network systems.
- Standards-setting bodies.

- Distributors and related groups such as installers, maintenance services, etc., who are 'warmcd-up' by means of items in the trade press, briefing sessions at trade conferences and so on well before product launch.
- Regulators and lawmakers, since legal or regulatory factors may inhibit diffusion of technologies. For instance, British Telecom was subjected to considerable criticism around the use of its chatline/talkabout service (which allowed several people to join a 'telephone party' – and which resulted in some adults paying huge bills for their children's calls, as well as some moral outrage as to the topics and purposes of conversations), and this is one of the factors deterring it from a renewed effort to promote multiway consumer messaging services.
- Organized social actors, such as consumer associations which are frequently cautious about the introduction of new technologies, especially where questions of individual privacy, or of new distribution of financial costs are involved.
- Consumers themselves may be provided with information about, and images of, products that are not yet available. Very rarely does such provision of images of products well before their release seem to be employed for consumer feedback. Such feedback may nevertheless be forthcoming (e.g. negative reactions have been apparent in letters to newspapers responding to some press coverage of home automation).

Images of future products and of future consumption patterns play a mobilizing role in the development of constituencies behind new consumer products.

Sometimes the functionality of the product is believed to be so evident that dilation upon patterns of use is unnecessary. Such restricted use of product images may well be the norm for many products which offer one discrete function, such as the portable electronic bibles, translators, pulse meters and chess games that are featured in kaleidoscopic profusion in the catalogues that are delivered with credit card statements.

Even at early stages of product development, there is considerable incentive to produce more articulated visions of consumption – albeit frequently of a highly rudimentary form. For designers themselves, this can be part of the process of selecting among alternative product specifications. For the wider constituency it can be critical, not only to building confidence in the potential creation of a market, but also to defining the envisaged market. For instance, whether a product such as CD-I is to be seen as a games-playing device, an educational device, an adjunct to the TV, or a super home computer can be important in winning the support of particular parts of the potential constituency. It may help raise funds from public organizations to have a device presented as being for serious applications, or as helping marginalized social groups; and likewise, the efforts of complementary producers to orient their efforts in particular directions might be influenced.

In the home automation field at least, 'interaction among producers was
. . . more influential in shaping evaluations of the feasibility of products
than more direct consumer feedback . . . the enthusiasts, including some
major firms, were successful at winning over the majority to consider
the plausibility of the innovation' (Cawson *et al.* 1989: 7). Here an
influential forum for exchanging views over an extended period had been
constituted – a NEDO Task Force. More common are the less intensive
encounters at conferences, trade association meetings, and sometimes
through standards-setting bodies and the like. A variety of media (trade
press, etc.) also circulate ideas about products and markets. The Home of
the Future consortium in the UK was initially organized by a consultancy
group (Applied Futures), who argue that value change drives social change,
and that we are witnessing a shift from subsistence to other-directed and
autonomous value groups. Different scenarios, based upon the degree of
dominance of each of the latter groups, were used for brainstorming and
more serious analysis of product concepts. The group is planning to exhibit
products aimed at the year 2000, in Milton Keynes in 1992.

A PERFECT AND ABSOLUTE BLANK?

'Other maps are such shapes, with their islands and capes!
But we've got our brave captain to thank'
(So the crew would protest) 'that he's brought us the best –
A perfect and absolute blank!'
                    (Lewis Carroll, *The Hunting of the Snark*)

Since, in general, consumer feedback is given little weight in early stages
of product development, the map of consumer opinion is a total and
absolute blank. But the Snark-hunters draw on other sources of information
concerning the market. A major source of inspiration is simply monitoring
what other suppliers are putting on the market, what turns out to be
successful or a failure, and what patterns of use appear to be associated
with new products. Thus firms routinely scan products which already offer
some of the functions associated with the envisaged product. In particular,
they will be interested in trying to locate points of weakness in these existing
products, such as rising costs or points where further functionality could be
added. To quote one of our interviewees: 'we know we have this technology
that can do this: now, where's the market for it? We look at the existing
product and ask where the market gaps are, and whether we can match
these to a technology.'

Trends in the use of products are covered less systematically, but some are
widely cited. During our study we were frequently pointed to the supposed
shift to more interactive use of media. Examples of this included, especially,
flicking between TV channels using a remote control (sometimes known

as 'zapping'), and using teletext systems enthusiastically (again usually using remote controllers). Such trends are seen as creating a body of consumers ready for more interactive modes of consumption. Suppliers accordingly design remote controls for products of many sorts (CD-I has a control handset modelled to that of a TV controller), and consider ways of facilitating – or living with – consumer zapping practices that may develop with new products.

Much of the knowledge of such trends in products and markets is derived from reading the technical and trade press, and from commissioning reports from consultants as to key developments.

Such sources also provide coverage on more quantitative trends in purchasing patterns and motivations. Diffusion curves of consumer products may be used to depict the early development of markets for an existing product; to show that a major new product can take off in a matter of a few years (as in the case of audio CD systems), so that there would be scope for rapid market expansion or to suggest that the market is waiting for the next exciting attraction.

Beyond the diffusion process, evidence may be accumulated as to social trends that might prompt more discontent with existing products, or make innovations more appealing. For example, greener attitudes might lead people away from the wasteful use of paper and towards electronic media. Broad trends in attitudes and values are studied by several consultants, whose views are reproduced in the media, and which are widely attended to. Common themes include versions of post-industrial theory (shift to higher needs, more interest in personal development, more environmental consciousness), postmodern theory (more fragmentation of demand, requirements for personalized products, divorce of image from initial attachments), and related themes such as the self-service economy or the information society.

Such data and arguments provide substantiation, of a sort, for views of the size of markets and speed of their development, for the product itself and for complementary products. They are also used to forecast patterns of usage in terms of, for instance, frequency of use, whether isolated or convivial, luxury or basic. And they may be used to support forecasts of the ways in which the product as an artefact is liable to be manipulated (the levels of interactivity and the sorts of interface desired, for example).

The media are used as a source of information on product and market trends, and of popularized versions of social scientific analyses. As well as simply relaying impressions about changing use of consumer products, media commentary often adds evaluations and perspectives from the journalist or from 'straw polls' that have been conducted, often warning about possible fears associated with new technologies, and complaints addressed to innovators.

Even more common is introspection as to desired products and functions and the innovator's direct experience of existing facilities. Such experience may well be shaped directly or indirectly by media coverage. Suppliers often tie the rationale for a particular type of product function to their own experiences, or to other people's experiences that have been communicated to them. For instance, one project leader for a major home automation project made a personal case for a more efficient home. It would be convenient to identify himself to the house upon entry, since it could then select his preferred environments, saving time in setting devices. It would be 'more intuitive' to have dimmer-type switches on remote control devices according to his own preferences. He would personally welcome lights and heating reducing as bedtime neared, and coming on (together with music) to wake him up.

Industry lore takes various forms. As well as circulation of personal experiences and vignettes like those discussed above, there is transmission of evidence from research and consultancy studies: 'I heard at a conference that . . . .' 'There's an American survey somewhere which shows that . . . .' Such sharing of information is part of the building of consensus about the interpretation of market trends, the strategies of competitors (especially the dreaded Japanese), and the viability of products. One variety of industry lore is views of different markets. For instance, home automation will, it is said, appeal in Japan because of the predilection for having one's hot tub turned on when one gets back from the office, not to mention a fear of embarrassment generated by having to turn away in person a hawker at the door. Another variety is stories of IT heroes and horrors: individuals may be keen to draw analogies between themselves and – or to distance themselves from – pioneering figures like Clive Sinclair, Chris Curry, Alan Sugar. Products and marketing strategies are frequently situated in terms of earlier experiences: 'This is not another Prestel' is a common statement, and reference is also made to the home computer boom-and-bust of the mid-1980s, the losers in the standards wars for video cassette recorders, and a number of other horror stories.

Presentations of mock-ups and prototypes are used in product exhibitions at trade shows and 'Ideal Home'-type exhibitions, from which feedback may be elicited. Demonstration sites have been long important for constructing visions of the home of the future, and there are currently several European 'smart house' sites. Video has also been used as a means of product presentation: in addition to the US Smart House video mentioned above, a tacky Japanese video of the fully wired home – with North American actors – was doing the rounds in the mid-1980s. Such presentations are often part of the constituency-building effort, and are intended to persuade potential partners of the feasibility of the product idea, or (as in the case of the Home of the Future being constructed in Milton Keynes) to provide firms with experience in working together. They can also be used as sources of feedback on product performance, where questions can be asked as to how attractive it is, what sort of price people would pay for it, what technical and other niggles there are. Such feedback on the basis of concrete visions, albeit from a limited number of atypical observers, is widely thought to be more revealing than asking hypothetical questions of conventional market research samples. In the words of an interviewee such feedback 'can establish whether you've got a product which is plainly laughable, and you may amend your offering fairly considerably . . . . It very rarely tells you that a product will be a success, at best it stops you making some obvious mistakes.'

Home automation does seem to have attracted a number of market research studies – in the UK and US at least these have been carried out on behalf of industrial consortia, which may indicate that they are more oriented to mobilizing potential collaborators than directly aiding product design, costing, and release strategies. In the US there have been surveys showing that a sizeable proportion of consumers would be willing to pay a target amount more for new homes in order to gain specific features (energy conservation, convenience, safety being the highest rated). But there have also been rather deeper focus group studies which reveal rather complex attitudes to 'smart house' ideas. The RMDP (1989) UK study for NEDO, *Automating the Home*, based on literature reviews and a series of focus group discussions, reported that 'attitudes to home automation are open and uncertain . . . home automation services appear the sensible next steps in domestic services, but this is countered by anxiety over invasion of privacy and other social changes' (p. 6). These complex ideas parallel uncertainty about the nature of the product: there is a variety of terminological labels with distinctive connotations: 'smart house', 'intelligent home', 'home bus', 'homenet', 'home automation', 'domotique', 'batimation', etc.

ALMOST TOO GOOD TO BE TRUE?

'It's a Snark!' was the sound that came first to their ears,
And seemed almost too good to be true.
Then followed a torrent of laughter and cheers
Then the ominous words 'It's a Boo –'
                    (Lewis Carroll, *The Hunting of the Snark*)

Evidence as to market development and the scope for new products may be used to help select among alternative product configurations. This selection task is not merely a process of rational choice between clearly defined product alternatives. When major aspects of the product have been clarified, and agreed upon, attention may turn to product details – such as a page-based or scrolling electronic mail system, a voice or text interface to a home appliance, a CD-I system packaged as part of a rack product or sold as a stand-alone. But frequently there are more fundamental questions to be addressed, whose open-endedness makes the creation of radically new products resemble the hunting of the Snark. It makes the process one where vision and exhortation play as critical a role as the purely technical aspects of design. And because of the very big stakes that can be associated with the answers to these questions, in terms of individual careers and corporate finances, and in terms of eventual market shares, the process resembles Snark-hunting in another respect. One may call a Boojum into being – and then one's hopes (and career prospects) may well softly and silently vanish away.

Open-ended questions can only remain open for so long. If the constituency is to act in a concerted fashion, there will be increasing requirements for clarity about the central features of the product. Innovation theorists talk of 'design paradigms', dominant accepted ideas of what the product looks like – how the controls work, what size and shape is typical, and so on (Teece 1986). Early in the product's life, there is typically competition between different types of design, and it is not clear which will come to dominate. In the consumer sphere, the conflict between different VCR standards in the early take-off of this new consumer product is a case in point. Prestel was a premature effort to set a design paradigm for new consumer telecommunications services (Thomas and Miles 1990).

Such a design paradigm is typically selected by market processes, out of a range of alternatives that consumers are confronted with. At an earlier stage, the market is a market of ideas rather than of concrete products, and the currency is not consumer expenditure, but the commitment of business resources. A paradigm is formed, or at least there is an effort to form a commonly accepted idea of what the product will be and what it will do. This may be more or less fuzzy. It may be debated explicitly, or left largely unexamined, when 'common sense' appears to dictate that there is no doubt, for instance, that a particular product is an audiovisual entertainment accessory, a home appliance, etc. But quite often the nature of the product is the focus of continuing uncertainty and even conflict: the term 'paradigm' hardly seems appropriate for such Snark-hunting.

This unstable state of affairs characterizes the products we have been focusing upon in our study, especially home automation. The scope for supplying new types of functionality through the development of new products based on IT, or the transfer of industrial-type products to consumer applications, was recognized. But the very general types of functionality that are made possible have to be related to the activities people carry out in everyday life, and have to be packaged together to form specific products with particular sets of functions and other design characteristics. Uncertainties as to the nature of the product – Is it a Snark? Where? Are we mistaking a Boojum for a Snark? – serve as pointers to uncertainties as to consumption styles.

Images of consumers and of consumption are integral to the debates about the nature of the product, its identification as a true Snark. There are relatively few cases where an image of consumption can be said to have directly inspired a line of product development – except where individuals have identified their own requirements in an everyday situation, or those of a special group (e.g. physically disabled people). More often, knowledge of technology, rather than of the market, is the source of product ideas. Early recognition of product development opportunities commonly inspires a search for market possibilities.

Despite the very limited use of formal market research, there is considerable interchange under way as to the processes underlying consumer behaviour, and the consequent development of markets. This 'continuous chatter' affects product design and release strategies, and is critical to the establishment of the sociotechnical constituencies which lie behind most major product innovations. The interchange extends well beyond the suppliers, and is actively used in attempts to bring about desirable outcomes. Most of us remain as spectators to these interchanges, if we are privileged to have access to them at all before the products themselves are released into the market. Without wishing to urge that everyone should get involved in Snark-hunting, it might well be worth considering how a wider range of social actors, with a wider range of objectives, might constructively join in this process, whose results are so intimately entangled with our everyday lives. It might even turn out to be the case that more social participation in the generation of new consumer technologies would lessen the risk of running into Boojums.

ACKNOWLEDGEMENTS

This paper is a product of a project entitled 'Delivering IT into the home', funded by the Economic and Social Research Council as part of the 'New Technology and the Firm' initiative. We gratefully acknowledge the support we have received for this project from the ESRC, and the various industrial managers who have given us time for interviews.

REFERENCES

Cawson A., Haddon, L. and Miles, I. (1989) 'Delivering IT into the home: interim report', University of Warwick workshop of DTI/ESRC project on New Technologies and the Firm, October 1989.
Freeman, C. and Soete, L. (eds) (1987) *Technology and Full Employment*, London: Pinter Publishers.
Gershuny, J. I. and Miles, I. (1983) *The New Service Economy*, London: Frances Pinter.
Klein, G. (1977) 'Discontent in American science fiction', *Science Fiction Studies* 4 (1): 3–13.

Miles, I. (1988) *Home Informatics*, London: Pinter Publishers.

Miles, I. *et al.* (1990) *Mapping and Measuring the Information Economy*, Boston Spa: British Library LIRR77.

Molina, A. (1989a) *The Social Basis of the Microelectronics Revolution*, Edinburgh: Edinburgh University Press.

——(1989b) 'Transputers and transputer-based parallel computers: sociotechnical constituencies and the build-up of British–European capabilities in IT', *Research Policy* 19: 308–33

Mulder, R. J. (1991) 'ISDN: the European perspective', *Communications International* June 1991: 54–62.

Schneider, V., Charon, J.-M., Miles, I., Thomas, G. and Vedel, T. (1991) 'The dynamics of videotex development in Britain, France and Germany: a cross-national comparison', *European Journal of Communication* 6(2): 187–212.

Teece, D. (1986) 'Profiting from technological innovation', *Research Policy* 15(6): 285–305.

Thomas, G. and Miles, I. (1990) *Telematics in Transition*, Harlow: Longmans.

Tomlinson, A. (1990) 'Consumer culture and the aura of the commodity' in A. Tomlinson (ed.) *Consumption, Identity and Style*, London: Routledge, 57–73.

Tucker, D. G. (1978) 'Electrical communications', in T. Williams (ed.) *A History of Technology*, Oxford: Clarendon Press, 1220–67.

Watson Brown, A. (1987) 'The campaign for high definition television', *Euro-Asia Business Review* 6(2): 3–11.

Williams, T. (ed.) (1978) *A History of Technology*, Oxford: Clarendon Press.

Wilson, G. B. L. (1978) 'Domestic appliances', in T. Williams (ed.) *A History of Technology*, Oxford: Clarendon Press, 1126–49.

Chapter 5

Explaining ICT consumption
The case of the home computer

Leslie Haddon

The main aim of this chapter is to illustrate the vital group processes in the consumption of the home computer which occur outside the home, but which have a clear bearing on the experience of this 'domestic' technology.

The first part of the chapter briefly outlines the main qualitative analyses of the consumption of the micro. The second part draws upon my research on home computers in Britain. Based mainly on interviews conducted within the microcomputer industry, this study documented the (unexpected) appearance of the home micro as a consumer electronic and its dramatic popularity during the early 1980s (Haddon 1988a).

Finally, the chapter explores how insights from different approaches to consumption may be related to each other and to the issues surrounding the home computer. The last section provides some examples of the questions which might be raised within family-oriented studies that would complement the empirical material on the role of the micro within wider social networks.

RESEARCH ON THE MICRO

In the early 1980s, Sherry Turkle examined the first years of microcomputer use in the US (Turkle 1984). For Turkle, the micro was only one of a family of technologies, including larger computers and devices such as games machines, which created enticing electronic worlds. These could be peculiarly evocative, prompting reflection upon consciousness, personality and the social world. Turkle aimed to chart this process at work among different social groups, noting how metaphors (e.g. the mind as a computer program) disseminate from technical cultures to wider audiences.

Although *The Second Self* contains various brief historical outlines, the bulk of the discussion deals with psychological processes, illustrated through individual case studies. The nature of the individual's encounter with computers is framed in relation to the user's developmental process, referring to theories of cognition and of the self. Such analyses of technology may have their uses in sensitizing us to the possible consumer experiences and readings of these artefacts as texts. However, Linn points out that this artefact text is credited with too much power, too great an influence, and that Turkle is perhaps overenthusiastic about its potential (Linn 1985; McNeil 1989). Linn points to (a) the fact that other texts (e.g. advertising 'hype') influence interpretations of the computer and (b) that the micro as text can be more polysemic, including being open to more negative interpretations.[1]

In fact, Turkle's account of the nature of the micro is based on, and illustrated by, people's (usually positive) description of their experience, and hence her book is also a study of actual 'consumption'. The main criticism here from both Linn and McNeil is the lack of context in which such readings of the artefact/text arise. Although Turkle makes some reference to the way in which a positive experience of the micro amongst some hobbyists arises from a wider sense of alienation at work and to Hacker culture, for the most part the social location and immediate circumstances of her case studies are only sketchily provided.

While it is desirable to study the specificity of different technological forms, the degree of uniqueness which has been claimed for the micro has also been questioned. For example, Turkle's discussion of the microcomputer's 'holding power' reflects the theme contained in a number of contemporary writings, such as Bolter's 'Grammatical Man'. These stress that the computer constitutes a qualitative leap in terms of the way it will affect our very way of thinking (Bolter 1984). This emphasis on the extraordinary nature of computers opens the way for the discourses on 'computer addiction'. In fact, it was these very concerns about the micro's unique addictive powers which sparked the work of Margaret Shotton on 'computer dependency' (Shotton 1989).[2] Also based on a psychological analysis, this research ultimately plays down claims about the exceptionality of the micro – for example, showing that people with an intense interest in computers usually had intense interests in other activities long before the micro entered their lives.

In contrast to these more psychologically oriented approaches, the recent doctoral thesis of Reva Shapiro provides an account which is firmly rooted in a symbolic interactionist/'social construction of reality' tradition (Shapiro 1988). Like Turkle, this study covers the early period of computer hobbyism in the US, but now the emphasis is on entering the *social world* of computing. That is to say, she examines the process of becoming a computer user, of learning the values, rules and perspectives of what comes close to being called a subculture.

David Skinner's current research includes work on computer clubs which notes that 'home' computing is really a much broader social activity. He also examines overarching IT discourses, and shows how these discourses were experienced by individuals and families, creating a fear of being 'left behind', and a sense of participating in social events by involvement in the computer boom.

More recent work (Haddon and Skinner 1991) has focused on the way in which the home computer was developed and marketed as an open-ended, multifunctional device. This research shows how producers and consumers constantly searched for and tried to construct the 'usefulness' of this mass market product after it had been developed and launched. This is not without precedent, although it may be more common to the new ICTs aimed at the home.[3]

Domestic consumption

Family life has been touched upon in a number of the above studies, as well as in my own research (Haddon 1990). But generally there has been little detail on the meaning added to cultural objects such as the micro specifically through family dynamics.

We are just starting to see more systematic documentation of the family context. The Mass Communications Research Centre's longitudinal study provides a more extensive time dimension following changes in family purchases and use over five years, and has already pointed to issues such as the policing of the micro's use (Murdock et al. 1986 and chapter 9). Jane Wheelock (chapter 6) charts the diverse patterns of use and perceptions of the 'family computer'. Meanwhile, the theoretical work at CRICT has helped to sensitize researchers to the various dimensions of family dynamics in which we can locate the home micro and other ICTs (Silverstone et al. 1989 and chapter 1).

In relation to accounts of the popularity of technologies and to gender issues, these studies are important for a number of reasons. First, family interaction provides an important context at the point of entry of the micro into the home. As we shall see below, studying wider social group interaction may help to explain the popularity of the micro in terms of generating interest in end-users. But acquisition is a process in own right, where the entry of the product into the home is mediated by others.

This is especially clear when buying 'for the family', or 'for the children', where parents are trying to make sense of what is best for their offspring and anticipate how the potential purchase will affect family life and its own image of itself. But even where adults, more often male, buy machines for themselves, my interviews have indicated that the considerable expense involved still had to be justified to others. It is possible to evaluate the micro in various ways, given undercurrents of concern about addiction and the disruption of family cohesion, and the view that the computer is just a toy of no serious use. These themes may all emerge in the negotiation which takes place in families before acquiring this technology.

Second, most of the studies discussed earlier referred to the construction of an individual's identity, either via the experience of interaction with the technology or membership of the wider social world of computing. A further dimension to be welcomed is provided by accounts of this process of identity formation in relation to families, both *vis-à-vis* other family members and in terms of the family's collective identity in relation to the outside world.

Third, family studies are central to our understanding of what exactly is involved in the process of accommodation and resistance to, and regulation of, domestic ICTs over time. This significance of this issue is already clearly signalled in the current research projects – e.g. in terms like the 'domestication' of technology (Silverstone *et al.* 1989; Hirsch 1989).

THE BROADER RELEVANCE OF CONSUMPTION STUDIES

Several observations can already be made about the broader relevance of current research on the micro. First, some writers have already noted some of the implications for the innovation research literature. For example, Murdock points out that

> in contradistinction to the diffusion of innovations model which presents the home computer as a simple technological commodity with a stable identity defined by its applications, we view it as a site of struggle between contending discourses, notably those emanating from government and the education system on the one hand and from the entertainment industry on the other. This struggle is regularly played out in conflicts between parents and children as to the proper use of the machine.
>
> (Murdock 1989: 233)

Shapiro also devotes some time to challenging the limited role given to users in the innovation process, even by those writers who acknowledge the role of users in 're-inventing' or modifying industry products (Shapiro 1988: 21–6). She argues that in the early days of the micro, extremely active hobbyists influenced the directions in which the micro developed and negotiated the very form of the innovation. Indeed, the degree of grassroots influence in the early formation of this industry and family of products was considerable compared to, say, compact disc innovations.

Even when the micro became more established, it is arguable that user influence extended beyond that of merely altering given products and finding new uses – both activities being captured in notions such as that of 'social innovation' (Gershuny 1983). For example, the fact that users concentrated on games rather than employing the micro for multiple applications partially changed the micro's very identity from multipurpose computer to games machine. To use the language of cultural studies, users, albeit with the collaboration of some parts of the computer industry, 'appropriated' the micro, helping to transform the meaning of the artefact.

A second area where the various forms of research on consumption have a broader relevance is where they can feed into frameworks for thinking about future innovation. This might mean using the material to add to and go beyond current debates on what counts as 'socially useful production' (Collective Design/Projects 1985). But equally, the analyses from these studies could inform the thinking of current producers of IT products. There is ample scope for enriching producers' understanding of such areas as family dynamics (see chapter 4).[4]

One example of a more specific theme where production and consumption studies can work together is in relation to 'moral panics'. This notion, derived from the sociology of deviance (Cohen 1973), refers to the process by which public concerns and anxieties are constructed around a particular phenomenon such as mods and rockers, or the effects of horror comics (Barker 1984). Such panics can equally well emerge in relation to technologies, for example worries about computer addiction and about the antisocialness of becoming isolated through microcomputer use.

A few years ago the computer industry was up in arms about the BBC's QED programme which dramatized this concern once more. A flurry of letters to the trade press discussed the need to combat this image.[5] Given that similar fears have emerged in the past in relation to television destroying the quality of family life, we need to develop an analysis of how producers try to manage the way in which their products become symbolic of and embroiled in concerns about trends in everyday life.

CONSUMPTION OUTSIDE THE FAMILY

Previous research on television has provided perhaps the most important route into studying ICTs in the home (Murdock *et al.* 1985; Silverstone *et al.* 1989). One key argument raised about television in particular is that it is important to understand the family context of consumption because television is an essentially domestic medium (Morley and Silverstone 1990: 32) – we watch TV primarily in our homes. But we have to be careful of using this starting point when considering other ICTs. TV is arguably exceptional in this respect. It is not a work tool on the whole, except perhaps for on-site training. And although educational TV programmes are viewed in schools, TV's role in this context is modest. However, other ICTs, such as the micro, have a role outside the home which may play an important part in the overall experience of these products, and one which may be less visible from family-based studies.

BOYS AND HOME COMPUTERS[6]

My first focus is on the 'computer talk' which constitutes part of boys' interest in micros – a facet which is not picked up by statistical measures of usage in the home. While this talk may not occur so routinely within the family as discussion of TV programmes, it has been incorporated into the somewhat amorphous boys' 'culture' of school and leisure. This section outlines the nature of computer and games talk and charts how, for a time, discussion of computers achieved a particularly high level as a form of participation in the micro boom.

The development of computer talk

The 1983 surge in computer sales was complemented by the way in which home computers became an object of classroom discourse. This itself contributed to my interviewees' desire for a machine and their sense that micros were 'getting popular'. One boy, who had been one of the few with an earlier interest in computing, described the change:

> Well, in my class there was me and my friend in the second year [1982] we were the only ones who used to use the computers initially. And when there was the form period, occasionally we'd talk about something on the computers. After Christmas in the third year [1983] I remember a lot of people talking about computers and in the fourth year we took a survey and found that about 20 per cent of the people [in the class] had a computer. [It provided] more better conversation in a way. I mean, at that point, when the computer was pretty popular about a third of the class talked about them. That's quite a lot compared to what most people usually talk about.

That interest in, and the topicality of, computing appears to have peaked a few years ago. By the time of my interviews and observation in 1985–6 there was far less talk, which itself helped create the feeling that the boom had died down. But while computing's profile may now be lower, its presence, especially within the relationships of a smaller core group of enthusiasts, has by no means faded away. Like the sales of hard- and software, computer talk had become established and routinized – it forms a normal part of male classroom discourse.

The nature of computer talk

This talk often amounted to a perpetual, joking rivalry over computers, where boys derided the features of the micros which belonged to their peers: some said that they always 'insulted each others' computers'. But apart from this competitive banter, there were topics which were regularly discussed. The most common themes related to games, but also included evaluation of hardware and non-game software products, the next purchases to which the boys aspired, the cost of products and where to buy them. They traded news about who might be buying or selling equipment or software, or tales of how they had acquired products cheaply. In other words, computer talk was similar to talk about toys, music or other products of interest among these peers.

The interests of some of the boys extended beyond this level. By keeping in touch with general developments in computing as well as being aware of its history, certain boys were identified as self-styled 'experts'. One interviewee, for example, even tried to re-enact the earlier role of the 'hacker' in small ways, such as programming in solitude in the evening. In this endeavour, the current equivalent of the challenge of breaking into telecommunications systems had become breaking into protected software. Such 'experts' promoted computer activities in the school. In much the same manner as some adult computer buffs, these more enthusiastic boys lamented the fact that much of classroom discussion was limited to games.

Games talk could also be competitive, emphasizing superior skills in terms of the scores which had been achieved, the relative size of the boys' game collections, and who possessed the latest games. As games had become a 'cultural industry' like the music one, newsworthy talk also covered items such as which games had recently been released and were in vogue, what features they possessed, and what might be in the pipeline from the arcades or as a conversion from another machine format.

A second set of knowledges mobilized in games talk related to actual playing, and was very much the type of discussion material which might be expected at the arcade. This involved tips, such as how to get onto the next screen – that is to say, the next part of the game. Peers supplied information concerning the problems which would be encountered in that next stage. There was advice concerning what players needed to acquire or achieve early on in preparation for these later sections of a game. The boys traded suggestions about tactics, and offered warnings about the manoeuvres which one could expect from electronic opponents, about the hazards which could 'hurt' the side which the player controls and about aspects which were harmless.

Murdock refers to the way in which the customizability of products has a bearing on the scope for creativity and self-presentation (Murdock 1989: 234). While the need for a level of competence in computing provided some constraints, the very programmability of the micro provides ample potential for self-expression. Most boys attempted programming at some stage, and it remained a continuing activity for a few. Furthermore, home brew products could be shown to and discussed with peers, especially the games and games' special effects. Any such initiatives were judged by a different standard from the slicker commercial products and these amateur productions offered a wider audience the chance to participate in suggesting ideas for improvements. Many of my interviewees were proud of their contemporaries' achievements and their own involvement in that process, referring back to the days when there were reports of schoolboy success stories through games-writing.[7]

Commercial products could also be amenable to intervention, which differentiated computer games from their precursor; video games. This option sparked off a certain amount of trade in information about the 'Pokes' which enabled users to affect the program's structure – for example, allowing players to work through all the stages of the game in order to see what would be encountered later and to explore all the areas in which the action took place.

Computer talk reflected the boys' experience of a new cultural industry which was geared to promoting interest in the latest releases. Various producers clearly had some bearing upon the ways in which boys experienced home computing and games playing, as exemplified by the fact that so much of classroom talk was based on reading computer magazines. But ultimately this male youth also made creative use of the raw material – they made their own culture through the way they used 'talk' about micros and about games, through developing and changing products and even more clearly through the activities to which we now turn.

Computer-related activities

The organized exchange of software within school was definitely something which software producers had not intended, and against which they have campaigned with limited success since the early 1980s. The particular form which has caught most attention is the copying of software, made easier by twin-deck cassette recorders. But this should not obscure the fact that boys have also borrowed each other's purchased software for fixed amounts of time ever since games first appeared. In effect, male youth (and many adults) are purchasing software collectively, whereas the industry would much prefer that they did so individually.

One form of visible computer 'event' in the class is the occasional games-playing competition, although for the more basic machines such occasions are inhibited by the problem of arranging access to TVs. School clubs could sometimes be turned into games-playing locales, depending on the extent to which they were policed by the teacher in charge. But since school on the whole provided only limited opportunities for playing games in company, meeting in the homes of friends or visiting relatives was a key way to try out the latest games.

In addition to the venues of home and school, playing and exchanging games took place in a range of public locations. For a minority of boys, the computer clubs which had arisen during both the late 1970s and early 1980s constituted one such meeting place. These boys' demand for a 'space' for games purposes sometimes transformed the clubs from their original function of developing computing skills. Hence, some of the old guard in these clubs soon expressed disappointment that the motivation of the boys was not the same as that of earlier hobbyists. Occasionally the 'serious' clique abandoned the site altogether, switching to meeting at a member's house.

By visiting arcades, the boys could keep in touch with the latest games available on the coin-ops. The home computer equivalents of these venues were the shops and department stores which sold micros and software. While some shop managers seemed to regard playing as beneficial to sales, others have already started to adopt tactics to prevent the conversion of their areas into alternative arcades – for example, by periodically turning off the computers. The same mixed feelings apply to the computer shows, where a number of exhibitors have expressed ambiguity about the extent to which the hordes of players monopolizing machines may be deterring other, less game-orientated, custom.

All these public settings provided an opportunity to try out products, to play in collective settings and to make contact with those who shared an interest, which could mean a chance to exchange games and other software. By appropriating space the boys, albeit perhaps relatively few boys, were very visible to the various producers of hardware, software and magazines. It is little wonder that those in the industry could easily assume that micros and games-playing were a totally male domain, and show surprise that girls demonstrated any interest at all. The actual situation is far more complex.

Girls and home computers

One reason for detailing the nature of boys' collective interest is because this dimension did not appear to exist for girls. Available statistics show that, although the involvement is less than that of boys, girls actually use computers – mainly for playing games. Like the boys, the girls are not simply isolated users. For instance, they play with other family members and with friends who visit their homes. However, that was mainly the limit of their interest. The currency which computer talk and games play had among some young male peers appeared to be absent in the case of girls, which means that the experience of the activity was very different.

For example, these machines were not an object of girls' classroom talk in the same way as for the boys. This is not to say that the girls are never willing to discuss games or micros and when they did so the verbal exchanges included joking about each other's competences and tastes. But other topics of conversation had greater primacy:

People talk about what they did last night . . . video, you know. They don't talk about computers. Not unless, like, in computer studies. Yes, that's when you talk about computers. Like, sometimes we're on a computer doing our work and we say, 'Oh yeah, I've got this game', you know . . . and all this. But apart from that we don't really talk about computers. Like someone might say to you out of the blue, 'Have you got one?'. You say, 'Yeah', and that's it.

One corollary was that there was little in the way of computer-related activities such as exchanging software – that was left to brothers. Some girls had watched TV programmes such as 'Microlive', keyed in program listings or read library books for clues about programming. A few of the girls had even read computer magazines from time to time, especially if bought by someone else in the house. More usually, the girls relied on brothers to inform them about the latest game. Mainly, the girls 'just played' the games which were available – a range of choice which was not, on the whole, within their control. Hence, the majority of games played were of the fast, arcade-style action games reflecting the general predominance of this genre.

Few girls visited or played games in the various public sites which were geared to microcomputers – and when they did, attendance was not so much with peers as with family. For instance, one girl described how she regularly played in the arcades with her brothers when the family spent weekend holidays in Kent. This resembles the pattern whereby the few wives who ever came to computer clubs had done so with husbands as part of 'family leisure'.

History of games consumption

This outline of boys' collective consumption in the 1980s needs lastly to be placed within a broader history. The home computer provides an instance where we have to be sensitive to the interrelationship of different technological forms, specifically of computing and of interactive games. These were to provide the micro with a dual heritage and identity.

The problem with a number of accounts of the home micro is that they trace its genealogy solely through the history of the computer industry (e.g. Freiberger and Swaine 1984). At least Turkle provides a brief discussion of games history before noting the similarity of games to other computer programs. But that account does not include a thorough review of the history of games consumption.[8] I believe that the general neglect of games leads to a blinkered view of the micro, since only part of the identity of the home computer actually derives from computing. In part the home micro, at least in Britain, is a games machine, and so bears the legacy of this lineage.

As documented more fully elsewhere, interactive games are intimately connected to the precursors of current microcomputers (Haddon 1988c). Games became established, especially as demonstration programs, within the computing field and were thus familiar to and reproduced by the early hobbyists in the late 1970s and early 1980s. In addition, games as a whole, as well as particular game genres, were transferred from the computers to the arcade in the form of coin-operation games machines. As a replacement for pinball, the new games machines were incorporated into the existing social activities of amusement parks, and many of the other public sites where coin-op machines were found. These were mainly young male preserves. Although games were played individually, the activity remained grounded within the social life of the peer group. The talk, rules and rituals of game play carried over both into the experience of home-based video games machines and later home computers.

Some commentators would have us believe that games became popular by default, since there were no better applications for the type of machine which appeared in Britain. This is not so. Games and games-playing have a history in their own right, and it is only by appreciating the development of consumption outside the home and family settings that we can make sense of both the popularity of micros and the different forms of male and female interest in them.

THE INTERFACE WITH FAMILY STUDIES

Like the other research in this area, the dimensions outlined here provide only a partial account of the experience of the micro, and indeed of the gender issues with which I am concerned. For example, we might also want to ask how the specific identity of the micro as a frontier technology was constructed through its own design and related texts, and how this affected male and female response to the product (Haddon 1990). And in relation to the family, it would be important to investigate how parents, as gatekeepers over the entry of the micro into the home, saw the product differently in relation to the futures of their male and female children.

But this research on the experience of the micro outside the domestic sphere does cast some light on 'home' computing. I now turn to the questions one might ask within family-based research which connect with some of the points raised in the above account of boys' collective interest in these computer products.

In her critique of the work of Paul Willis, McRobbie noted that his stress on the stance and self-image of male youth in street life, in school and on the shopfloor neglects the question of how this integrates with the lads' experiences within the home (McRobbie 1980: 41). It is possible to raise the equivalent point here for at least some of the boys who develop the role of experts in relation to their peers (or teachers), or who even see themselves as 'hackers'. How is this role supported or hindered within the family? After all, buying magazines, software, hardware, books, travelling to computer fairs, etc. may require financial support, or parents might be expected to comment on how their children spend their own savings. Then there are questions concerning parental support, or lack of it, in terms of the encouragement of expertise, as well as the forms of regulation of time and space already noted above – especially if this hobby is deemed to be excessive or detrimental to other commitments.

We also have to consider family influence on what happens outside the home: in this case, on how computing or games-playing are viewed by parents as leisure activities. In contrast to the fears about isolation through computing, one mother interviewed in my pilot study talked about the positive way in which her shy son had made new contacts through this interest. So we have questions concerning the extent to which parents see the activities described above as constructive, or at least harmless, leisure, in comparison to other behaviour such as simply 'hanging around' with other boys. In this sense, is computing a relatively 'healthy' interest?

One extension of this theme concerns parental control over the movement of their children outside the home. There was certainly some concern expressed in the US during the 1970s about the corrupting influence of the arcades (Haddon 1988c). But what about the respectability of computer shows, shops and clubs which some of the boys visited? Certainly my own discussions with mothers and boys support Shotton's view that shops, at least, made ideal places for women to leave their children (and sometimes husbands) while on shopping expeditions (Shotton 1989: 2).

A final example of the type of question we might ask from family-based studies concerns parental reactions to the copying of software. When the copying of audio, video and written material is both easy and widespread, including in educational circles and the workplace (Chesterman and Lipman 1988), under what circumstances do parents see such computer copying as trivial and sanction it, and when does it raise parental concerns about children's perception of legality?

CONCLUSION

Family-oriented research on consumption is necessary, increasing our understanding of certain key issues. For example, it can highlight the negotiation surrounding the very entrance of new technologies into the home. Such research can indicate the relation of domestic consumption and identity, e.g. how perceptions of technological competences are built up through family interaction. These are significant dimensions of consumption which cannot so adequately be handled by research focusing on individuals on group processes outside the family.

The various approaches to the consumption of ICTs, including this focus on the domestic experience, have a broader relevance for other bodies of research. In particular, they show that 'adoption' and 'use', indeed, the nature of the product, is far more complex than is often portrayed in the innovation literature. Chapter 4 examines producer conceptualizations of family consumption which could, in future research, be contrasted with the material from studies of actual domestic consumption. Certainly, there is scope for the latter material to inform the whole innovation process.

The case of the home computer, however, indicates some of the types of limitations of family-based studies, showing how complementary research is required. The popularity, patterns of usage, the meaning and the gendered nature of the home computer arise in large part from processes outside the home. So-called 'home computing' cannot be viewed as an activity based solely in the home.

NOTES

1 However, even in this earlier work, Turkle makes a distinction between two experiences of the micro: those of 'hard' and 'soft' users. This forms a basis for discussing gender differences in usage. In her later work, Turkle starts to take into account the wider context beyond the machine, noting the masculine connotations that become attached to the technology by virtue of certain patterns of male usage – i.e. hacker culture (Turkle 1988).

2 All these claims are worthy of further deconstruction into their component strands. For example, some claim that the seductiveness of the micro lies in its 'interactive' quality. But now that computers are embedded in many products, we might in a few years' time see these concerns transferred to technologies such as CD-I, which we are currently examining at Sussex (cited in chapter 4).

3 The products now being examined in the Sussex project are also somewhat multifunctional and open-ended, with producers partly waiting to see what specific applications will prove popular.

4 Given the widespread acknowledgement of the wider capitalist structures in which ICT products emerge and are consumed, it may be controversial to enquire about the extent to which critical analysts should engage in some form of a dialogue with firms producing ICTs. For example, there are problems with simply acting as an intelligence gatherer for industry and then potentially losing control over the way those insights are interpreted and utilized. According to one scenario, academic participation in production might be providing just another means for capital to manipulate consumers. This is an issue for researchers such as my colleagues and myself who are already involved in such a dialogue and more debate would be welcomed.

5 BBC's 'QED' series showed the programme 'My Best Friend's a Computer' on 17 January 1990. Letters of indignation appeared in *Computer Trade Weekly* on 29 January, 19 and 26 February, culminating in the article by J. Minson (1990), 'You've never addict so good', *Computer Trade Weekly*, 5 March.

6 The following account is mainly based on observations in a computer club, separate interviews with boys from both that club and others, and interviews with a small sample of girls from a a neighbouring school. The age range was from 11 to 16. This material was supplemented from other sources, e.g. observations in shops, discussions with retailers and mothers and interviews with members of computer clubs.

7 In a number of respects, the domestic technology most resembling the micro

of the 1980s was the radio when it first appeared earlier this century. The particular parallel relating to this account is the press stories telling of the route to fame achieved by some amateur radio enthusiasts and how this affected the hobbyists' romantic perception of their activities (Douglas 1986).

8 The early PREST work on attitudes to new technologies, and the Mass Communications section of that report also refer to the importance of games history (Murdock *et al*. 1985).

REFERENCES

Barker, M. (1984) *A Haunt of Fears: The Strange History of the British Horror Comics Campaign*, London: Pluto Press.

Bolter, D. (1984) *Turing's Man: Western Culture in the Computer Age*, London: Duckworth.

Chesterman, J. and Lipman, A. (1988) *The Electronic Pirates: DIY Crime of the Century*, London: Comedia/Routledge.

Cohen, S. (1973) *Folk Devils and Moral Panics*, London: Paladin.

Collective Design/Projects (1985) *'Very Nice Work If You Can Get It': The Socially Useful Production Debate*, Nottingham: Spokesman.

Douglas, S. (1986) 'Amateur operators and American broadcasting: shaping the future of radio', in J. Corn (ed.) *Imagining Tomorrow: History, Technology, and the American Future*, Cambridge, Mass.: MIT Press.

Freiberger, P. and Swaine, M. (1984) *Fire in the Valley: The Making of the Personal Computer*, Berkeley: Osborne/McGraw-Hill.

Gershuny, J. (1983) *Social Innovation and the Division of Labour*, Oxford: Oxford University Press.

Griffin, C. (1985) *Typical Girls: Young Women from School to the Job Market*, London: Routledge & Kegan Paul.

Haddon, L. (1988a) 'The roots and early history of the UK home computer market: origins of the masculine micro', Ph. D. thesis, Imperial College, University of London.

——(1988b) 'The home computer: the making of a consumer electronic', *Science as Culture* 2: 7–51.

——(1988c) 'Electronic and computer games: the history of an interactive medium', *Screen* 29 (2): 52–73.

——(1990) 'Researching gender and home computers', paper given at the workshop on Technology and Everyday Life: Trajectories and Transformations, University of Trondheim, Trondheim, Norway, May.

Haddon, L. and Skinner, D. (1991) 'The enigma of the micro: lessons from the British home computer boom', *Social Science Computer Review* 9 (3): 435–49.

Hirsch, E. (1989) 'Households, technology and the domestication process: some relationships between family culture and ICT', paper from the PICT workshop on Culture and the Study of ICT, Centre for Research on Organisations, Management and Technical Change, University of Manchester.

Linn, P. (1985) 'Microcomputers in education: living and dead labour', in T. Solomonides and L. Levidow (eds) *Compulsive Technology: Computers as Culture*, London: Free Association Books.

McNeil, M. (1989) 'Turing's men, cyborgs and wise women: information technology, gender and culture', paper given at the PICT Gender and IT workshop, Eastbourne, 30–31 May.

McRobbie, A. (1980) 'Settling accounts with subcultures: a feminist critique', *Screen Education* 34: 37–49.

Morley, D. and Silverstone, R. (1990) 'Domestic communication: technologies and meanings', in *Media, Culture and Society* 12: 31–55.

Murdock, G. (1989) 'Critical inquiry and audience activity', in B. Deruin, L. Grossberg, B. O'Ceefe and E. Wartella (eds) *Rethinking Communication*, vol. 2, London: Sage.

Murdock, G., Hartmann, P. and Grey, P. (1985) 'Everyday innovations', in *Public Acceptance of New Technologies*, vol. 2: *Appendices I–V*, Manchester: PREST, University of Manchester.

——(1986) 'Home truths', *Times Higher Educational Supplement*, 7 March.

Shapiro, R. (1988) 'Analytical portraits of home computer users: the negotiation of innovation', Ph. D. thesis, University of California.

Shotton, M. (1989) *Computer Addiction? A Study of Computer Dependency*, London: Taylor & Francis.

Silverstone, R., Morley, D., Dahlberg, A. and Livingstone, S. (1989) 'Families, technologies and consumption: the household and information and communication technologies', CRICT Discussion Paper, Brunel University.

Turkle, S. (1984) *The Second Self: Computers and the Human Spirit*, London: Granada.

——(1988) 'Computational reticence: why women fear the intimate machine', in C. Kramarae (ed.) *Technology and Women's Voices: Keeping in Touch*, London: Routledge & Kegan Paul.

Chapter 6

Personal computers, gender and an institutional model of the household

Jane Wheelock

There are two sides to the process whereby families adopt personal computers. Computer usage diffuses between the household and outside state and market institutions. It also spreads between family members within the household. The focus of this chapter is on gender and generational differences in the process of the adoption of personal computers arising from a pilot study of thirty-nine families in a peripheral region of the national economy. The study was undertaken in Washington New Town in the north-east of England during 1989.[1] The domestication of personal computer technology is considered in the light of an Institutionalist theory of value. The study of the process by which judgements about values are made in the context of the dynamic process of technological accumulation is seen as fundamental.

The analysis of the interrelationships within and between families (in the informal or complementary economy) and between families and the formal economy is undertaken using a model of the domestic economy developed from an empirical study of household work strategies in a post-industrial economy (Wheelock 1990a). The study, then, is concerned with the extent to which families' personal distribution systems coincide with the distribution systems of market and state institutions in perpetuating gender differences in access to computers.

Interest in the regional dimension of the information revolution is justified in terms of several aspects of the disparities between north and south. Large-scale unemployment for extended and even indefinite periods, and the consequent enforced leisure, make the north-east an important focus for studying the social and cultural aspects of drastic economic restructuring, and provide a case study for what a leisure society might really mean. Available data underline the particular crisis of the north-east in relation to unemployment, but in addition there has been a dramatic shift in the structure of employment itself. A pattern of full-time male employment has increasingly been replaced by one of part-time and female employment, and the Wearside local economy can be seen as a particularly marked example of the movement towards 'post-Fordist' flexibility in the labour market. If we turn to information and communications resources within the household, the relatively sparse data available indicate that ownership of three key items, telephones, personal computers and video recorders, is more widely spread in the south than in the north, providing further evidence of disparities.

Washington is part of the Wearside Travel to Work Area, and though the new town's growth (including the location of the Nissan car plant) has done something to offset the long-term decline in the traditional local industries of coal, shipbuilding and engineering, the Wearside economy remains dependent on a limited range of industries. Unemployment rates on Wearside have continued at up to twice the national average since 1971, and also well above the rates for the northern region.

The thirty-nine families interviewed had an average of 2.3 children living at home, with the majority (nineteen families in all) having two children. Thirty-five families contained secondary school-aged children, but three families had only adult children. Nine of the thirty-nine families had only boys in them and nine had only girls. The vast majority of both men and women left full-time education at school-leaving age, but four of the husbands went on to obtain degrees, while three of the wives completed teacher-training courses. The expected gender discrepancies arose in that, whilst only eight men had no qualifications at all, eighteen of the women had none. In terms of employment status, two husbands were no longer in the labour market and two were unemployed, one long term. Nine of the wives were currently not in the labour market, with one wife as a full-time student. As one would expect, whilst all the men in employment were working full-time, of the twenty-nine women working in the labour market, eighteen were part-time.

AN INSTITUTIONAL MODEL OF THE HOUSEHOLD

The model I propose to use was developed as an outcome of a study of household work strategies in the context of the type of economic restructuring that has taken place in the northern and Wearside economies. It is a model which places primary emphasis on the production role of the household. Given that much of the research into technology and the household has made use of purely consumption approaches, the aim is to bring a new perspective to bear on the empirical evidence available.

The household is a productive economic institution, which, like the firm, produces goods and services with a tangible economic value and employs labour and capital. The difference is that 'The producer produces *for* the household; the consumer produces *within* the household' (Burns 1977: 61). This contrast between producer and consumer indicates how the household is excluded from the ideology of the market, for the household acquires only such goods, and provides only such services, as it deems necessary.

To take account of total economic activity, the formal sector can be contrasted with the complementary economy, which in turn can be subdivided into two sectors: the irregular economy and the social economy. The social economy itself consists of two subsectors, many of whose tasks may be undertaken in either the household sector or in the voluntary sector (see Fig. 1). Broadly speaking, the division between the formal and the complementary economy follows the line between measured and unmeasured economic activity. Just as the formal economy has two sectors – one private and marketed, the other a non-marketed state sector – so too does the complementary economy. These are the marketed irregular sector and the non-marketed social economy.

The output of the social economy is not sold on the market, and its labour is unpaid. The institutions of the social economy are self-generated informal ones, which operate independently of regular economic institutions, and can be characterized as personalized institutional forms. There are essentially two sorts of institutional relations in the social economy: intra-household relations and inter-household ones. In the latter case work is unpaid, but it is undertaken between households. It is here that the computer networks of teenage boys can be located, for example.

I have contrasted the formal economy with the complementary economy because the latter plays precisely that role: it complements the formal economy. The complementary sector is neither parasitic nor residual, and it operates in the interstices of formal institutions, not as an alternative society but as a complementary economic activity to the formal. So, for example, while the state and the private sector within the formal economy may have taken on some aspects of the production and reproduction of labour power (such as education, training, pension provision and health), the household sector still retains much of its responsibility here. This is of considerable relevance when we consider the role of personal computers in the family. I shall specifically be examining the role that home computers play in producing and reproducing labour power.

The household, as the unit of reproduction, must apply its working activities to earning and to supplying directly goods and services through self-consumption. Household work strategies require the individuals who make up this unit to negotiate and decide a balance between work for income and for self-consumption. These decisions will, however, be made in the light of the social and gender recompositions brought about by the process of international economic restructuring. Yet the labour process within the household also involves the adoption of a personalized lifestyle. Indeed, one of the hallmarks of the social economy is that it allows the development of a personal lifestyle, based on home-centred values, which may be at variance with economic rationality (Wheelock 1990c). It has, indeed, been remarked that an important feature of home computers as consumer durables is their 'self-referential' character. In contrast, the

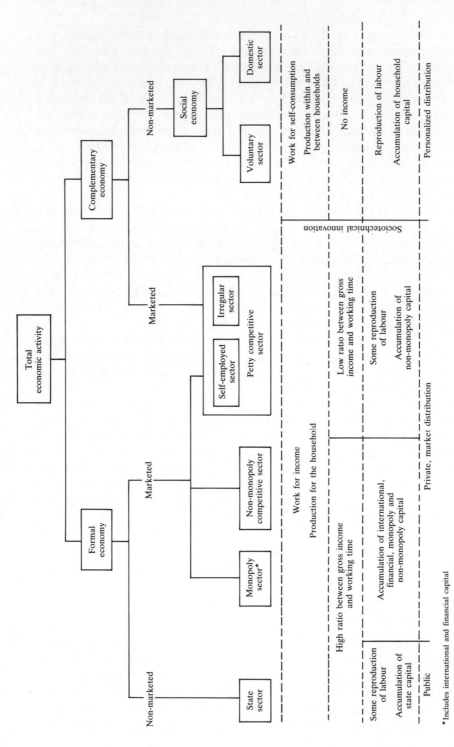

Figure 1 Selected characteristics of economic sectors

*Includes international and financial capital

marketed sectors of the economy satisfy private, rather than personal, needs, needs which are directly circumscribed by market-based values. To what extent do computers, in providing for entertainment needs, answer to private needs too?

Gershuny (1978; 1983) puts forward a theory of sociotechnical innovation which provides a framework for linking the domestic sector to the formal economy. He points out that the connection between needs and economic demand is not a direct one, but rather mediated by technology. A sociotechnical innovation is one where the means by which a need is satisfied changes, so that households' demand for commodities change too. There are new modes of provision for particular needs; and instead of catching the bus to work, people buy cars which they drive themselves. Home computers also provide an example of a sociotechnical innovation, but with the problem that the need that is being met is not fully clear, despite the importance of its entertainment function.

Sociotechnical innovations like the private motor car, television, video recorders, washing machines, freezers, microwave ovens and PCs have a two-fold effect. First, the new modes of provision for particular needs affect the structure of the economy through final demand, while second, they influence the division between paid and unpaid time and thus household activity patterns. Gershuny's theory suggests not merely an interrelation between the household sector and the formal economy, but that the domestic sector may well be a causal factor for economic development. Such a shift to the domestic provision of services also has important gender implications, of which Gershuny is aware, although he does not develop them. Some of these implications with respect to home computers as a sociotechnical innovation will be developed in this chapter.

THE DIFFUSION PROCESS BETWEEN FAMILIES AND OUTSIDE INSTITUTIONS

PCs as consumer durables

The last section has already suggested that the purchase of consumer durables comprises an important aspect of the relation between the formal and the complementary economy, and that the domestic sector thereby accumulates substantial amounts of household capital. The sample families were untypical both in the lower than expected proportion who owned their own houses, and a higher than expected range of consumer durables.[2] It is perhaps surprising that ten families have had two PCs, three have had three and one family has had as many as eleven. Indeed, six families had either two or three home computers currently working in their households. It could be said that in identifying households which have PCs, one is finding families who tend to purchase consumer durables generally and brown goods in particular, regardless of other measures of socioeconomic status.

Further aspects of the purchase of home computers as consumer durables were that the vast majority of PCs purchased were at the cheapest end of the market. The Sinclair Spectrum 48k machine was by far the most popular, both as a first purchase, and amongst all types bought by families. It is also interesting to note the date when a family's first PC was acquired. Whilst the boom in home computers has been seen as over by the mid 1980s, 23 per cent of the sample families purchased their PCs in 1985 and a further 36 per cent in 1986 and 1987.[3]

Families purchased a perhaps surprising amount of additional hardware and peripherals. Almost half the families had bought an extra television, with two of these buying two extra ones. Forty-six per cent of families had bought extra cassette players, with six families buying multiple tape recorders. It is also interesting that thirty-four families had set aside special places for their PCs, with twenty-four PCs to be found in bedrooms, especially children's bedrooms.

These basic features of domestic investment in relation to personal computers can be considered in the light of Gershuny's concept of a sociotechnical innovation. So far, we can best view home computers as a new mode of provision for entertainment needs. Two important issues for individual families then arise: How far can expenditure on the new hardware (and software) be afforded, and how does the new type of brown good affect the pattern of leisure provision within families in competition with the old? Such issues are also of importance for the macroeconomy in terms of their implications for overall levels of demand for new and older forms of consumer durables, and their implications for private sector borrowing.

An evident feature of the sample families is that purchase of one or more home computers has also been a stimulus to further purchase of more traditional brown goods, such as TVs and tape recorders. On the one hand this must provide reassurance for world manufacturers of apparently competing entertainment hardware, yet on the other it raises real questions of affordability and debt for less well-off households. There was indeed evidence of financial constraints operating in a number of the Washington households, and these may be a factor behind the sample families being relatively late purchasers of PCs.

Unlike the study undertaken in the early 1980s by Murdock, Hartmann and Gray, my own sample of computer users was relatively unconstrained by other household members wanting to watch television at the same time as the computer was being used, due on the one hand to multiple ownership of televisions and on the other to PCs frequently being set up in rooms which were not the main living room. Patterns of leisure activity did not appear to relate to the negotiated needs of the whole family, and in particular could be divided between the desires of adults and those of children.

Prior experience of computers

Ownership and use of home computers are considered of importance for outside institutions in a way that other domestic technologies are not. It is to this more unusual aspect of the PC as a sociotechnological innovation that I now turn. With respect to the experience of computers that individual members had before the family purchased a PC, gender differences between husbands and wives are very apparent, in that twice as many wives (26) as husbands (13) had no prior experience at all.

Children's prior experience of computers at school did not show the same gender differentiation as their parents' generation. Murdock *et al.* (1986) have suggested the importance of networks in making use of personal computers. It is interesting that in the Washington sample the generational pattern is reversed when it comes to prior experience at relatives' or friends' houses: there is no gender difference between husbands and wives here, but a large difference between sons (15) and daughters (5).

Taking on an educational role

Let me now turn to the role that personal computers are perceived to play with regard to the education and training of children. Whilst this is usually seen as the responsibility of the state or of the employer, families – and perhaps particularly middle-class families – have always played their part in producing and reproducing labour. It is, however, important to keep in mind that home computers may not actually provide what families expect of them in this respect. In part this ties in with the arguments of Turkle (1984), who develops the idea that it is the meaning of the computer rather than what it does that is significant.

Commentators have, of course, already pointed out that home computers are often purchased with the idea in parents' minds that access to a computer at home will enhance educational and job prospects for their children. Indeed, Leslie Haddon (1988) analyses how important it has been for British manufacturers to emphasize the educational aspects of PCs in their advertising campaigns. Interestingly, amongst the Washington sample, it was not only parents who anticipated improved prospects for their children, but also children who saw prospects for themselves.

Almost half of the parents remarked on the possibility that a home computer could improve either the educational or the employment prospects of their children. For many this was couched in fairly general terms. For example, Mr Taylor, a process worker, saw the potential in terms of the future employment prospects for his 15-year-old twin sons, where computer competence would be required, and purchased an Amstrad CPC 464 in 1986.[4] Mrs Jarvis, a single parent and part-time cleaner, saw a future in IT for her 14-year-old son in particular, and indeed he hopes to join the

RAF and work in communications, having already sent for the necessary application papers a year ago. Mrs Ellis, a part-time cashier whose husband is an assembly worker, sees no relevance to her life of their 48K Spectrum, other than increasing the opportunities for her daughter (11) and son (9) in a world where 'new technology is everywhere'. Mr Young, a telephone engineer, was more specific: he saw their PC as developing the typing skills of himself and his two daughters aged 10 and 11, providing an interesting gender contradiction, especially considering that there is also a 13-year-old son in the family. Other parents feel that a home computer will make their children 'feel comfortable' with PCs at school.

In a number of cases such general hopes seem to have been justified in terms of what children have actually achieved, although the link between parental hopes and the effect on children is not necessarily a direct one, especially since the vast majority of children had some contact with computers at school. Mr and Mrs Reed, a gas engineer and housewife respectively, bought a 48K Sinclair Spectrum in 1986 for their daughters, now aged 16, 13 and 6. The biggest impact of the computer has been their surprise and pleasure in their youngest daughter's apparently natural aptitude for the machine.

It is also interesting that, in a quarter of the families, children are explicit about the prospects that they see for themselves in acquiring computer competence at various levels, although it is noticeable that only two daughters are involved, in respect of office and keybord skills alone. When we turn to sons there is far more variety. For example, one 19-year-old son sees the importance of business-related aspects of the use of computers. The 16-year-old son of a single parent whose mother used to be a part-time barmaid is currently hoping to train and work on computers, and will shortly be starting a YTS scheme involving computers. Other sons, who anticipate going into careers as varied as banking, the police and the RAF, all see computer knowledge as important.

PCs and the entrepreneurial culture

I have just been examining the perceived and actual roles that PCs play in the complementary economy with regard to education and training of the future workforce. In the Washington sample I also found a number of parents who considered that their home computer would develop their own skills and employment potential. I want now to turn to the role that the complementary economy plays in the social reproduction processes of capitalism through the development of adult human capital, whether for employment or self-employment. To what extent has the entrepreneurial culture penetrated the household in the form of perceptions that home computers can develop parental occupational skills?

There were sixteen households in all where the importance of PCs for parental aspirations was mentioned, sometimes with respect to both partners. Since their hopes for themselves are often rather more concrete than those for their children, it is easier to identify whether they have been fulfilled. A grouping of parents can be attempted on this basis. First, there are those who have some rather general perceptions of the relevance and usefulness of a familiarity with computers for employment or self-employment. For example, Mrs Webster, who is at present a full-time factory hand, was the guiding force behind the family purchase of a home computer. Although her husband has some experience of computers at work, it is she who shows considerable interest in their home computer. Mrs Webster has the idea that in the longer run, if she develops some familiarity and skills with the computer, there may be opportunities for her to move over to the white-collar side at work.

A further three husbands have some hopes of self-employment in the future, and see an ability to use a personal computer as a relevant and important skill. One is currently an educational psychologist. Another, Mr Hardy, is a manager in the motor trade, a third is a crane driver.

At the same time there are other adults whose perceptions have not been fulfilled. Mr and Mrs Edwards, who work as production manager and office administrator respectively, are both aware of the neccessity of some computing knowledge in relation to their work. However, both husband and wife have many commitments, including community and sports activities, and find that their time is limited.

A further group have specific requirements of their home computers, and their skills are still being developed. Mr and Mrs Shaw are an interesting example. He is a civil servant and local councillor, whilst she is a part-time doctor's receptionist. They have an Amstrad 464 purchased on advice from a computer-knowledgeable friend, with the intention of filing and indexing Mr Shaw's local councillor correspondence. He is disappointed at his own lack of time and inclination, or prioritizing of work load, to accommodate harnessing the capacity of the PC. It is Mrs Shaw who organizes and assists with their children's computing time, and she now feels less apprehensive about the fact that the surgery's filing system may be computerized. Mr Shaw now hopes to learn in tandem with his daughters.

A final group of adults actually use their home computers for work or self-employment purposes. As might be expected, this group fits the stereotype of the professional doing keyboard work at home. Mr Kirkham, a physics department laboratory technician, built his first home computer himself in 1977, and has had eleven machines at home at various stages since then. He uses one of the three machines he now has every night, often preparing work for the next day. Finally, Mr Jones, who is a technical manager, has a sideline in breeding and selling British butterflies all over the country. He has purchased a second Sinclair Spectrum specifically for word processing associated with this hobby and self-employment activity. Indeed, he has some thoughts of making this into a full-scale business, and sees the PC as important in this respect.

PCs and the social economy

The final aspect of the interrelation between households and outside institutions that I wish to consider briefly is that of households with one another in respect of home computers. As other commentators have pointed out, the most noticeable aspect of the social economy and PCs is the gender-specific networks that are established between boys, especially teenagers. The Washington sample was no exception here. True, a small proportion of husbands and wives socialize using computer games, but only one daughter played with friends from outside the home rather than with other family members.

Otherwise, it was only boys who had networks of friends with whom they played, exchanged games and socialized through computers. Many also belonged to computer clubs, some helped their friends with computer problems. However, if there was more than one son in a family, it was often the case that only one was an enthusiast. Whilst some sons lost interest as they grew older, others maintained their enthusiasm. One unemployed 19-year-old is utterly absorbed in the whole process and practice of using the Sinclair Spectrum that his parents own, yet has no thought of taking a course in computing.

In other words, with respect to boys, home computers do not promote a more privatized environment, as Rothchild (1983) suggests, but rather encourage more socializing by them. Indeed, figures from the Washington sample indicate that, for sixteen sons, their PC has increased social interaction, whilst it has done the same for only seven daughters, four husbands and three wives. It has also reduced TV viewing time for twenty sons, and for twelve daughters, though it has also increased viewing for three daughters. The PC does, however, increase time watching IT programmes, again with a degree of gender differentiation. Thus, although there was more socializing, there is a shift in its locus to the domestic environment, and the presence of a computer often increased time spent at home, particularly for boys, and albeit on a seasonal basis.

DIFFUSION WITHIN THE HOUSEHOLD

According to Jonathan Gershuny's definition, a sociotechnical innovation occurs when the means by which a need is satisfied changes. What is perhaps unique about home computers is the fluidity of the need that is being met by them. As Haddon (1988: 28) points out in a historical study which begins by focusing on hobbyists, the 'self-referential' nature of PCs is crucial here: 'You bought the machine for itself, to explore it, rather than for what it could do.' In highlighting the links between the household and other institutions in the diffusion of computer knowledge, the last section largely focused on perceived and actual ways in which PCs answer to families' desires to supplement the education and training provided by the formal economy. Such self-improvement fits in well with the entrepreneurial culture. As we turn to the diffusion process within the household, the more widely accepted aspect of home computers, as a new mode of provision for leisure needs, comes to the fore. Yet leisure and educational needs are not contradictory, for many leisure pursuits can be regarded as having an educational element.

In considering the process of adoption and diffusion of a new consumer electronic within the household, we are concerned first with the development of a personalized lifestyle. The family and its members go through a process of self-correcting value judgements against a background of the technological change embodied in the availability of home computers on the consumer goods market. Second, a personalized system of distribution for the sociotechnical innovation will develop within the household. As Judy Wajcman (1989) suggests, brown goods represent the technology of leisure, and one would thus expect to find gender divisions in their development, ownership and use. Let me now examine these two interrelated processes of changes in lifestyle and in the system of distribution in the study families.

For whom was the first computer mainly bought at the time of purchase? In the largest number of cases (16) it was bought for the children of the family. It is, however, interesting that in a further eight cases the computer was purchased for sons, even though there were also daughters in the family. In contrast, only one machine was bought for a daughter where there were also sons. In seven cases the computer was for the whole family. Whilst three machines were bought for husbands only, there were other PCs for use by the rest of the family.

Who was actually the main user of the PC once it was bought? Again, children are the largest category, followed closely by the whole family as main user. Noticeably more sons (6) than daughters (1) are the main users. More husbands (seven in all) play with their children than do wives (only one), and this fits in with evidence that, whilst fathers take a part in child care, it is often in the form of a special occasion. In this case fathers are using a glamorous and expensive tool, a consumer electronic that is frequently perceived as male gendered.

What about changing usage by individual family members? On purchase, daily usage was highest amongst sons, and higher than daughters, as well as higher amongst husbands than wives. Daily usage has, since purchase, declined amongst all family members. However, usage three to five days a week has increased amongst boys and girls, but particularly so for the former, whilst that for parents has declined. There has been a very marked increase amongst adults not using the machine at all, and fifteen wives did not use it at all even on purchase.

There are again interesting gender and generational features in how family members actually learn to use their home computers. Eleven wives have not learned to use the computer at all, whilst only two husbands have not, one of whom works away from the north-east. Of the thirty-two husbands who have learned, only seven were not self-taught compared with fourteen of the wives. Where did wives learn, then? Nine learned from their husbands, nine from their sons, and three from their daughters. In contrast, none of the husbands learned from their wives, though there was a similar dependence on children, where eight learned from sons, three from daughters.

The younger generation learned through networks of friends and relatives, especially the sons, twenty-seven of whom learned from this source, although twelve daughters were also involved here. In the older generation, too, networks are more important for husbands than for wives. This provides a further indication of the importance of the social economy in the diffusion of computer knowledge. Some children also learned from their parents; as might be expected, more fathers (9) than mothers (3) did the teaching, though in three families it was a joint parental effort. There were also eight families in which children taught each other.

Let me now turn to some contrasting cases in order to highlight possible factors and mechanisms which might give rise to change in the gender stereotypes which have been found in the adoption process of home computers by families in both the older and younger generations. It must of course be remembered that families will already incorporate gender-differentiated practices. For example, although a lack of willingness to undertake domestic work by their husbands will encourage women to limit their work in the paid economy (see Yeandle 1984), a large minority of wives in the sample were working part-time but some were full-time housewives, thus facilitating a traditional division of labour in the household. Four of the men were not working, and it is interesting that in these cases only one wife was also not in employment, enabling a non-traditional division of labour in three families (see Wheelock 1990a).[5] However, the material possibility of flexibility in gender roles is far from the only factor determining a shift in roles, and ideology and traditional views must also be kept in mind (Wheelock 1990c).

Among the older generation, it is possible to compare interested husbands with interested wives, as well as comparing those who are not interested. Lack of time is a constraint for both husbands and wives, though husbands seem more likely to mention the limitations imposed by paid work. For example, although Mr Walker bought a Dragon with his own business in mind, when that failed, he found that his work as a carpet salesman took up too much time for him to use the machine. His wife has no time either, because they have a 9-month-old baby as well as two children of secondary school age and she has a part-time job too. In addition, many wives are simply not interested in the PC, expressing sentiments such as 'It's a glorified toy' or that 'It doesn't relate to my lifestyle'. In contrast, Mr Potts, a lorry driver, finds that his hobbyist activities in CB radio and PCs 'make life worth while'.

With regard to the family computer, as in other spheres relating to the domestic, the wife may act as facilitator, or even as a manager of the home environment. Gender-segregated leisure may be an accepted facet of the different roles of men and women. Mr Pollard, who has been unemployed for ten weeks, has become almost a fanatic. He is currently working on his family tree, and hopes to store, catalogue and file it on the computer. He has recently made contact with computer buffs, meeting them regularly to exchange information. His wife (a part-time home help) has noticed how her life has been affected by the PC in that Mr Pollard now shares his time less with the rest of the family, including herself. However, despite her own lack of interest, Mrs Pollard is grateful that her husband has an interest during his unemployment.

Whilst Mrs Hardy, who has had some experience of computers at work, is not intimidated by their PC, she has no time to play on it, with two children and a full-time job, nor can she see a relevant use for the machine. It is, however, she who is expected to order software from the PC magazine, and organize maintenance or repairs. There is, then, some contradiction in the fact that, although wives are generally less interested in the home computer, and use it less than their husbands, their traditional production role in the household means that they may nevertheless take on a teaching and managing role with the new piece of technology.

It has already been shown that both wives and husbands may either hope to, or actually, use their PC for work or training-related purposes. It is, however, probably true that men use the machines more intensively both for work and for leisure, something that must be linked with the traditional gender segregation of work roles in our society. There were certainly no female hobbyists like Mr Potts or Mr Kirkham. However, there were a few wives who really enjoyed leisure use of the family machine.

It is now time to turn to the activities of children. In the majority of families where there are both sons and daughters, a gender-segregated pattern of PC usage is common. It is nevertheless important to note that in eight families, sons and daughters seem both to make considerable use of the computer. In some cases, this may be due to parental encouragement. In another household, the computer has recently been moved from the 13-year-old son's room to the 11-year-old daughter's, so that 'trouble occurs' when the son wants to use it and the daughter, for whatever reason, denies him access. Location may be a factor promoting more equal usage in this family.

Generalizations about the more common occurrence of gender-segregated practices between children in a small pilot study are fraught with difficulty, for different types of family structure and different ages of children may be as important as differences between girls and boys. Nevertheless, it is noticeable from the Washington sample that many girls seem to have opted out of using the family computer to a greater or lesser extent, and that this is often on the basis of gender-related perceptions of relevant skills. Thus, in the Peel family, Mr Peel and his 13-year-old son were initially the prime users of their Commodore +4, and although the 15-year-old daughter was slightly interested, this was mostly in typing skills. She now has a typewriter and uses the PC only very occasionally. The 16-year-old daughter in the Carr family initially thought their 48K Sinclair Spectrum might be useful for office skills and future work, but she is now more interested in hairdressing.

In other cases, daughters are squeezed out of using the computer by their brothers, sometimes aided by their parents. The 14-year-old son in the Carr family is now the main user of the PC, along with his father, with whom there is some conflict over the machine. He helps his younger sisters, aged 8 and 4, with the PC, but this is when he allows them to use it. In the Potts family, Mrs Potts and her 11-year-old daughter go to dancing classes together as a response to her hobbyist husband. Nor are the daughter's interests encouraged since she is without a TV, and so is unable to use the PC whenever she wishes. She has to wait until her 14-year-old brother will allow her to borrow his, and, as he is fairly interested himself, this does not happen often.

If we contrast interested sons with interested daughters, we immediately find a huge difference in numbers. In some half a dozen families there were daughters who were positively interested in the home computer, while there were eighteen families with boys who were positively interested. Sons, as we have already seen, are often involved in computer networks, whilst none of the daughters appeared to be. A proportion of sons is labelled as 'computer addicts' or as being 'glued to the screen', whilst none of the daughters calls forth this kind of comment. Sons may well perceive employment spin-offs from computer competence; daughters often seem to abandon such thoughts.

From those families where girls are interested, there would appear to be four possible facilitating factors: the encouragement of parents, or of the school, the fact that brothers have lost interest in the PC, or the absence of sons in the family. We have already seen examples of these factors at work in some of the families considered. Perhaps a particularly significant factor is that there are nine families where young children (aged 6 or under) are using the family computer, and of these, seven are girls. They may be helped by older brothers, by parents, or they may have learnt in nursery, but early introduction to computers would seem to be useful in counterbalancing gender differentiation in usage and access within the family.

CONCLUSIONS

The institutional model of the household that has been used here provides insights into the interactions between the personal distribution system operating within families and the distribution systems of market and state. The traditional division of labour found in the formal economy is reflected in the older generation, where male parents have more prior experience of computers than their wives. Amongst their children, the state distribution system has, through the schools, overcome gender differences in prior experience. However, when we look at how computer knowledge is acquired and transmitted via the social economy, a much more contradictory process seems to be at work. Use of networks of friends and relatives shows no gender differentiation in the older generation, yet a very strong bias towards boys in the younger generation. This also increases boys' socializing, and shifts its locus towards the home; traditionally both are features of girls' experience.

Two other mechanisms provide links between the domestic and the formal economies. First, the household purchases consumer durables from the market, where the computer is a new mode of provision for entertainment needs. There was some evidence that the Washington households which owned PCs tended to purchase more brown goods than other measures of their socioeconomic status might imply. The development of any change in personal lifestyle for family members depends on the system of distribution operating within the household. In both learning about and using PCs, there were marked generational and gender characteristics, with a strong bias both towards children and towards males.

Second, households see their PCs as a production as well as a consumption good, albeit in an often rather generalized way. In contributing to the production and reproduction of labour, computers are seen as making for the kind of self-improvement so beloved of our enterprise culture. Again, we find both gender and generational features – parents have hopes that access to a computer at home will assist their children both at school and when they move into the labour market, but amongst the children themselves we find that boys have far clearer goals in this respect than girls. This of course reflects the reality of the division of parental work between the formal and complementary economies, where wives tend to work shorter hours in paid employment.

The process by which judgements about values with regard to personal computers are made is thus part of a complex interaction between formal and complementary economic institutions. The outcome is in part a reproduction of traditional gender and generational distribution patterns in the two sectors, in part a modification of them.

NOTES

1 The sample of families interviewed was not a representative one, being intended as a pilot study of families with children who also owned PCs. A cluster method was used to supplement contacts found through local comprehensive schools. I should like to thank Cath Bell for doing the interviewing.
2 These factors may of course be related to each other. Further details are available in Wheelock (1990b).
3 It is, however, possible that earlier purchasers in Washington were no longer using their machines and so were unlikely to come forward for interview. Cultural lag might also be part of the explanation.
4 The names of respondents have been changed to preserve anonymity.
5 In contrast with my own work on Wearside, Morris (1985) finds little evidence of changes in the domestic division of labour in the context of redundancy in South Wales.

REFERENCES

Burns, S. (1977) *The Household Economy*, Boston: Beacon Press.
Gershuny, J. (1978) *After Industrial Society*, London: Macmillan.
——(1983) *Social Innovation and the Division of Labour*, Oxford: Oxford University Press.
Haddon, L (1988) 'The home computer: the making of a consumer electronic', *Science as Culture* 2: 7–51.
Mingione, E. (1985) 'Social reproduction of the surplus labour force', in N. Redclift and E. Mingione (eds) *Beyond Employment: Gender, Household and Subsistence*, Oxford: Blackwell, 14–54.
Morris, L. (1985) 'Renegotiation of the domestic division of labour in the context of redundancy', in B. Roberts, R. Finnegan and D. Gallie (eds) *New Approaches to Economic Life*, Manchester: Manchester University Press, 400–16.
Murdock, C., Hartmann, P. and Grey, P. (1986) 'Home truths', *Times Higher Education Supplement*, 7 March.
Redclift, N. and Mingione, E. (eds) (1985) *Beyond Employment: Gender, Household and Subsistence*, Oxford: Blackwell.
Rothchild, J. (1983) 'Technology, housework and Women's Liberation: a theoretical analysis', in J. Rothchild (ed.) *Machina Ex Dea*, New York: Pergamon Press, 79–93.
Turkle, S. (1984) *The Second Self: Computers and the Human Spirit*, London: Granada.
Wajcman, J. (1989) 'Domestic technologies', paper presented at Gender and IT workshop, Cambridge University, May.
Wheelock, J. (1990a) *Husbands at Home: The Domestic Economy in a Post-industrial Society*, London: Routledge.
——(1990b) 'Personal computers, gender and an institutional model of the household', paper presented at ESRC/PICT workshop, Brunel University, May.
——(1990c) 'Families, self-respect and the irrelevance of "rational economic man" in a postindustrial society', *Journal of Behavioural Economics* 19 (2): 221–36.
Yeandle, S. (1984) *Women's Working Lives*, London: Tavistock.

Chapter 7

The meaning of domestic technologies

A personal construct analysis of familial gender relations[1]

Sonia Livingstone

THE FAMILY, GENDER AND DOMESTIC TECHNOLOGIES

> Home ownership and state suburbanization have opened up a new
> lifestyle based on family possession of consumer durables.
>
> (McDowell 1983: 157)

In this chapter, I explore the ways in which families account for their
use of domestic technologies. The family may be characterized in terms
of dynamic properties emergent from the interaction between members.
Family dynamics are expressed and managed through shared goals, family
myths, rules and routines, conflicts and tensions, and its frameworks for
explanation and understanding (Byng-Hall 1978; Reiss 1981; Olson *et al.*
1983). These properties affect the ways in which families variously construe
the relationships between individual members of the family and between
the family and the social world.

The accounting practices through which people understand and explain
the role of domestic technologies in their lives reflect their gender relations
and family dynamics. Talk about the television or the telephone, for
example, is imbued with notions of who lets who use what, of moral
judgements of the other's activities, of the expression of needs and
desires, of justifications and conflict, of separateness and mutuality. The
purpose of analysing such talk is that 'while from a *theoretical* point of
view, human acts encode things with significance, from a *methodological*
point of view it is things-in-motion that illuminate their human and social
context' (Appadurai 1986: 5). Domestic practices are not only revealing,
they are also constitutive: 'consumption is the very arena in which
culture is fought over and licked into shape' (Douglas and Isherwood
1978: 57).

SYMBOLIC MEANINGS AND EVERYBODY OBJECTS

> It is clear that between what a man calls *me* and what he simply calls
> *mine*, the line is difficult to draw.
>
> (James 1890: 291)

Relatively few empirical studies have explored people's everyday experiences of consumption. Psychologists generally focus on interactions between people, not recognizing that social life takes place in a material context with which people also conduct meaningful interactions. Yet people are 'no longer surrounded by other human beings, as they have been in the past, but by *objects*' (Baudrillard 1988: 29). Davidson (1982) notes how these objects are changing ever faster, exacerbating the task of making sense of them. How do material objects come to acquire social meanings and how are they incorporated into everyday experiences?

When discussing the significance of 'home', Putnam describes 'an interweaving of personal imagination, lived relationships and shaped surroundings' (1990: 7). Csikszentmihalyi and Rochberg-Halton (1981) studied exactly this in their ethnographic study of 'the meaning of things' to eighty-two Chicago families. They identified a range of uses of domestic objects: symbols which mediate conflicts within the self (see also Turkle 1984), signs which express qualities of the self, signs which mediate between self and others, and signs of social status. For Prentice (1987), these represent symbolic functions of possessions, which he distinguishes from the instrumental functions identified, for example, in a study of the meaning of personal possessions in old age (Kamptner 1989). Kamptner emphasized the importance of objects in exercising personal control over the social environment (see also Furby 1978).

Csikszentmihalyi and Rochberg-Halton (1981) identify two modalities for the symbolic functions which organize the relation between people and things: differentiation, 'separating the owner from the social context, emphasizing his or her individuality' (ibid.: 38); and similarity, where 'the object symbolically expresses the integration of the owner with his or her social context' (ibid.: 39). While the dynamic between these two forces is fundamental to a sense of self, their study of possessions led Csikszentmihalyi and Rochberg-Halton to claim that the balance differed between people. Most notably, men and younger people expressed a more differentiated sense of self in relation to possessions while women and older people tended more towards similarity or other-orientation. Dittmar (1989) also showed how for men the meaning of possessions was more self-oriented and instrumental, while for women possessions were used to express more symbolic, other-oriented functions.

How people make sense of their domestic circumstances has implications for their experiences of frustration or satisfaction, of potency or passivity, of individuality or connectedness, and it underpins their desire to maintain the status quo or to negotiate change. Putnam argues that 'an understanding of home becomes a means for organising the world and orienting our passage through it' (1990: 7). More broadly still, Kelly, the originator of personal construct theory, claims that 'much of [a person's] social life is controlled by the comparisons he has come to see between himself and others' (1963: 131).

Douglas and Isherwood discuss processes of 'cognitive construction' (1978: 65) in consumption, resulting in what Miller has termed 'consumption work' – 'that which translates the object from an alienable to an inalienable condition' (ibid.: 190). This work of appropriation includes 'the more general construction of cultural milieux which gives such objects their social meaning' (ibid.: 191). By making sense of consumer durables in their lives people also realize the 'essential function of consumption [which] is its capacity to make sense' (ibid.: 62). How does making sense of domestic technologies contribute to the construction of gender relations in the family?

A PERSONAL CONSTRUCT APPROACH

Various theoretical approaches might illuminate the ways families account for their domestic practices. From family therapy, a focus on family myths would reveal the shared belief system which sets out members' roles, responsibilities, and scripts for action (Byng-Hall 1978). From social psychology, a study of people's attitudes towards new technology (Breakwell and Fife-Shaw 1987) or social representations (Moscovici 1984) of technology or patterns of attribution and explanation (Antaki 1988) in the family might predict family interaction around domestic technologies.

The present research adopted Kelly's (1955) personal construct approach, for this offered a theory and method which allowed exploration of the different perspectives of different family members and which meshes with the ethnographic concerns of the larger project of which this research is part (Silverstone et al. 1989). A personal construct analysis asks about the nature of people's constructions of domestic technologies. One may also ask about the relation between the construct systems of husband and wife and the relation between the private, personal and the public, shared construct systems. Putnam notes that 'research into the meaning of home repeatedly throws up the same basic terms; privacy, security, family, intimacy, comfort, control' (Putnam 1990: 8). Key questions remain: How are these terms related to different objects? What significance do they have for those who use them? How are they differently used by family members? How do they fit into diverse construct systems?

Personal construct theory (Kelly 1955; 1963; Bannister and Fransella 1971) focuses on the ways in which people actively construct their phenomenological world. It argues that people only know the world through systems of constructs which serve to categorize and connect events. The notion of the construct is central: 'each personal construct is based upon the simultaneous perception of likeness and difference among the objects of its context' (Kelly 1955: 560). Meaning is generated through contrastive judgements of similarity and difference. Psychological functioning is determined by the ways in which a person applies constructs. For example: Over what range of elements is a construct typically applied? To what is a construct implicitly or explicitly opposed? How do one person's constructs relate to another's? How complex or rigid or permeable is someone's construct system?

Through their construct systems, people may be understood to be striving to impose order and certainty on a fragmented and constantly changing world. Broadly speaking, personal construct theory studies what Bourdieu terms the 'practical mastery of classification' (1984: 472), where classification can be understood in terms of spatial relations such as opposition, difference, similarity, spread, and so forth. This practical mastery implies nothing about reflexivity or principled understanding of the classification, but rather concerns 'the sense of social realities that is . . . what makes it possible to act *as if* one knew the structure of the social world, one's place within it and the distances that need to be kept' (ibid.: 472).

THE RESEARCH METHODOLOGY

The personal construct research described here forms part of a larger, multi-method project on family use of domestic technologies (Silverstone *et al.* 1989; see also chapters 1 and 13, this volume). The larger project investigated a broad range of questions concerning household uses of domestic technologies. The families in the study were selected so as to vary on dimensions of social class, occupation, location and religion, but to be roughly comparable in composition, age and possession of consumer durables. Sixteen families were studied in depth, using a range of methodologies including diaries, maps of domestic space, ethnographic observation, and interviews about viewing habits (Silverstone *et al.* 1989). The personal construct interviews were designed to complement the other methods used, offering an individual and phenomenological analysis of the ways in which husbands and wives separately experienced and accounted for their domestic technologies. I conducted separate in-depth interviews with the husband and wife in each of the sixteen families (all names have been changed). Each interview lasted some 45 minutes, each was taped, and each took place in relative privacy in the family home.

The interviews were based on the 'personal construct interview' designed by Kelly (1955; see Fransella and Bannister 1977). This elicits key constructs (descriptive words or phrases) through which people frame their understanding of, in this case, domestic technologies. Husbands and wives were separately asked to identify the similarities and differences between a set of objects (persons, technologies, etc.). Respondents sorted the technologies into similar categories and explained the basis of their grouping. Second, they compared arbitrary groups of three technologies to 'find the odd one out' (the 'triadic method'), again explaining the reasons for their choice. This comparison task was conducted flexibly so that interesting or unclear distinctions could be pursued. The interview was opened with the general injunction to think about moods, feelings and associations rather than about the uses of technologies (How do you feel when you use X? What makes you prefer relaxing with X to Y? What does Z mean to you?). Although some participants were initially surprised by the task, they found it reasonably accessible.

This chapter offers an interpretative rather than a statistical analysis of the personal construct interviews (Adams-Webber 1989), focusing on the personal constructs of husbands and wives as revealed through their accounts of their use of domestic technologies and analysing these in terms of the categories of gender and family dynamics. Clearly, additional themes also emerged from the interviews, different analytic categories could be applied to the data, and further links could be made with other methods used across the larger research project than can be discussed here (see chapter 13).

GENDERED TALK ABOUT TECHNOLOGIES

In so far as objects function as extensions of the self, invested with personal and family meanings, the language with which people discuss their technologies tells us of their identities, their needs and desires, their ways of interpreting the world and of relating to each other (Lunt and Livingstone, 1992). While in many ways women and men shared a discourse for describing their possessions, there were also important differences. Although most domestic technologies are used by both husband and wife, they may be used differently and hence they are often understood differently. For example, both watch television but may do so at different times of day and for different programmes; both use the telephone, but often for quite different types of calls; both listen to the radio, but to accompany different activities. The differences in their accounting for and understanding of these technologies may be broadly characterized in terms of four key constructs: necessity, control, functionality, sociality.

Necessity

Compared with men, the women talked more explicitly about the importance of domestic technologies in their lives. Common constructs included 'lifeline', 'would miss it', 'important', 'use a lot', and 'essential', and these were opposed to such constructs as 'luxury', 'could manage without it', and 'rarely use'. Women described how technologies helped them – with their chores, with childcare. They described the convenience provided by technologies with relief, shuddering at their vision of domestic life without them:

> 'Lifesaving, dear, lifesaving, particularly that [washing machine] comes first, followed by that [tumble drier], followed by the telephone. Stereo record player comes next. Without them I couldn't survive. They are my lifelines.'
>
> (Shirley Lyon)

> 'I couldn't live without it [washing machine]. . . . I couldn't live without that either [freezer] . . . washing machine – I've got no option. It's got to be used whether I like it or not.'
>
> (Lynn Irving)

> 'The only way I can get through what I have to do.'
>
> (Christine Dole)

As is generally the case (Oakley 1974; Henwood *et al.* 1987), the woman was mainly responsible for housework in all of the families studied. Women's particular emphasis on the necessity of white goods reflects the relative lack of distinction for women between work and home (as Morley (1986) and others have argued, for men the home is primarily the site of leisure). If work-related objects are construed as necessary and entertainment objects are more often seen as luxuries, then for women the home is seen more in terms of necessity, and threats to the home (frequently imagined through the question 'Could I live without it?') place them more in jeopardy. The additional objects construed in terms of necessity can be understood as compensating for the frustrations of housework – the telephone to combat isolation, the stereo as an essential source of pleasure, a cassette player to return one's sense of self. These are necessary because, as Oakley (1974: 223) argues, 'the housewife cannot get any information about herself from the work she does'.

Control

It seemed at first as if women were more concerned about control in relation to technologies:

> 'I like the video because it gives you control over when you watch things.'
>
> (Gloria de Guy)

> 'The telephone I hate. . . . Once I'm actually on the phone I don't mind

it so much, it's the fact that it rings and interrupts you. . . . you don't have control over it.'

(Sarah Green)

Women talked more often of being 'in control of it' or 'it gives you control over things'. On the other hand, the construct of control, used in a different sense, was important for men. They valued the challenge posed by domestic technologies (especially home computer, electric drill) and talked in terms of the potential rewards offered ('challenging', 'stimulating', 'gives a choice', 'achievement'):

'[I use the computer] when I want to be a bit more active than just sitting down and watching, but actually want to do something a bit more . . . stimulating.'

(Daniel Dole)

'I genuinely enjoy ironing. . . . It's peaceful, it's a feeling of you're actually achieving something.'

(Paul de Guy)

Clearly, 'control' can mean different things to different people. For women, control refers more to keeping potential domestic chaos at bay, keeping things under control, having control over things. For men it means allowing the expression of expertise, permitting the exercise of control or power. This difference is also seen in the frequent use of the construct of functionality.

Functionality

Men tended to emphasize that technologies are 'purely functional'. By their frequent use of constructs such as 'functional', 'utilitarian', 'a tool', they focus their attention less on the role of the object in their lives and more on the inherent properties of the object. Commonly, technologies are described in terms of their technical features. For example, many men differentiated between audio and visual media, or they emphasized what connects with what, or what properties an object has, or how modern the technology is:

'You get more out of them [television and video], of course, you get sound and vision as well, it's more real as well. . . . I do think of it in compartments like that [audio versus visual].'

(Mark Lyon)

'I mean quite often the television's on and I'm not taking any notice of it, in fact it's quite often on and nobody's watching it, the reason being it's not good for the television to keep switching it on and off I mean that's a technical thing.'

(Frank Irving)

'That's functional [the telephone]. . . . For example, I ring my brother if I want to ask if I can borrow his sledgehammer. . . . I don't really want to know what he did yesterday and I don't tell him what I did yesterday. . . . As I say, it's purely functional.'

(Paul de Guy)

However, women are also concerned with the utility of objects, often assessing their 'convenience' or whether they 'make things easier'. Their concern is how the object allows them to function in their everyday lives. They thereby acknowledge the contextual meaning and value of objects for them: they tend to refer outwards to domestic practices when justifying object use rather than pointing out its inherent properties, its modern features or its price tag.

This pattern of accounting may provide men with a sense of inevitability, of consensual support for their consumer choices and values, while women may have to work harder to justify why their particular circumstances warrant a new purchase. One possible consequence is that men may more easily disguise, or not recognize, psychological reasons for product use. For example, one may claim to prefer television to radio because the provision of both audio and visual channels is obviously more relaxing, while another man may feel the absence of a visual channel makes his stereo more relaxing. Yet maybe the former also finds television relaxing because it dominates the living room, ensuring that his needs are prioritized, while the latter finds music on the headphones relaxing because he is thereby cut off from the demands of his children.

The women interviewed seemed more aware that their choices of possessions and their talk about these possessions were revealing. For men, meanings seemed to lie within the object, not within their lives, and were thus presented as obvious and natural. Maybe these gender differences reflect more general differences in the accounting practices of those who have more or less power. After all, 'inequality in the wider society meshes with inequality within the household' (Pahl 1989: 170).

It was also apparent that both men and women tend to employ a passivized discourse for technology use which tends to delete them as the agent, reflecting a perceived lack of control (Trew 1979). Decisions, preferences and meanings were frequently reified and attributed to the technologies rather than construed as a reflection of themselves or their situation. Televisions just 'go on', for adults rarely confess to switching them on, radios 'come on' in the morning automatically, washing machines 'have to' be used, stereos have become too cumbersome to use:

'Television might go on usually when [his son] comes in. . . . It doesn't get turned off necessarily.'

(Keith Mitchell)

'It's so fiddly nowadays to use a record. . . . In this day and age records are a drag to put on and put a stylus on, then clean them.'

(Frank Irving)

'The television tends to be on.'

(Mark Lyon)

Sociality/privacy

Domestic technologies appear to play at least two distinct roles in social interaction: they may facilitate interaction between people, and they may substitute for that interaction, providing instead a social interaction between person and object. In general, men talked more of technologies providing a substitute for social contact (using constructs such as 'keeps me company', 'stops me feeling lonely') or an alternative to social contact ('when I'm by myself'). For them, the key technologies which carry these social meanings are the radio, Walkman and television.

'While I work in the living room I usually have the television without any sound . . . the television in the background when I'm doing other things . . . relieving tension.'

(Gerald Green)

In contrast, for women technologies were often seen to facilitate social contact ('sociable', 'lifeline'). Consequently the key technologies were the telephone and the car. For women, the telephone was a vital source of emotional involvement, a connection with friends and family. They generally discussed the telephone with enthusiasm and pleasure. Even the microwave and dishwasher could be included under this construct of sociality, by creating spare time for socializing:

'It's [telephone] a connection to other people, other worlds, prevents me from being isolated. And if you can't get to see people, you can chat to them. So I enjoy the fact that it's there, to be in contact with people.'

(Lynn Irving)

As Csikszentmihalyi and Rochberg-Halton (1981) argued, the uses of objects to differentiate oneself from others and to connect oneself to others both confer selfhood, but they result in a different psychological balance between individuality and communality. This is clearly seen in women's enthusiasm for the telephone, when they feel real, alive:

'Talking on the telephone is really being, just myself, you know, to listen to who is on the telephone.'

(Linda Bell)

'I love that. I love talking on the telephone. I enjoy a chat on the telephone. . . . I'd phone all over the world if it wasn't so expensive. I'd be busy all the time.'

(Lynn Irving)

This contrasts strongly with men's frequently expressed hostility towards or lack of interest in the telephone, often construed in terms of functionality (where properties inherent to the telephone make it an unattractive device):

'The telephone is used – well, the telephone is just a random gadget – it's either used or it's not used. It's either used because there's a need to use it or it's used because somebody else is using it and we have to be at the receiving end. . . . I don't much use the telephone unless I have absolutely to use it. . . . She's the dominant user of the phone. And probably accounts for about 75 per cent of the cost of use. So that's not really an area I'm terribly into – it's absolutely totally utilitarian for me. It's only used because there's a need to use it.'

(Frank Irving)

For men, calls are 'just functional', to make arrangements, or they represent the interruption of work into the domestic space. Consequently, men regard the telephone with irritation, suspicion and boredom, they see little point in chatting on the phone, avoid initiating a call, and often prefer not to answer an incoming call.

Presumably, through this relation between constructs and technologies, men are not here rejecting communal or shared aspects of self. Instead, it seems likely that they balance the dynamic between differentiation and similarity through the use of different social situations, most notably work, and different technologies. Moyal (1990) shows how the telephone is more important for women who depend on a, typically female, social support network. Moreover, the telephone is needed by women for their social role of kin-keeper for the family, a function not always understood by husbands (revealing how different construct systems may lead to misunderstanding or tension):

'She may use it [the telephone] because she wants to talk to a friend – there's no need to talk to her friend, but she will use it to talk to her friend. Whereas for me it is not a tool of entertainment, it's just simply used because I need to use it.'

(Frank Irving)

'However, my wife can spend about five or six hours on the telephone. . . . I find it quite irritating the way some people go on and on.'

(Paul de Guy)

Different experiences and roles within the home result in differing construct systems. These in turn may result in misunderstandings over, for example, what is or is not necessary:

> 'I would like to get one [washing machine] but my husband said it's not really necessary. . . . [use the launderette?] They just ruin them [clothes], it crumples them, too difficult to iron and some of them you won't be able to use it again . . . so I prefer to wash it by hand.'
>
> (Linda Bell)

PUBLIC AND PRIVATE MEANINGS OF THINGS

In the world of marketing and advertising, of public discourse, of social representations (Moscovici 1984), it could be argued that a masculine discourse is predominant (e.g. Gilligan 1982). Public meanings of things often concur with the ways in which men account for or understand them. For example, the television is publicly defined as an 'entertainment medium', and men construe it similarly as 'relaxing', 'interesting', 'enjoyable'. There is little public acknowledgement that, for many women, television is of little interest ('It doesn't bother me'), except for particular genres (most notably soaps, which offer experiences of sociality or communality (Livingstone 1988)):

> 'I hardly ever use it [video]. . . . It doesn't bother me. Neither does the television. I'm not terribly fussed . . . two or three programmes a week I especially watch.'
>
> (Shirley Lyon)

Women's relative lack of expressed interest may be masked by the ratings figures, for they have it on for long hours to babysit the children, or because the children forget to turn it off, or to hear when their favourite programme comes on when they are in the kitchen. As Morley (1986) suggests, television is problematic for women because it demands inactivity in a space construed as both work and leisure. In this study, women often talked of the radio or cassette player with greater enthusiasm, yet in public discourse these are less valued objects, being cheaper, older, technologically less interesting. Similarly, the telephone is publicly seen through men's constructs – as functional, providing a service, there for emergencies, a gadget with fancy dials and extra functions. British Telecom's Beattie ridicules the woman who chats on the phone, while the men are resigned, distant (although some recent advertising is more clearly targeted towards women, for whom social contacts are 'only a phone call away').

These public representations enter the private relations between men and women in various ways (see Morley 1986). When the construct

systems of husband and wife differ significantly, the relative power of
these public representations may preclude recognition of the woman's
needs or desires, making the negotiation of product purchase especially
difficult for women:

> 'We [self and husband] basically don't like the same programmes. And he
> also goes out to work at night so I will choose my own programme. . . .
> He has first choice normally. . . . He won't watch in the bedroom . . .
> but in the lounge I can see it properly – in our bedroom it's awful [green
> screen].'
>
> (Lynn Irving)

Yet when asked if they might replace the bedroom television with the
defective screen, he says:

> 'No, no, no, there's not any need for it. We just don't have to watch
> the television.'
>
> (Frank Irving)

Constructs also direct perception and attention. Thus the woman's activities
may often go unrecognized, while the man's activities are made public
for him:

> '[he] is not household-oriented, he doesn't realize what needs to
> be done.'
>
> (Shirley Lyon)

Women often organize their time to support this: in the Simon family, the
woman gets up at 6 a.m. to do all the washing and ironing before the family
rises, rendering the housework as invisible for her husband as it is in the
public mind (Oakley 1974). Similarly, men may claim that 'we' rarely use
the radio, when in fact she has it on all day while doing the housework,
only turning it off when he returns in the evening to watch television.

Public representations may also provide external legitimation for the
husband's desires, allowing him to override her account of their needs:

> 'I'd like a compact disc player but that's a bone of contention . . . well,
> she thinks of it as being a bit of a luxury, but eventually, when I'm ready
> to buy one I will get one and that will be the end of the matter. So I will
> get one.'
>
> (Frank Irving)

They may further be used to justify his exercise of power within the home,
circumventing her activities or wishes:

> 'I would like to use it [electric drill] but my husband won't allow me. . . .
> He won't allow me to use that, he did it for me, if I ask him if I could do
> it when he's out or at work he says, "Oh don't touch them or whatever,

I can do it for you". . . . He said only a man could do that, but mind you if he's not around I know that I could use it.'

(Linda Bell)

Generally, the present findings concur with Pahl when, after interviews with husbands and wives separately, the wives claimed that, 'in general, husbands were likely to perceive a greater degree of sharing [of economic resources] in marriage than wives, who were more aware of conflicts of opinion and interest' (Pahl 1989: 169). At times, neither husband nor wife may perceive conflict, for both share the public construction of domestic activities. For example, both men and women talk of white goods (used almost exclusively by women) as 'time savers' which 'make life easier' (for her). Yet this need not imply that the interests of both men and women are served. The shared, public representation may render beyond question the issue of whether or not, for example, 'clothes must be changed every day', and 'cannot wait' (Lynn Irving). However, as many have noted (Oakley 1974; Davidson 1982; Cowan 1989), 'labour-saving devices' often increase labour and leisure time is lost, as women do so much 'necessary' washing, or use the 'convenient' microwave to cook for each member of the family separately as they come home.

Do different construct systems result in conflict? Interestingly, neither men nor women talk of objects they use little: men are silent about the sewing machine, and often about the washing machine; women have nothing to say about the drill or, often, the hi-fi. The use of different constructs for the same technology – for example, women construe the telephone as involving and the television as uninteresting while for men the converse is often true – may or may not generate conflict. Conflict is sometimes expressed over future purchases, where couples compete for resources. Indeed, technology acquisition is often seen as the resolution to acknowledged family problems. In the Lyon family, the wife is longing for her own cassette player so as to retreat to her bedroom and escape the family chaos, to regain her own peace and sense of individuality. In the Dole family, both husband and wife wish for a video camera to record their children, particularly as one child may not survive long: their desired technology expresses their desire for family cohesion under threat.

FAMILY DYNAMICS: COHESION AND SEPARATION

While clear gender differences in accounting for use of domestic tech-nologies were apparent across the sample of families studied, the incon-sistencies or contradictions within the pattern were not insignificant. To understand these, we must recognize that the gender relations studied were constructed and expressed in the context of family dynamics, and that these dynamics will, for psychological, social and historical reasons, vary between families. In particular, cohesion and dispersal, with their more extreme forms – enmeshing and disengagement – represent a key family dynamic (Reiss 1981; Olson *et al.* 1983) around which the complex relationship between gender and domestic technologies, among other things, is played out in everyday life. This interpersonal dynamic parallels the intrapsychic dynamic between similarity and differentiation in the construction of the self in relation to others (Csikszentmihalyi and Rochberg-Halton 1981). Such complexities and contradictions in gender relations in constructions of domestic technologies may be illuminated by considering the dynamics of the family, focusing here on the degree of cohesion or separation between the husband and wife.

For example, the Dole family differs from the general picture in that the wife tends not to construe the telephone in terms of a lifeline or connection to others. Nor does she distance herself from the television. Similarly, he feels little antipathy towards the telephone, and shares her interests in the television. They talk of each technology in similar rather than contrasting ways, talking of 'we', rather than 'I'. Their shared pattern of accounting for object use reflects their shared, cohesive family dynamics, which in turn derive from the 'real work' they do together at home fostering children. The telephone plays a special role for them in connection with the fostering work, so maybe the 'functionality' of the telephone overrides the alternative construction of 'sociality'. Maybe, too, the closeness of their interests and roles overcomes the loneliness and frustrations which might otherwise colour her position as housewife.

> 'Normally we'd either be all in the front room, together as a family, at the end of the day, the one time when certainly the two older ones would be with Mum and Dad, tidying up the loose ends as to what had happened at school and what was going to happen tomorrow. . . . On the telly we'd be more likely to watch a documentary-type factual piece of information . . . particularly if about children, the social side of things, which for the last eight years as foster parents we have obviously been very involved in. So all that sort of thing is of great interest to both of us, great interest, it's no hard work listening to at all. . . . She goes for the soaps more, that's not to say I'll walk out of the room when *Coronation Street* is on. If they're on, and I'm in the room, then I'm just as likely to sit down and see what's going on.'
>
> (Daniel Dole; she confirms this view)
>
> 'I don't actually use it [telephone] to chat on but I use it to arrange things on. You know, if I want to talk to somebody, I'll phone them up and ask when we can get together.'
>
> (Christine Dole)

In contrast, the Lyon family lives, as she describes, 'like ships in the night'. Their views of their technologies are quite different, they talk of 'I', not 'we', and they disagree in their priorities for product purchase, having very different construct systems – he thinks television is 'more real'; she wants a cassette player 'to keep me sane'. Their separation, however, is due in part to the fact that both work outside the home, and they rarely see each other. Consequently, she too differs from the general picture, for example not liking to chat on the telephone, although she does value it as a lifeline when he works away from home. In this case, her pleasures and attention are, with the exception of her children, focused away from the home, for her work provides an alternative reality in which she is noticed, valued, and in satisfying social contact with others.

A final example concerns a traditional, role-segregated couple (the de Guy family). She appears to have positively embraced the housewife role. As with the examples above, she too lacks enthusiasm for leisure activities, using rather neutral constructs about the telephone and television, for example. She comes alive talking about housework:

> 'I fight against things which take away from all aspects of housework. I actually like cooking, I like washing up, I enjoy it. . . . I'd rather just do as I go along . . . hygienic.'
>
> (Gloria de Guy)

She also appears to exercise the traditional notion of indirect female power (Williams and Watson 1988), being very concerned to control the domestic space. For example, she threw out their previous stereo system because it 'was not compatible with the room'; as her husband notes, 'she loves the grass to be this high – 2 cm high'. She chooses what they will buy, and even though she knows that his hi-fi was 'his main love before we married', she says:

> '[he wants compact disc] I shall try to dissuade him, I can't see the point. . . . He would love to have the more advanced product, but I don't think it's so important, and he tends to like to keep me happy, so we're not getting it for now.'
>
> (Gloria de Guy)

Although they talk in terms of 'we', their constructs are quite different and they disagree about many things (he likes constant background noise, she prefers patches of music; he bought a computer for the children, she disapproves of 'learning through play'). Again, her focus of key constructs on white goods particularly, neglecting brown or entertainment goods, can be understood in the context of their family dynamics.

FAMILY DYNAMICS AND THE ROLE OF DOMESTIC TECHNOLOGIES

The changing and expanding market for domestic technologies may influence the options families face when negotiating their relationships and domestic practices. Twenty or thirty years ago, when bedrooms were more commonly left unheated, families owned only one television set, and videos were unheard of, one can see that the main living room had considerable symbolic importance as the locus of family life (Morley 1986; Putnam 1990). Today, domestic space and the range of domestic objects have changed dramatically (McDowell 1983; Forty 1986; Madigan and Munro 1990): many families heat all their rooms, bedrooms may be used in the day, families have multiple televisions, even multiple videos and telephones, and numerous radios and cassette players – typically more radios than people. If television once brought the family together around the hearth, now domestic technologies permit the dispersal of family members to different rooms or different activities within the same space.

In our study, some families did not have the option of multiple technologies or multiple rooms. The Bell family is relatively poor, and tends to draw together around the television in the living room. The Mitchell family is also poor, but often chooses to switch off the one set in their one warm room in order together to support their son in his work or play. In contrast, all six members of one family in the pilot study (Silverstone *et al.* 1989) watched *Neighbours* every day, but each on separate sets or at different times, and they did not see this common experience as an occasion for conversation or sharing. The White family provides music centres and televisions for each child in his or her bedroom and construes this positively in terms of encouraging independence and individuality.

Families differ in the balance struck between cohesion and dispersal. Domestic space, leisure time, financial resources, and ownership of technologies all combine to permit different arrangements of family life (Lunt and Livingstone, in press). Further research should ask whether technologies are used to facilitate family cohesion and unity or family dispersal and diversity, how families negotiate their choices and what implications their understandings and decisions have for family life, technology use and gender relations.

NOTE

1 An earlier version of this chapter was presented at an ESRC/PICT workshop, 'Domestic consumption and information and communication technologies', 18–19 May 1990, CRICT, Brunel University, and at the annual conference of the International Communication Association, June 1990, Dublin. Thanks to Peter Lunt for comments on an earlier version.

REFERENCES

Adams-Webber, J.R. (1989), 'Some reflections of the "meaning" of repertory grid responses', *International Journal of Personal Construct Psychology* 2: 77–92.

Antaki, C. (ed.) (1988) *The Analysis of Everyday Explanations*, London: Sage.

Appadurai, A. (1986) 'Commodities and the politics of value,' in A. Appadurai (ed.) *The Social Life of Things: Commodities in Cultural Perspective*, Cambridge: Cambridge University Press, 3–63.

Bannister, D. and Fransella, F. (1971) *Inquiring Man*, Harmondsworth: Penguin.

Baudrillard, J. (1988) 'Consumer society', in M. Poster (ed.) *Jean Baudrillard: Selected Writings*, Cambridge: Polity Press, 29–56.

Bourdieu, P. (1984) *Distinction: A Social Critique of the Judgement of Taste*, translated by Richard Nice, London: Routledge & Kegan Paul.

Breakwell, G. M. and Fife-Shaw, C. (1987) 'Young people's attitudes towards new technology: source and structure', in J. H. Lewko (ed.) *How Children and Adolescents View the World of Work*, New Directions for Child Development, no. 35, San Francisco: Jossey-Bass, 51–67.

Byng-Hall, J. (1978) 'Family myths used as defence in conjoint family therapy', *British Journal of Medical Psychology* 40: 239–50.

Cowan, R. S. (1989) *More Work for Mother: The Ironies of Household Technology from the Open Hearth to the Microwave*, London: Free Association Books.

Csikszentmihalyi, M. and Rochberg-Halton, E. (1981) *The Meaning of Things: Domestic Symbols and the Self*, Cambridge: Cambridge University Press.

Davidson, C. (1982) *A Woman's Work is Never Done: A History of Housework in the British Isles 1650–1950*, London: Chatto & Windus.

Dittmar, H. (1989) 'Gender identity-related meanings of personal possessions', *British Journal of Social Psychology* 28: 159–71.

Douglas, M. and Isherwood, B. (1978) *The World of Goods: Towards an Anthropology of Consumption*, Harmondsworth: Penguin.

Forty, A. (1986) *Objects of Desire: Design and Society, 1750–1980*, London: Thames & Hudson.

Fransella, F. and Bannister, D. (1977) *A Manual for Repertory Grid Technique*, London: Academic Press.

Furby, L. (1978) 'Possessions: towards a theory of their meaning and function throughout the life cycle', in P.B. Baltes (ed.) *Life-span Development and Behavior*, New York: Academic Press, 297–336.

Gilligan, C. (1982) *In a Different Voice: Psychological Theory and Women's Development*, Cambridge, Mass.: Harvard University Press.

Henwood, M., Rimmer, L. and Wicks, M. (1987) *Inside the Family: The Changing Roles of Men and Women*, London: Family Policy Studies Centre, occasional paper no. 6.

James, W. (1890) *Principles of Psychology*, New York: Holt, Rinehart & Winston.

Kamptner, N. L. (1989) 'Personal possessions and their meanings in old age', in S. Spacapan and S. Oskamp (eds) *The Social Psychology of Aging*, London: Sage, 165–96.

Kelly, G. A. (1955) *The Psychology of Personal Constructs*, vol. 2, New York: Norton.

——(1963) *A Theory of Personality: The Psychology of Personal Constructs*, New York: Norton.

Livingstone, S. M. (1988) 'Why people watch soap opera: an analysis of the explanations of British viewers', *European Journal of Communication* 3: 55–80.

Lunt, P.K. and Livingstone, S.M. (1992) *Mass Consumption and Personal Identity*, Milton Keynes: Open University Press.

McDowell, L. (1983) 'Urban housing and the sexual division of labour', in M. Evans and C. Ungerson (eds) *Sexual Divisions: Patterns and Processes*, London: Tavistock, 142–63.

Madigan, R. and Munro, M. (1990) 'Ideal homes: gender and domestic architecture' in T. Putnam and C. Newton (eds) *Household Choices*, London: Futures, 25–30.

Miller, D. (1987) *Material Culture and Mass Consumption*, Oxford: Blackwell.

Morley, D. (1986) *Family Television: Cultural Power and Domestic Leisure*, London: Comedia.

Moscovici, S. (1984) 'The phenomenon of social representations', in R.M. Farr and S. Moscovici (eds) *Social Representations*, Cambridge: Cambridge University Press, 3–70.

Moyal, A. (1990) 'Women and the telephone in Australia: study of a national culture', paper presented at the Annual Conference of the International Communications Association, Dublin, June.

Oakley, A. (1974) *Housewife*, Harmondsworth: Penguin.

Olson, D.H., McCubbin, H.I., Barnes, H.L., Larsen, A.S., Muxen, M.J. and Wilson, M.A. (1983) *Families: What Makes them Work*, Beverly Hills: Sage.

Pahl, J. (1989) *Money and Marriage*, London: Macmillan.

Prentice, D.A. (1987) 'Psychological correspondence of possessions, attitudes and values', *Journal of Personality and Social Psychology* 53: 993–1003.

Putnam, T. (1990) 'Introduction: design, consumption and domestic ideals', in T. Putnam and C. Newton (eds) *Household Choices*, London: Futures, 7–19.

Reiss, D. (1981) *The Family's Construction of Reality*, Cambridge, Mass.: Harvard University Press.

Silverstone, R., Morley, D., Dahlberg, A. and Livingstone, S.M. (1989) 'Families, technologies and consumption: the household and information and communication technologies', CRICT Discussion Paper, Brunel University.

Trew, T. (1979) 'What the papers say: linguistic variation and ideological difference', in R. Fowler, B. Hodge, G. Kress and T. Trew (eds) *Language and Control*, London: Routledge & Kegan Paul, 117–56.

Turkle, S. (1984) *The Second Self: Computers and the Human Spirit*, New York: Simon & Schuster.

Williams, J. and Watson, G. (1988) 'Sexual inequality, family life and family therapy', in E. Street and W. Dryden (eds) *Family Therapy in Britain*, Milton Keynes: Open University Press, 291–311.

Chapter 8

Living-room wars

New technologies, audience measurement and the tactics of television consumption

Ien Ang

THE PROBLEM OF THE AUDIENCE

In February 1990, Walt Disney Studios decided to prohibit cinema theatres in the United States from airing commercials before screening Disney-produced movies. The decision was made because the company had received a great number of complaints from spectators who did not want to be bothered by advertising after having paid $7.50 for seeing a film, leading the company to conclude that commercials 'are an unwelcome intrusion' to the filmgoing experience (Hammer 1990: 38). Of course, Disney's decision was informed by economic motives: it feared that commercials before films would have a negative effect on the number of people willing to go to the movies, and thus on its box-office revenues. As a result, the issue of in-theatre advertising is now a controversial one in Hollywood.

This case clarifies a major contradiction in the institutional arrangement of the cultural industries. More precisely, the conflicting corporate interests represented by two types of consumption are at stake here: a conflict between media consumption on the one hand, which is the profit base for media companies such as Disney, and the consumption of material goods on the other, presumably to be enhanced by the showing of commercials. In this case, the conflict inheres in the very logic of cinema spectatorship as a consumer activity, both economic and cultural. Films are discrete media products, to be watched one at a time by consumers who pay a fixed entrance fee in advance in order to be able to see the film of their choice. In this exchange, commercials are not included in the bargain. On the contrary, it is suggestive of the controversial social meaning of advertising that commercials are seen to hurt rather than enrich the value of cinemagoing. In the cinema, the consumption of the film is to be clearly marked off from the selling of goods and services through advertising, both in the experience of the film consumer and in the economic logic of the industry.

The situation is altogether different with television. The very corporate foundation of commercial television rests on the idea of 'delivering

audiences to advertisers'; that is, economically speaking, television programming is first and foremost a vehicle to attract audiences for the 'real'
messages transmitted by television: the advertising spots inserted within and
between the programmes (e.g. Smythe 1981). The television business, in
other words, is basically a 'consumer delivery enterprise' for advertisers. So,
in the context of this structural interdependence of television broadcasters
and advertisers, television consumption takes on a double meaning: it is
consumption both of programmes and of commercials; the two presuppose
one another – at least, from the industry's point of view. Once a consumer
has bought a TV set, (s)he has bought access to all broadcast television
output, and in exchange for this wholesale bargain (s)he is expected to
expose herself to as much output as possible, including most importantly
the commercials which in fact make the financing of the programmes
possible. This merging of the two types of consumption is corroborated
in the occurrence of one single activity, a presumably one-dimensional type
of behaviour: 'watching television'. This complex intermingling of economic
conditions and cultural assumptions with regard to television consumption is
a necessary precondition for the construction of an institutional agreement
about the exchange value of the 'audience commodity' that is bought and
sold. As is well known, this agreement is reached through the intermediary
practice of audience measurement, producing ratings figures on the basis of
the amount of 'watching television' done by the audience. These figures are
considered to be the equivalent to box-office figures for cinema attendance
(see, e.g., Meehan 1984; Ang 1991).

But this equivalence is fundamentally problematic, as I will try to show
in this chapter. Undertaken by large research companies such as Nielsen
and Arbitron in the United States and AGB in Britain and continental
Europe, audience measurement is an entrenched research practice based
upon the assumption that it is possible to determine the objective size of the
'television audience'. However, recent changes in the structure of television
provision, as a result of the introduction of new television technologies
such as cable, satellite and the VCR, have thrown this assumption of
measurability of the television audience into severe crisis. The problem
is both structural and cultural: it is related to the fact that 'watching
television' is generally a *domestic* consumer practice, and as such not at
all the one-dimensional, and therefore measurable, type of behaviour it is
presumed to be.

The domestic has always been a contested terrain when it comes to the
regulation of consumption. It is a terrain which, precisely because it is
officially related to the 'private sphere', is difficult to control from outside.
Of course it is true, as the young Jean Baudrillard (1988 [1970]: 49)
once stated, that '[c]onsumption is not . . . an indeterminate marginal
sector where an individual, elsewhere constrained by social rules, would
finally recover, in the "private" sphere, a margin of freedom and personal

play when left on his [*sic*] own'. The development of the consumer society has implied the hypothetical construction of an ideal consuming subject through a whole range of strategic and ideological practices, resulting in very specific constraints, structural and cultural, within which people can indulge in the pleasures of leisurely consumption.

Indeed, it is important to note that the day-to-day, domestic practice of television consumption is accompanied by the implicit and explicit promotion of 'ideal' or 'proper' forms of consumer behaviour, propelled by either ideological or economic motives and instigated by the social institutions responsible for television production and transmission.[1] More generally, the acceptance and integration of television within the domestic sphere did and does not take place 'spontaneously', but was and is surrounded by continuous discursive practices which attempt to 'normalize' television viewing habits.

For example, Lynn Spigel (1988) has shown how American women's magazines in the late 1940s and early 1950s responded to the introduction of television in the home with much ambivalence and hesitation, against the background of the necessity for housewives to integrate household chores with the attractions (and distractions) promised by the new domestic consumer technology. Through the advice and suggestions put forward in these magazines, they helped establish specific cultural rules for ways in which 'watching television' could be managed and regulated without disturbing the routines and requirements of family life.

However, precisely because the home has been designated as the primary location for television consumption, a 'right' way of watching television is very difficult to impose. As Roger Silverstone (1990: 179) has put it, '[t]he status of television as technology and as the transmitter of meanings is . . . vulnerable to the exigencies, the social structuring, the conflicts and the rituals of domestic daily life'. The domestic is a pre-eminent site of everyday life and the everyday is, according to Michel de Certeau, the terrain in which ordinary people often make use of infinite local tactics to 'constantly manipulate events in order to turn them into "opportunities"' (1984: xix). 'Watching television' can be seen as one everyday practice that is often tactical in character, articulated in the countless unpredictable and unruly ways of using television that elude and escape the strategies of the television industry to make people watch television in the 'right' way. And as we shall see, the home environment only reinforces the proliferation of such tactics in the age of new television technologies.

However, the fact that television consumption has been historically constructed as taking place within the private, domestic context has paradoxically also been quite *convenient* for the television industry. Precisely because the activities of 'watching television' take place in a site unseen, behind the closed doors of private homes, the industry could luxuriate in a kind of calculated ignorance about the tactics by which consumers at home constantly subvert predetermined and imposed conceptions of 'watching television'.

Again, the cinema provides a suitable comparison. Because the cinema audience is gathered together in a public theatre, spectators' reactions to the screen are immediately available and therefore not easily ignored. For example, Disney's decision to ban commercials in theatres was, at least in part, a response to observations that audiences have booed and hissed a Diet Coke commercial in which Elton John and Paula Abdul sing the soft drink's praises (Hammer 1990). Similar audience resistance in front of the television screen at home, however, remains largely invisible to the outsider. At the same time, it seems fair to suspect that television viewers are in a far better position to avoid messages they do not want to be subjected to than cinema spectators, who are trapped in their chairs in the darkened theatre, enforced to keep their gaze directed to the large screen. After all, television viewers have the freedom to move around in their own homes when their TV set is on; there is no obligation to keep looking and they can always divert their attention to something else whenever they want to. But it is precisely this relative freedom of television audiences to use television in ways they choose to which has been conveniently repressed in the industry's imaginings of its consumers.

This repression is reflected in the rather simplistic methods of information-gathering used by ratings producers to measure the size of the television audience (or segments of it). Historically, two major audience measurement technologies have dominated the field: the diary and the setmeter. In the diary method, a sample of households is selected whose members are requested to keep a (generally, weekly) diary of their viewing behaviour. At the end of the week the diaries must be mailed to the ratings firm. In the second case, an electronic meter is attached to the television sets of a sample of households. The meter gives a minute-by-minute automatic registration of the times that the television set is on or off, and of the channel it is turned on to. The data are transmitted to a home storage unit, where they are stored until they are accessed by the central office computer during the night. The meter data, which only indicate numbers of sets on, form the basis for what are called 'gross ratings', while the diary data, which are more cumbersome to produce because they presuppose the active co-operation and discipline of viewers of sample homes in filling out their individual diaries, are used to compose demographic information about audiences for specific programmes.[2]

It should be noted that these methods of measurement are grounded upon a straightforward behaviourist epistemology. 'Watching television' is implicitly defined as a simple, one-dimensional, and purely objective and isolatable act. As Todd Gitlin (1983: 54) has rightly remarked in relation to the electronic setmeter, 'The numbers only sample sets tuned in, not necessarily shows watched, let alone grasped, remembered, loved, learned from, deeply anticipated, or mildly tolerated'. In other words, what audience measurement information erases from its field of discernment is any specific consideration of the 'lived reality' behind the ratings. In the quantitative discourse of audience measurement TV viewers are merely relevant for their bodies: strictly speaking, they appear in the logic of ratings only in so far as they are agents of the physical act of tuning-in. More generally, the statistical perspective of audience measurement inevitably leads to emphasizing averages, regularities and generalizable patterns rather than particularities, idiosyncrasies and surprising exceptions. What all this amounts to is the construction of a kind of streamlined map of 'television audience', on which individual viewers are readable in terms of their resemblance to a 'typical' consumer whose 'viewing behavior' can be objectively and unambiguously classified. In other words, in foregrounding the stable over the erratic, the likely over the fickle, and the consistent over the inconsistent, ratings discourse symbolically turns television consumption into a presumably well-organized, disciplined practice, consisting of dependable viewing habits and routines.

Imagining television consumption in this way is very handy for the industry indeed: it supplies both broadcasters and advertisers with neatly arranged and easily manageable information, which provides the agreed-upon basis for their economic negotiations. The *tactical* nature of television consumption is successfully disavowed, permitting the industry to build its operations upon an unproblematic notion of what 'watching television' is all about. This, at least, characterized the relatively felicitous conditions of existence for (American) commercial television for decades.

TECHNOLOGY AND MEASUREMENT

Since the mid-1970s, however, an entirely different television landscape has unfolded before the viewer's eyes, one characterized by abundance rather than scarcity, as a result of the emergence of a great number of independent stations, cable and satellite channels. This, at least, is the situation in the United States, but it also increasingly characterizes European television provisions. By 1987, 49 per cent of American homes had been connected to a basic cable system, giving them access to cable channels such as MTV, ESPN and CNN, while 27 per cent had chosen to subscribe to one or more pay cable channels, such as Home Box Office. All in all, thirty or more channels can be received in 20 per cent of American homes. Furthermore, after a slow start the number of homes with VCRs had grown exponentially in the early 1980s, reaching about 50 per cent in 1987 (*TV World* 1987). This multiplication of consumer options has inevitably led to a fragmentation of television's audiences, which in turn has led to a perceived inadequacy of the figures provided by the existing ratings services. What's happening in the millions of living rooms now that people can choose from so many different offerings? Consequently, diverse branches of the industry began to call for more finely tuned audience information, to be acquired through better, that is, more accurate measurement.

This call for better measurement was articulated by criticizing the prevailing techniques and methods of measuring the television audience: the diary and the setmeter. For example, the proliferation of channels has acutely dramatized the problems inherent to the diary technique. Suddenly, the built-in subjective (and thus 'unreliable') element of the diary technique was perceived as an unacceptable deficiency. David Poltrack, vice-president of research for CBS, one of the three major US networks, voiced the problem as follows:

> It used to be easy. You watched $M*A*S*H$ on Monday night and you'd put that in the diary. Now, if you have thirty channels on cable you watch one channel, switch to a movie, watch a little MTV, then another program, and the next morning with all that switching all over the place you can't remember what you watched.
>
> (Quoted in Bedell Smith 1985: H23)

And officials of the pop music channel MTV complained that their target audience, young people between 12 and 24, consistently comes off badly in the demographic data produced through diaries, because 'younger viewers tend not to be as diligent in filling out diaries as older household members' (quoted in Livingston 1986: 130). In short, agreement grew within the industry that the possibilities of 'channel switching' and 'zapping' (swiftly 'grazing' through different channels by using the remote control device) had made the diary an obsolete measurement tool. Viewers could no longer be trusted to report their viewing accurately: they lack perfect memory, they may be too careless. In short, they behave in too capricious a manner! In this situation, calls for a 'better' method to obtain ratings data began to be raised; and better means more 'objective', that is, less dependent on the 'fallibilities' of viewers in the sample. A method that erases all traces of wild subjectivity.

The video cassette recorder has also played a major destabilizing role in the measurability of the television audience. 'Time shifting' and 'zipping' (fastforwarding commercials when playing back a taped programme) threatened to deregulate the carefully composed TV schedules of the networks. This phenomenon has come to be called 'schedule cannibalization' (cf. Rosenthal 1987), a voracious metaphor that furtively indicates the apprehension, if not implicit regret, felt in network circles about the new freedoms viewers have acquired through the VCR. Through the VCR, the tactical nature of television consumption clearly begins to manifest itself. In response, the industry demanded the measurement of the VCR audience: it wanted answers to questions such as: How often is the VCR used by which segments of the audience? Which programmes are recorded most? And when are they played back?

In the face of this growing demand for more accurate and more detailed information about television consumption, the ratings business has now come up with the 'people meter', a new audience measurement technology that was introduced in the United States in 1987.[3] The people meter is supposed to combine the virtues of the traditional setmeter and the paper-and-pencil diary: it is an electronic monitoring device that can record individual viewing rather than just sets tuned in, as the traditional setmeter does. It works as follows.

When a viewer begins to watch a programme, (s)he must press a numbered button on a portable keypad, which looks like the well-known remote control device. When the viewer stops watching, the button must be pressed again. A monitor attached to the television set lights up regularly to remind the viewer of the button-pushing task. Every member of a sample family has her or his own individual button, while there are also some extra buttons for guests. Linked to the home by telephone lines, the system's central computer correlates each viewer's number with demographic data about them stored in its memory, such as age, gender, income, ethnicity and education.

There is definitely something panoptic in the conceptual arrangement of this intricate measurement technology (Foucault 1979), in that it aims to put television viewers under constant scrutiny by securing their permanent visibility. This is attractive for the industry because it holds the promise of providing more detailed and accurate data on exactly when who is watching what. The people meter boosts the hope for better surveillance of the whole spectrum of television-viewing activities, including the use of the VCR. Smaller audience segments may now be detected and described, allowing advertisers and broadcasters to create more precise target groups. New sorts of information are made available; hitherto hidden and unknown minutiae of 'audience behaviour' can now be detected through clever forms of number-crunching (see, e.g., Beville 1986a and 1986b).

Still, the existing versions of the people meter are by no means considered perfect measurement instruments, as they still involve too much subjectivity: after all, they require viewer co-operation in the form of pushing buttons. A professional observer echoes the widespread feelings of doubt and distrust when he wonders:

> Will the families in the sample really take the trouble? Will they always press the buttons as they begin watching? Will they always remember to press their buttons when they leave the room – as when the telephone rings, or the baby cries?
>
> (Baker 1986: 95)

It should come as no surprise, then, that furious attempts are being made to develop a so-called *passive* people meter – one with no buttons at all – that senses automatically who and how many viewers are in front of the screen. For example, Nielsen, the largest ratings company in the US, has recently disclosed a plan for a rather sophisticated passive people meter system, consisting of an image-recognition technology capable of identifying the faces of those in the room. The system then decides first whether it is a face it recognizes, and then whether that face is directed towards the set (unfamiliar faces and even possibly the dog in the house will be recorded as 'visitors'). If tested successfully, this system could replace the imperfect, push-button people meter by the mid-1990s, so Nielsen executives expect (*San Francisco Chronicle* 1989). In short, what seems to be desired within the television industry these days is a measurement technology that can wipe out all ambiguity and uncertainty about the precise size of the audience for any programme and any commercial at any given time.

This recent utopian drive towards technological innovation in audience measurement can be interpreted as a desperate attempt to repair the broken consensus within the television industry as a whole as to the meaning of 'watching television'. Indeed, from the industry's perspective, a kind of 'revolt of the viewer' seems to have erupted with the emergence of the new television technologies: 'watching television' now appears to be a rather undisciplined and chaotic set of behavioural acts as viewers zip through commercials when playing back their taped shows on their VCRs, zap through channels with their remote controls, record programmes so as to watch them at times to suit them, and so on. 'After years of submitting passively to the tyranny of [network] television programmers, viewers are taking charge', comments American journalist Bedell Smith (1985: H21). This 'taking charge' can be seen as the return of the tactical nature of television consumption to the realm of visibility, shattering the fiction of 'watching television' as a simple, one-dimensional and objectively measurable activity which has traditionally formed the basis for industry negotiations and operations.

In other words, what has become increasingly uncertain in the new television landscape is exactly what takes place in the homes of people when they watch television. Reduction of that uncertainty is sought in improvements in audience measurement technology, with its promise of delivering a continuous stream of precise data on who is watching what, every day, all year long. But beneath this pragmatic solution lurks an epistemological paradox.

For one thing, as the macroscopic technological 'gaze' of audience measurement becomes increasingly microscopic, the object it is presumed to measure becomes ever more elusive. The more 'watching television' is put under the investigative scrutiny of new measurement technology, the less unambiguous an activity it becomes. 'Zipping', 'zapping', 'time-shifting' and so on are only the most obvious and most recognized tactical maneouvres viewers engage in in order to construct their own television experience. There are many other ways of doing so, ranging from doing other things while watching to churning out cynical comments on what's on the screen (see, e.g., Sepstrup 1986). As a result, it can no longer be conveniently assumed – as has been the foundational logic and the strategic pragmatics of traditional audience measurement – that having the TV set on equals watching, that watching means paying attention to the screen, that watching a programme implies watching the commercials inserted in it, that watching the commercials leads to actually buying the products being advertised.

To speak with de Certeau (1984), it is that which happens beneath technology and disturbs its operation which interests us here. The limits of technology are not a matter of lack of sophistication, but a matter of actual practices, of 'the murmuring of everyday practices' that quietly but unavoidably unsettle the functionalist rationality of the technological project. In other words, no matter how sophisticated the measurement technology, television consumption can never be completely 'domesticated' in the classificatory grid of ratings research, because television consumption is, despite its habitual character, dynamic rather than static, experiential rather than merely behaviourial. It is a complex practice that is more than just an activity that can be broken down into simple and objectively measurable variables; it is full of casual, unforeseen and indeterminate moments which inevitably make for the ultimate unmeasurability of *how* television is used in the context of everyday life.

The problem I refer to here has been foreshadowed by a classic study by Robert Bechtel et al. (1972), who in the early 1970s observed a small sample of families in their homes over a five-day period. Ironically, the method these researchers used is very similar to that of the passive people meter. The families were observed by video cameras whose operation, so the researchers state, was made as unobtrusive as possible: 'There was no way to tell [for the family members] whether the camera was operating or not. The camera did not click or hum or in any way reveal whether it was functioning' (Bechtel et al. 1972: 277). More important, however, were the insights they gained from these naturalistic observations. Their findings were provocative and even put into question the very possibility of describing and delineating 'watching television' in any simple sense as 'a behaviour in its own right': they asserted that their 'data point to an inseparable mixture of watching and nonwatching as a general style of viewing behavior', and that 'television viewing is a complex and various form of behavior intricately interwoven with many other kinds of behavior' (ibid.: 298–9). Logically, this insight should have led to the far-reaching conclusion that having people fill out diaries or, for that matter, push buttons to demarcate the times that they watch television is principally nonsensical because there seems to be no such thing as 'watching television' as a separate activity. If it is almost impossible to make an unambiguous distinction between viewers and non-viewers and if, as a consequence, the boundaries of 'television audience' are so blurred, how could it possibly be measured?

This study was certainly ahead of its time, and its radical consequences were left aside within the industry, because they were utterly unbearable in their impracticality.[4] Instead, technological innovations in audience measurement procedures is stubbornly seen as the best hope to get more accurate information about television consumption. Still, in advertising circles, in particular, growing scepticism can be observed as to the adequacy of ratings figures, no matter how detailed and accurate, as indicators for the reach and effectiveness of their commercial messages. For example, there is a growing interest in information about the relationship between television viewing and the purchase of products being advertised in commercials. After all, this is the bottom line of what advertisers care about: whether the audiences delivered to them are also 'productive' audiences (that is, whether they are 'good' consumers). For example, in more avant-garde commercial research circles the search for ever more precise demographic categories, such as the people meter provides, has already been losing its credibility. As one researcher put it:

> In many cases, lumping all 18–49 women together is ludicrous. . . .
> Narrow the age spread down and it still can be ludicrous. Take a 32$1/2$ year-old woman. She could be white or black, single or married, working or unemployed, professional or blue collar. And there's lots more. Is she a frequent flier? Does she use a lot of cosmetics? Cook a lot? Own a car? Then there's the bottom line. Do commercials get to her? These are the items the advertiser really needs to know, and demographic tonnage is not the answer.
>
> (Davis 1986: 51)

The kind of research that attempts to answer these questions, currently only in an experimental stage, is known as 'single source' measurement: the same sample of households is subjected to measurement not only of its television viewing behaviour but also of its product purchasing behaviour (see, e.g., Gold 1988). Arbitron's ScanAmerica, for example, is such a system. In addition to measuring television viewing (using a push-button people meter device), it supplies sample members with another technological gadget: after a trip to the supermarket, household members (usually the housewife, of course) must remove a pencil-size electronic 'wand' attached to their meter and wave it above the universal product code that is stamped on most packaged goods. When the scanning wand is replaced in the meter, the central computer subsequently matches that information with the family's recent viewing patterns, thus producing data presumably revealing the effectiveness of commercials (Beville 1986b; *Broadcasting* 1988). Needless to say, this system is technically 'flawed' because it necessitates even more active co-operation than just button-pushing. But the tremendous excitement about the prospect of having such single-source, multi-variable information, which is typically celebrated by researchers as an opportunity of 'recapturing . . . intimacy with the consumer' (Gold 1988: 24) or getting in touch with 'real persons' (Davis 1986: 51), indicates the increasing discontent with ordinary ratings statistics alone as signifiers for the value of the audience commodity.

Similarly, one British advertising agency, Howell, Henry, Chaldecott and Lury (HHCL), has recently caused outrage in more orthodox circles of the advertising industry by launching a strong attack on the common practice of selling and buying advertising time on the basis of people meter ratings statistics. In an advertisement in the *Financial Times* it showed a man and a woman making love in front of a television set while stating: 'Current advertising research says these people are watching your ad. Who's really getting screwed?' (see Kelsey 1990).[5] HHCL's alternative of getting to know the 'real consumer', however, is not the high-tech method of computerized single-source research, but more small-scale, qualitative, in-depth, focus group interviews with potential consumers of the goods to be advertised.

What we see in this foregrounding of qualitative methods of empirical research is a cautious acknowledgement that television consumption practices, performed as they are by specific individuals and groups in particular social contexts, are not therefore generalizable in terms of isolated instances of behaviour. If anything, this marks a tendency towards a recognition of what could broadly be termed the 'ethnographic' in the industry's attempts to get to know consumers. This ethnographic move is in line with a wider recent trend in the advertising research community in the United States and elsewhere to hire cultural anthropologists to conduct 'observational research' into the minutiae of consumer behaviour that are difficult to unearth through standard surveys (Groen 1990) – an interesting and perhaps thought-provoking development in the light of the growing popularity of ethnography among critical cultural researchers![6]

CONCLUSION

What are we to make of these developments? To round off this chapter, then, some concluding remarks. First of all, it is important to emphasize that a research practice such as audience measurement is constrained by strict institutional pressures and limits. We are dealing here with an industry with vested interests of its own. Market research firms are for economic reasons bound to respond to changes in demand for types of research on the part of media and advertisers. Furthermore, it is important to stress the *strategic*, not analytic, role played by research in the organization and operations of the cultural industries. Research is supposed to deliver informational products that can serve as a shared symbolic foundation for industry negotiations and transactions, and epistemological considerations are by definition subservient to this necessity. Thus, innovations in audience measurement should be understood in this context: in the end, market-driven research will always have to aim at constructing a 'regime of truth' (Foucault 1980) that enables the industry to improve its strategies to attract, reach and seduce the consumer. In this respect, recognition of some of the tactics by which viewers appropriate television in ways unintended and undesired by programmers and advertisers may under some circumstances be beneficial, even inevitable, as I have shown above. But the interests of the industry cannot and do not permit a complete acceptance of the tactical nature of television consumption. On the contrary, consumer tactics can be recognized only in so far as they can be incorporated in the strategic calculations of media and advertisers. In other words, despite its increasing attention to (ethnographically oriented) detail, market research must always stop short of acknowledging fully the permanent subversion inherent in the minuscule but intractable ways in which people resist being reduced to the imposed and presumed images of the 'ideal consumer'.

If we take full account of this inherently tactical nature of television consumption, however, we must come to the conclusion that any attempt to construct positive knowledge about the 'real consumer' will always be provisional, partial, fictional. This is not to postulate the total freedom of television viewers. Far from it. It is, however, to foreground and dramatize the continuing dialectic between the technologized strategies of the industry and the fleeting and dispersed tactics by which consumers, while confined by the range of offerings provided by the industry, surreptitiously seize moments to transform these offerings into 'opportunities' of their own – making 'watching television', embedded as it is in the context of everyday life, not only into a multiple and heterogeneous cultural practice, but also, more fundamentally, into a mobile, indefinite and ultimately ambiguous one, which is beyond prediction and measurement. But this idea, which if taken seriously would corroborate the adoption of a fully fledged ethnographic mode of understanding, is epistemologically unbearable for an industry whose very economic operation depends on some fixed and objectified description of the audience commodity. Therefore, it is likely that technological improvement of audience measurement will for the time being continue to be sought, stubbornly guided by the strategically necessary assumption that the elusive tactics of television consumption can in the end be recaptured in some clearcut and hard measure of 'television audience', if only the perfect measurement instrument could be found.[7]

De Certeau speaks of a 'strange chiasm':

[T]heory moves in the direction of the indeterminate, while technology moves towards functionalist distinction and in that way transforms everything and transforms itself as well. As if the one sets out lucidly on the twisting paths of the *aleatory* and the metaphoric, while the other tries desperately to suppose that the utilitarian and *functionalist* law of its own mechanism is 'natural'.

(de Certeau 1984: 199)

Meanwhile, American film producers worry that, as advertising in cinema theatres proliferates, more would-be moviegoers will stay at home and watch the film on video. Advertisers, unrelentingly in search of new ways to reach their potential consumers, have not been too keen on putting their commercials on video tapes, reportedly because they distrust one element missing from cinemas: the fast-forward button (Hammer 1990).

NOTES

1 This statement should not be interpreted monolithically. Discourses of audience produced by and within television institutions are certainly neither homogeneous nor without contradiction. In my book, *Desperately Seeking the Audience* (1991), I specifically discuss the differing assumptions about the 'television audience' and its sustaining 'viewing behaviour' as operative in the historical practices of American commercial television and European public-service television, respectively.

2 For a comprehensive overview of the audience measurement industry in the United States, see Hugh M. Beville Jr (1985).

3 I discuss extensively the introduction of the people meter in the American television industry in Part II of *Desperately Seeking the Audience*. The people meter is currently seen as the standard technology for television audience measurement in countries with developed (i.e. commercial, multichannel) TV systems, including most West European countries and Australia.

4 The study was part of the huge Report to the Surgeon-General's Scientific Advisory Committee on Television and Social Behavior, which was commissioned to establish facts about the effects of television violence. Even in that context, however, Bechtel *et al.*'s (1972) project was marginalized. As Willard Rowland (1983: 155) has noted,

[a]s provocative as this research was, its design violated so many of the normal science requirements for acceptable survey research that it had little impact on the major directions taken by the overall advisory committee program. Indeed this study was permitted only as a way of testing the validity of survey questionnaires. The somewhat radical theoretical implications of its findings were largely overlooked at all levels of review in the project.

5 The evidence dug up by HHCL was already substantiated in an earlier, IBA-funded research by Peter Collett and Roger Lamb (1986), similar in set-up to Bechtel *et al.*'s (1972) study, in which they confirmed the widespread occurrence of 'inattentive viewing' in the home.

6 For a more substantial discussion of the politics of ethnography in audience research, see Ang (forthcoming).
7 In this respect, it is interesting to note that the American national TV networks, faced with declining viewing figures for their programmes, are now insisting on the incorporation of television viewing *outside* the home (in bars, college dormitories, hotels and so on) in Nielsen's audience measurement procedures (Huff 1990).

REFERENCES

Ang, Ien (1991) *Desperately Seeking the Audience*, London: Routledge.
——(forthcoming) 'Ethnography and radical contextualism in audience studies', in Lawrence Grossberg, James Hay and Ellen Wartella (eds) *Towards a Comprehensive Theory of the Audience*, Chicago: University of Illinois Press.
Baker, William F. (1986) 'Viewpoints', *Television/Radio Age*, 10 November.
Baudrillard, Jean (1988) 'Consumer society' [1970], in his *Selected Writings*, Stanford, Calif.: Stanford University Press, 29–56.
Bechtel, Robert B., Achelpohl, Clark and Akers, Roger (1972) 'Correlates between observed behavior and questionnaire responses on television viewing', in E. Rubinstein, G. Comstock and J. Murray (eds) *Television and Social Behavior*, vol. 4: *Television in Day-to-Day Life: Patterns of Use*, Washington, D.C.: United States Government Printing Office, 274–334
Bedell Smith, Sally (1985) 'Who's watching TV? It's getting hard to tell', *New York Times*, 6 January.
Beville Hugh M., Jr (1985) *Audience Ratings: Radio, Television, Cable*, Hillsdale, N.J.: Lawrence Erlbaum.
Beville, Mal (1986a) 'People meter will impact all segments of TV industry', *Television/Radio Age*, 27 October.
——(1986b) 'Industry is only dimly aware of people meter differences', *Television/Radio Age*, 10 November.
Broadcasting (1988) 'Arbitron to go with peoplemeter', 27 June.
Certeau, Michel de (1984) *The Practice of Everyday Life*, translated by Steven Randall, Berkeley: University of California Press.
Collett, Peter and Lamb, Roger (1986) *Watching People Watching Television*, London: Independent Broadcasting Authority.
Davis, Bob (1986) 'Single source seen as "new kid on block" in TV audience data', *Television/Radio Age*, 29 September.
Foucault, Michel (1979) *Discipline and Punish*, translated by Alan Sheridan, Harmondsworth: Penguin.
——(1980) *Power/Knowledge*, ed. Colin Gordon, New York: Pantheon.
Gitlin, Todd (1983) *Inside Prime Time*, New York: Pantheon.
Gold, Laurence N (1988) 'The evolution of television advertising–sales measurement: past, present and future', *Journal of Advertising Research* 28(3): 18–24.
Groen, Janny (1990) 'Consument thuis per video begluurd', *De Volkskrant*, 20 January.
Hammer, Joshua (1990) 'Advertising in the dark', *Newsweek*, 9 April.
Huff, Richard (1990) 'New Nielsen study boosts numbers', *Variety*, 26 November.
Kelsey, Tim (1990) 'The earth moves for the ratings industry', *The Independent on Sunday*, 18 February.
Livingston, Victor (1986) 'Statistical skirmish: Nielsen cable stats vex cable net execs', *Television/Radio Age*, 17 March.
Meehan, Eileen (1984) 'Ratings and the institutional approach: a third answer to the commodity question', *Critical Studies in Mass Communication* 1(2): 216–25.

Rosenthal, Edmond M. (1987) 'VCRs having more impact on network viewing, negotiation', *Television/Radio Age*, 25 May.

Rowland, Willard (1983) *The Politics of TV Violence*. Beverly Hills: Sage.

San Francisco Chronicle (1989) 'New "people meter" device spies on TV ratings families', 1 June.

Sepstrup, Preben (1986) 'The electronic dilemma of television advertising', *European Journal of Communication* 1(4): 383–405.

Silverstone, Roger (1990) 'Television and everyday life: towards an anthropology of the television audience', in Marjorie Ferguson (ed.) *Public Communication: The New Imperatives*, London: Sage, 173–89.

Smythe, Dallas (1981) *Dependency Road*, Norwood, N.J.: Ablex.

Spigel, Lynn (1988) 'Installing the television set: popular discourses on television and domestic space, 1948–1955', *Camera Obscura* 16: 11–48.

TV World, 'The US is watching', September 1987.

Chapter 9

Contextualizing home computing
Resources and practices

Graham Murdock, Paul Hartmann and Peggy Gray

Along with the video cassette recorder, the Walkman and the compact disc player, home computers were one of the most conspicuous consumer products of the 1980s. From their first appearance at the beginning of the decade, they attracted an increasing amount of research aimed at finding out who was entering the domestic micro market and who wasn't, identifying barriers to adoption and how they might be overcome, and exploring what people were actually doing with their machines. This work, which began in the United States but spread rapidly to other advanced economies, employed a variety of methods, ranging from nationwide surveys (e.g. Danko and MacLachlan 1983) to studies of early adopters and computer enthusiasts (e.g. Dickerson and Gentry 1983; Hall *et al.* 1985) and ethnographies of computer households (e.g. Tinnell 1985). But beneath the differences of approach, virtually all these studies were united in viewing home computing activity in a radically decontextualized way. They shared this myopia with much of the new reception analysis that was emerging within mass media research over the same period (see Murdock 1989). Both currents of work focused on the practical activities of audiences and users but took little account of the way these activities were structured by the resources that consumers could draw upon, or were excluded from.

These resources are material, social and symbolic. Home computers are not just commodities that are traded for a price in the market. They are also the site of a continual cultural struggle over the meaning of the machine and its appropriate uses. In Britain, this has taken the form of a contest between offical discourses stressing home computing's educational and instrumental potentials, and commercial discourses promoting its entertaining, playful and expressive uses. Each discourse offers particular user identities, which intersect with the material resources and social relations inside and outside the household to produce specific patterns of use or disuse.

This chapter sets out to explore the relations between practices and resources, drawing on material gathered in the course of a longitudinal study of domestic communication technologies based on samples of just over one thousand households, drawn from four contrasted locations in the English Midlands.[1] All respondents were interviewed at three points in time about their use of media and new technology, including home computers. These indexical data were supplemented by focused interviews with computer users, drawn from the main samples. Because the detailed material presented here is not properly ethnographic, in the sense that it did not involve periods of observation outside the interview visits, it is necessarily limited in the issues it can raise about the relation of computing to household structures. At the same time, the fact that the interviewees were located through a large cross-sectional survey, provided access to a wider range of experiences than is usually the case with qualitative studies.

The period covered by the research, 1983 to 1987, coincided with the British home computer market's takeoff to growth. At the end of 1981 (when the first cheap, easy-to-use machines were launched) less than a quarter of a million households had a micro. By the spring of 1986, this figure had climbed to 3.06 million (*Marketing Week* 1986). Because the Midlands interviews were conducted over this crucial period, they provided clues to the complex interplay between the user careers of individuals and households and the general development of the home computer industry as a whole.

Most research on home computing has either ignored the diachronic dimension, and settled for a snapshot at a particular moment, or approached it from the point of view of the computer industry's interest in devising more effective marketing strategies (e.g. Venkatesh and Vitalari 1986). Work on the diffusion of innovations is a partial exception, however. This is centrally concerned with the social dynamics of adoption and use over time but until recently has paid little attention to material constraints, and no attention at all to the role of public discourse in organizing use.

MATERIAL RESOURCES: FROM DIFFUSION TO DIFFERENTIAL ACCESS

Writers in the 'diffusion of innovations' tradition are concerned with the processes whereby a novel object or practice comes to be adopted by the members of a society or social group and incorporated into everyday routines and practices (Rogers 1983). Diffusion models were orginally developed in relation to studies of agricultural innovations in rural America in the 1940s, in an attempt to explain why some farmers were more willing to adopt new techniques. After World War II they became one of the major theoretical linchpins of US-sponsored 'modernization' strategies in the Third World.

In the early 1980s, one of the key figures in developing the diffusion perspective, Everett Rogers, began to apply it to the spread of home computers in the United States. As a resident of southern California, living close to Silicon Valley, one of the major sites of commercial activity concerned with microcomputing, he was particularly well placed to observe its development as both an industry (see Rogers and Larsen 1984) and a market (e.g. Dutton *et al*. 1987). In seeking to explain patterns of adoption and use, Rogers and his co-workers originally focused on the interplay between the capacities and characteristics of the available machines – what they could do and how easy they were to use – and the personal needs and dispositions of users and potential users – what they wanted a machine for, whether they had any relevant skills or experience, and whether their attitude towards technology in general was positive or hostile. They paid comparatively little attention to the role of material resources in regulating market entry.

This was largely because their model took it for granted that everybody was a potential computer owner and that the diffusion curve would follow other major innovations in consumer electronics, such as the television set, with adoption trickling steadily down the income scale. This ignored the widening income gap and rising levels of unemployment produced by Reaganomics. As the decade wore on, however, research showed quite clearly that, despite a massive promotional effort, home computer ownership remained concentrated within the professional and managerial strata. The diffusionists accordingly modified their position, and accepted that 'differential access seems to be primarily based on income differentials across socio-economic status groups' (Dutton *et al*. 1988: 14). This pattern was repeated in other advanced capitalist societies (e.g. Jouet 1988). It was particularly marked in Britain, where the Family Expenditure Surveys revealed a clear linear relation between income and computer ownership. In 1986, for example, only 7.6 per cent of households with a weekly income of under £125 had a home computer, compared to 26.6 per cent of households in the income band £325–75 (see Murdock and Golding 1989).

The Midlands study confirms and extends this point. Economic capacity not only played a central role in determining whether or not a household entered the home computer market, it also shaped subsequent patterns of use in significant ways. A number of applications, such as word processing, are either made much more difficult or ruled out altogether if the machine owned is one of the cheaper models without a dedicated monitor or a printer. The last wave of the panel study, conducted in 1987, revealed that, despite the rapid growth of the Amstrad PCW range and the proliferation of relatively cheap IBM PC 'clones', the majority of computer households in the study still only had the machine they had first bought, more than half of which were basic Sinclair or Commodore models. Only one in four had traded up and acquired a more sophisticated model.

Behind these figures lay experiences of disillusion, particularly among those who had bought into 'the home computer revolution' in its first phase.

The limits of these early cheap machines were not obvious at first. On the contrary, as one teenager recounted, in 1983 when sales first boomed, they seemed exciting and full of possibility.

'I don't know really why, because it suddenly started didn't it, computers everywhere. The first one I ever saw was the [Sinclair] ZX81, which I thought was really good when I first saw it. It's nothing really is it? because it can only print the name on the screen.'

This restriction was a source of considerable disappointment to users who bought one thinking it could do more than it could.

'I wanted it as a word processor, but of course it's no good for that at all. I didn't appreciate it at the time. You can't get enough words on the screen, unless you get one that's about four or five times the price. . . . With this one you can only read four or five words across and you've had it. I just went round a bit and I thought, well this was the best for the price you know. I wanted it for a word processor and they said, "Oh yes they can do this" and "Oh yes they do that", you know. And of course it does, but not satisfactorily for proper use.'

Programming also proved to be a problem, with naive users often finding that it took far longer than they anticipated to master the skills they needed to pursue their own projects. As one young teacher explained: 'I quite enjoyed the programming side of it, but found that it was a lot of work to achieve very, very simple results. Although it was quite a challenge.'

Often initial enthusiasm dwindled rapidly, as in this account by a woman who had seen her husband and son lose interest:

'I think they thought they were going to do great things with it, and make programmes and use it in all sorts of ways. But then they realized what a long time it was going to be to learn to do this, and a long time putting the programme in. They haven't had the time.'

The problems of using the basic models to produce self-generated material were often compounded by two other material limitations.

One of the attractions of the early Sinclair and Commodore machines, besides their relatively low price, was the fact that they did not need a disc drive or dedicated monitor. They could be operated using a standard black-and-white television set as a display screen and a portable audio cassette recorder to load and store software. But both these selling points imposed important limitations on use. Whilst tape technology was cheap and convenient, it was not particularly robust in use and took a considerable time both to load programmes into the machine and retrieve stored material. Even in 1987, however, when the third wave of the Midlands survey was conducted, three-quarters of computer households still relied entirely on tape technology. An even higher proportion, 80 per cent, had computers without their own screens, and were still using a domestic television set for visual display facilities.

This was less of a problem where the machine was connected to a set reserved for the purpose and placed in a permanent location. As the survey results showed, however, this was a luxury that poorer households could not always afford. Because they were less likely to own a second or third television set, the home computer became a literal extension of the main set, competing with broadcast programming and video cassette recorder use for access to the screen. This meant that computing activity was restricted both spatially and temporally, with the keyboard and television set having to be connected and disconnected each time the machine was used. Not having an integral computer screen will become even more of a disadvantage if and when Britain's fifth terrestrial television channel comes on stream. This will employ the same frequency as home computers currently using a television set as a monitor and, though these machines could be re-tuned, the industry consensus is that most owners will not bother.

To sum up: the available evidence reveals a consistent relationship between patterns of home computer ownership and use and a household's income and class position. The more affluent the household the more likely it is to own a home computer and the more likely that this will be one of the more expensive and versatile machines with a built-in screen, a disc drive and a printer, capable of supporting a wide range of uses and applications.

The material resources at a household's disposal – in the form of discretionary income, domestic space and related technologies – can be said to be determinant in 'the first instance', in the sense that they establish the basic conditions of access to and exclusion from the various configurations of computing equipment (see Murdock 1989). To explain why this equipment is used in particular ways, however, or why it falls into disuse, we need to go on to explore the social resources at the user's disposal.

SOCIAL RESOURCES: NETWORKS AND DISCONNECTIONS

One of the strengths of the 'diffusion of innovations' perspective is its emphasis on the role of social networks in fostering and sustaining new practices. According to this argument, the maintenance of particular forms of computer use will depend in large part on access to other users who can offer advice, encouragement and practical support. Conversely, users who are isolated from or marginal to such networks may find it difficult to acquire competences and sustain interest over time. The centrality of networks emerged strongly from the Midlands data. As the following interview account makes clear, contacts can play an important role in providing back-up support at key moments.

'My friend down round the estate, who's got the same machine, which is useful because he has a lot of system software that I don't have. He's into computers as a job. It's useful. The other day when I was using the word processor, I was trying to save it. I had spent all morning keying it in. It's only an extract from a magazine. Started at 8 o'clock and finished about lunch. You make one mistake and it's rubbish. Terrifies you. Oh it's a swine to type in, and I wanted to make sure I'd save it. So, I saved a load of tape without turning the machine off. I then carried my tape recorder round to his machine to see if it would load on his machine. If it would then I was alright. So I was lucky, because if I'd turned it off I'd have wasted eight hours of work.'

Contacts also help to legitimate particular patterns of use through the swopping of information and anecdotes and exchanging software. Almost 60 per cent of the computer users interviewed in the Midlands study said that they often talked about computing to friends and acquaintances, and around half claimed to borrow and exchange software on a regular basis. Significantly, those with little or no contact with other users were more likely to have stopped using their machines once the initial novelty had worn off. They tended to live in households where no one had a job that involved using computers or gave them access to relevant expertise and contacts, and in neighbourhoods with relatively few other users. These patterns of social and spatial segregation interacted with the differential distribution of material resources described earlier to reinforce the disadvantaged position of users and would-be users in low-income households.

At the same time, we must be careful not to overstate the importance of class location. Computer use is also very strongly inflected by generation and gender. Among the Midlands sample, domestic micros were overwhelmingly concentrated in households with children and adolescents. By 1985, when the second wave of interviews was conducted, over a third (35 per cent) of 'nuclear families' had acquired one, as against 5 per cent of couples without children and 6 per cent of people living alone. When households with computers were asked to say who the main user was, only one in seven nominated a female. In fact, apart from a small number of adults in professional and managerial jobs, who mainly used their machines for work-related tasks, and a scattering of hobbyists, home computing was the province of children and teenagers and of boys rather than girls, a pattern confirmed by Jane Wheelock's recent research on Wearside (Wheelock 1990, and chapter 6). To explain these age and gender biases we need to go beyond the differential distribution of material and social resources, and explore the way the promotional discourses around home computing have drawn on activities and identities associated with youth and masculinity.

DISCURSIVE RESOURCES: THE MULTIPLE MEANINGS OF THE HOME MICRO

From its first entry into the British market, the home computer has been enmeshed in a web of competing definitions of uses and users, as the promotional discourses of the hardware and software industries (see Haddon 1988a) jostled for public attention with governmental discourses about information technology and education. By defining the micro's potentialities and pleasures in different ways, these discourses played an important role in structuring the ways it was used.

The push to market a micro for home use came initially from firms selling kits that purchasers assembled themselves. These began to appear in the late 1970s and were aimed firmly at committed hobbyists who wanted to explore the possibilities of the technology and had the competence to cope with the machines' far from 'user-friendly' characteristics, including the complete lack of pre-written software. They were, in Leslie Haddon's useful phrase, 'self-referring', in the sense that the pleasures they offered derived not from particular applications but from the possession of the technology itself and from solving the problems involved in getting it to perform.

This notion of the 'self-referring' machine was generalized by the British entrepreneur, Clive Sinclair, whose consumer electronics company had grown out of his own interest in inventing and brainstorming. He launched his first model, the ZX 80, in 1980, as a machine for learning to program on. Since there was no supporting software, this was more of a necessity than an invitation. Not surprisingly, it found its main market among enthusiasts with computer skills. They were also among the first to buy his second and more powerful model, the ZX 81, launched the following year. This extract from an interview captures the computer hobbyist's pleasure in possession particularly well.

> 'I caught the bug over ten years ago at college on the mainframe there. I was so keen that one summer holiday period I conned this company that I was just a little guy with a couple of "O" levels and I wanted to be an operator, and they trained me up. It was 8K. So, an expanded ZX 81 is more powerful. And this was a mainframe. This took up a whole room. I always thought one day I would have my own, you know. I just can't believe it now, I still haven't got over the shock.'

At the same time, the ZX 81 began to pick up sales in the general consumer market among households with little or no previous computer experience. Within twelve months of its launch, 400,000 had been sold, establishing it as the brand leader in the British home computer market. Its nearest rival was the VIC 20, produced by the American company, Commodore, which, like the Sinclair, used an ordinary domestic television as a display screen and a portable audio cassette recorder in place of a disc drive.

1981 also saw the launch of the government's scheme to put a microcomputer into every secondary school as part of its plan to help 'prepare children for life in a society in which devices and systems based on microelectronics are commonplace and pervasive' (Department of Education and Science 1981: 1). In line with the diffuse 'Buy British' policy in information technology, schools were directed to the machines manufactured by two domestic companies, Acorn and Research Machines. Acorn had a distinct advantage in this competition since the BBC's well-publicized computer literacy course, launched at the beginning of 1982, was built around their model. In October 1982, the Micros in Schools scheme was extended to primary schools, and once again Acorn was on the list of approved suppliers. This double seal of official approval, from the government and the BBC, gave a considerable fillip to Acorn's push into the general consumer market, and by the end of 1983 their machines had achieved sales of around 250,000.

Their marketing strategy resonated strongly with official discourse about the coming 'information age', and played on parents' hopes and fears about their children's future employment prospects. The advertisement for the second generation of Acorn machines is a good example. Headed 'Think of it as a downpayment on your child's future uniform', it featured a girl in her graduation robes, bathed in sunlight, standing in the cloisters of one of the country's ancient universities. The accompanying copy was addressed directly to parental worries.

> Your child's degree ceremony might seem a long way off. But the BBC Master Compact is equipment to help at every step of the way. Our new micro can provide your child with constant support throughout education, eventually graduating into business and professional use. Put it on your Christmas list. It should help to put a few letters after your child's name.

A contemporaneous advertisement, for the colour monitors aproved for use with BBC micros in schools, underlined this message, arguing that:

> This year, no less than 20,000 schools rely on the high resolution of Cub monitors to make computer-related education more clearly understood . . . . Now Microvite have made this same range available for home use . . . . It has never been more vital to ensure that your child has the benefit of the finest teaching aids . . . . The Microvite Cub is the colour monitor which your child will expect and is unlikely to out-grow.

These promotional appeals presented home computing as a form of rational recreation, in which domestic space becomes an extension of the classroom and the office, and the user practises 'useful' skills, gradually moving on to more complex tasks and becoming a fully functioning member of the computerized society.

This vision of the micro as an essential aid to educational and career advancement played a key role in encouraging parents to invest in one. Altogether, three-quarters of all the households in the Midlands survey that had a computer claimed to have purchased a machine with children and teenagers in mind. Many had gone out and bought one in much the same spirit as they might earlier have bought a set of encyclopedias. Its acquisition often coincided with the development of computer studies in school. Sometimes the push came from the children, as in this teenager's account of using his BBC micro:

> 'It was the time when everybody was getting a computer really, and I wanted one for school. So I thought I'd get one like the stuff I used at school, so I used it to get through my "O" level . . . . We did a project in the Fifth Form, which was handy, 'cause I could do it at at home you see.'

He also experimented with uses linked to his interests: 'what I used to like writing was sound programmes. Doing, you know, making? 'cause I used to have a music book and I used to type in. That's what I used to do a lot of.'

This form of micro use as rational recreation was the exception rather than the rule, however. With the prices of basic models starting at around £300, comparatively few families in the Midlands sample could afford an Acorn/BBC machine, and most therefore settled for one of the cheaper machines, in the belief that simply having one in the house would be beneficial. The following account is typical.

> *Son (14)* We didn't have anything to do with it. It was him over there [indicating the father]. We got in from school one day and he said, 'Right we're going to go and get a computer'.
> *Father* We'd obviously got a bit of spare cash like. I'd got some money coming at the end of the summer, and I said we'd go out and buy it at the beginning of the summer, didn't I?
> *Son* Yes.
> *Father* They were just about to start learning it at school when we got it, and I thought it wouldn't be fair if they got left behind . . . . I thought I could try it anyway, and then I found that I couldn't drive it at all [laughs].

In common with many parents with little or no knowledge of computers, this father hadn't realized that the cheaper machines were not well suited to educational applications. Their primary uses were being constructed by a quite different discourse.

The initial wave of parental decisions to buy a basic Sinclair or Commodore coincided with the point in time when the cheap micro was beginning to emerge as a games-playing machine. The major push in this direction came from the software companies rather than the hardware producers, several of whom feared that too close an identification with games would undermine the micro's status as a general-purpose machine. As the executive who handled Commodore's advertising campaign in the early 1980s put it: 'We wanted always to see our product as a proper piece of technology: but fun technology. We didn't want to see it as a toy' (quoted in Haddon 1988b: 71). By 1983, however, this precarious balance between 'proper' and playful uses had been tipped in favour of games-playing by the promotional activities of the entertainment entrepreneurs who were entering the software market. They saw home computer games as a logical extension of two other screen-based entertainment systems: the video games console that plugged into a domestic television set, and the coin-operated video games machines installed in amusement arcades.

In the United States, higher levels of disposable income combined with tax breaks encouraged households to invest in relatively powerful domestic computers, leaving a definable market niche for dedicated games consoles. Sales took off in 1975, when Atari launched its tennis game, 'Pong' and grew substantially after 1976, when reprogrammable cartridges were introduced. In contrast, the British console market started a little later and was undercut by cheap computers before it had a chance to establish itself. As a result, only 2 per cent of households had acquired a video games console by the end of 1982, compared to 15 per cent in the United States. Price was again a significant factor. In 1983, reprogrammable video consoles cost between £70 and £140, with games cartridges selling for between £20 and £30. By that time, consumers could purchase a basic Sinclair machine for less than £70, and select games from a rapidly expanding catalogue of titles for around £5 each. Moreover, the ubiquity of cassette recorders meant that games borrowed from other users could be copied for the price of a blank tape, despite the software manufacturers' best efforts to protect their sales with anti-piracy devices. Breaking these security systems became a popular pastime among computer hobbyists. For some, the main pleasure was in beating the system. Actually playing the game was secondary. As one teenager recounted: 'I must admit, I do have great fun trying to crack protection systems. But that's more to do with the fun of it, rather than anything to do with the programme once you've got it on tape.'

Other hobbyists, like this 21-year-old unemployed male, experimented with altering standard software and writing their own games. As he explained in interview:

> 'Games are nice to play, but I always have a go. I say, "I wonder if I could make that game", and then I try it myself. Sometimes people come and say "That's a nice programme. Did you buy it?" and I say "No, I made it" My talent seems to lie in making it look better . . . . For a start, I look for a different presentation, the title screen, etcetera, adding all little items like that . . . . One of me greatest achievements was writing me own adventure programmes, where I could slot in any adventure I wanted.'

Most users, however, were content to buy commercially produced games tapes. These drew on a range of sources, including the genres that had proved popular in the arcades.

Video games began to replace pinball machines in the arcades in the late 1970s. Their iconography was overwhelmingly masculine. Most were either simulations of glamorized male activities, such as flying a fighter aircraft or driving a Grand Prix racing car, or variants on the scenario where the player defended territory against enemy attack. The most famous of these games, 'Space Invaders', was introduced in 1979, to be followed by hosts of others. According to one American study, by the mid-1980s, women appeared in only 8 per cent of arcade games, and then mostly in passive roles (Toles 1985). The more polymorphous games such as 'Pac-Man', were less obviously gendered, but overall, the imaginary world of arcade games was overwhelmingly masculine. This bias was reinforced by the social organization of the arcades themselves and the fact that they had mostly been commandeered by adolescent male peer groups as arenas for competitive display.

This masculine orientation carried over into the home computer market when the most popular arcade games were adapted for domestic use. It was also evident in the other major games genres: sports and adventure games. Although some adventures drew on sources popular with girls as well as boys, such as J.R.R. Tolkien's fantasy, *The Hobbit*, many relied on predominantly masculine genres such as horror and science fiction (Skirrow 1986). A recent survey of Midlands teenagers, conducted in 1989, confirms the continuing gender bias of games-playing, with boys being twice as likely as girls to play once or twice a week and six times as likely to play three or more times a week.[2] Arcade games were still far and away the most popular genre, followed some way behind by simulations, sports and adventure games. There was also a strong age pattern, with games-playing falling away sharply by the age of 15, when activities outside the home become more central in peer group life. Nevertheless, it remains easily the most common use of micros by young people.

Despite its centrality, games-playing has never quite shaken off the connotations of addiction that surrounded the early arcade games. In 1981, the Labour MP George Foulkes narrowly failed to push through his 'Control of Space Invaders (and Other Electronic Games) Bill' in the House of Commons. Concern continued through the decade, but in 1988 a Home Office study concluded that there was no need for further legislation, and placed the responsibility for controlling adolescent use of arcades firmly on the shoulders of parents and managers (Graham 1988). Early worries about harmful 'effects' had already carried over into the domestic market, however, and home computer games were included in the terms of the 1985 Video Recording Act, which was introduced to regulate pre-recorded video tapes and eradicate the so-called 'video nasties'. Beneath these debates lay the familiar Victorian concern with the 'proper' use of leisure, and the continual clashes between contrasted definitions of rational recreation, trivial pursuits and dangerous pleasures.

By mid-decade, then, there were at least four major discourses around home computing, offering competing definitions of its potentialities and pleasures: the discourse of self-referring practice in which the machines appeared as a space for creative activity and problem-solving; the discourse of 'serious' applications related to the schoolroom and workplace; the discourse of games-playing and fun which presented the micro as another screen-based entertainment facility; and the discourse of righteous concern for the welfare of the young. These discourses provided the symbolic context within which the parents and children in the Midlands study negotiated and struggled over the uses of their machines.

MICROS AND MORAL ECONOMIES

The outcomes depended on the way households were organized as economic and cultural units, their moral economies (Silverstone 1991: 139, and chapter 1) and, in particular, on the structure of authority and the distribution of computing expertise among family members.

Parents familiar with computers sometimes made a determined effort to encourage 'serious' use, as in this mother's account of activities with her 10-year-old son and 12-year-old daughter:

> 'The first computer came when we had the children, even though my husband used to be a computer engineer and I use a computer at school with the children I work with. It is for educational purposes. We have always encouraged them. It is not just for playing games. Even when we had the Spectrum, before this Atari, we had a word processing package. They would write little stories, and we had a comprehension package, and a maths package, even when they were little. We all use the Atari. . . . We play games together. We have chess and so on.'

Other parents, even those used to working with computers, had given up an unequal struggle and accepted that the machine would be mainly used for games, though some rationed computer use in an effort to encourage their children to spend more time on 'improving' activities. As one mother (who taught computing in a secondary school) explained:

> 'On the whole they use it mainly for games, and therefore I do restrict how long they use it, because a lot of games I consider as not very worth while, and, like television, I believe in restricting what they do in some way.'

Other families resorted to more stringent measures, such as packing the computer away. As another mother related:

> 'We don't like to get it out too often because it's a temptation to them to give up their swotting. 'Cause once they start playing games, it's difficult to stop, we found that. . . . They are quite good and disciplined about it. They know that they've got work to do at the moment. So I say, "Right, we'll put it away".'

In all three of these cases, the parents attempted to exercise control over use, either positively or negatively. But, as the Midlands interviews revealed, this was much more difficult with older teenagers, particularly where the parents had little or no computer competence themselves. In these situations children could use their time on the micro to win space and privacy within the household and assert their separation and independence from their parents. This was particularly important in the case of fathers and sons, as in this account by a an unemployed man in his early twenties living at home. His father, a skilled tradesman, had never attempted to master the computer but valued practical expertise.

> 'It's a programme that's very simple to make. It just keeps jiggling through all the numbers. It's a system a lot have used to crack telephone numbers. 'Cause this place is ex-directory, and me dad said "You can't do it in a week", and I said, "Yes, I can". And using the number plan and the telephone book and a bit of guesswork as well, I located the number. And he says, "I backed you twenty pound that you can't do it in a week", he says. And I got my sister involved in as well, and we ended up taking forty pounds off him. Served him right.'

CONCLUSION

These tales from the field afford fleeting glimpses of complex processes, deeply embedded in the sedimented structures of families' interior lives. To tell these tales in the detail they deserve, we will certainly need better and deeper ethnographies of everyday consumption. But, as we have also argued, if we are interested in explanation as well as description, we will also need to look for better ways of linking these micro processes to the wider economic, social and symbolic formations that surround and shape them. We need more sensitive explorations of the continual traffic between public and private, interiors and exteriors, and of connections between user careers and the general trajectory of the computer industry, between biographies and history.

As we have argued, the British home computer market was divided, almost from the outset, into a 'serious' sector based around relatively powerful machines of the type being introduced into schools and offices, and a games-playing sector in which cheap computers became another extension of screen-based entertainment, often literally, since many families used a television set as a monitor. There is every sign that this bifurcation will continue. The recent *rapprochement* between the two leading personal computer companies, Apple and IBM, looks likely to consolidate their control over the market for 'serious' machines, whilst the Japanese companies, Nintendo and Sega, have revivified the market for dedicated games consoles, selling half a million units by the middle of 1991.

The Midlands data suggest that this industrial segmentation will be mapped onto social divisions, and that self-determined computing will remain concentrated in the relatively affluent and well-educated households of the professional and managerial strata, whilst the rest of the population are largely confined to participating in professionally crafted fantasies. They will have interactivity without power. The consequences of this situation for democratic participation, in a society increasingly organized around screen-based systems, deserves more extended discussion than it has so far received.

NOTES

1 The research was made possible by grants from Central Independent Television, the Economic and Social Research Council and the Research Board of Leicester University. We are grateful to all three organizations for their support.
2 This study, based on a survey of 460 11 to 15-year-olds in six schools in a Midlands town, was conducted by Mr Robert Cromwell in 1989 as part of his research for his doctoral thesis at the University of Loughborough.

REFERENCES

Danko, William D. and MacLachlan, James M. (1983) 'Research to accelerate the diffusion of a new invention: the case of personal computers', *Journal of Advertising Research* 23 (3): 39–43.
Department of Education and Science (1981) *Microelectronics Education Programme: The Strategy*, London: Department of Education and Science.
Dickerson, Mary and Gentry, James (1983) 'Characteristics of adopters and non-adopters of home computers', *Journal of Consumer Research* 10: 225–34.
Dutton, William H., Rogers, Everett M. and Jun, Suk-Ho (1987) 'The diffusion and

impacts of information technology in households', *Oxford Surveys in Information Technology* 4: 133–93.

Dutton, William H., Sweet, Patrick L. and Rogers, Everett M. (1988) 'Socioeconomic status and the diffusion of personal computing in the United States', paper presented to the conference of the International Association for Mass Communication Research, Barcelona, 24–8 July.

Graham, John (1988) *Amusement Machines: Dependency and Delinquency*, Home Office Research Study no. 101, London: HMSO.

Haddon, Leslie (1988a) 'The home computer: the making of a consumer electronic', *Science as Culture* 2: 7–51.

——(1988b) 'Electronic and computer games: the history of an interactive medium', *Screen* 29 (2): 52–73.

Hall, P.H., Nightingale, J.J. and MacAulay, T.G. (1985) 'A survey of microcomputer ownership and usage', *Prometheus* 3 (1): 156–73.

Jouet, Josiane (1988) 'Social uses of micro-computers in France', paper presented to the conference of the International Association of Mass Communication Research, Barcelona, 24–8 July.

Marketing Week (1986) 'Mediabank: videographics', 17 October.

Murdock, Graham (1989) 'Critical inquiry and audience activity', in Brenda Dervin, Lawrence Grossberg, Barbara J. O'Keefe and Ellen Wartella (eds) *Rethinking Communication* vol. 2: *Paradigm Exemplars*, London: Sage 226–49.

Murdock, Graham and Golding, Peter (1989) 'Information, poverty and political inequality: citizenship in the age of privatized communications', *Journal of Communication* 39 (3): 180–95.

Rogers, Everett M. (1983) *Diffusion of Innovations*, 3rd edn, New York: Free Press.

Rogers, Everett and Larsen, J.K. (1984) *Silicon Valley Fever: Growth of High-Technology Culture*, New York: Basic Books.

Silverstone, Roger (1991) 'From audiences to consumers: the household and the consumption of communication and information technologies', *European Journal of Communication* 6: 135–54.

Skirrow, Gillian (1986) 'Hellivision: an anaysis of video games', in Colin McCabe (ed.) *High Theory/Low Culture: Analysing Popular Television and Film*, Manchester: Manchester University Press. 115–42.

Tinnell, Carolyn S. (1985) 'An ethnographic look at personal computers in the family setting', *Marriage and Family Review* 8 (1–2): 59–69.

Toles, Terri (1985) 'Video games and American military ideology', in Vincent Mosco and Janet Wasko (eds) *The Critical Communications Review*, vol. 3: *Popular Culture and Media Events*, Norwood N. J.: Ablex, 207–23.

Venkatesh, Alladi and Vitalari, Nicholas P. (1986) 'Computing technology for the home: product strategies for the next generation', *Journal of Product Innovation and Management* 3 (3): 171–86.

Wheelock, Jane (1990) 'Personal computers, gender and an institutional model of the household', paper presented to the ESRC/PICT workshop on Domestic Consumption and Information Technologies, Brunel University, May.

Part III

Appropriations

Chapter 10

The Young and the Restless in Trinidad

A case of the local and the global in mass consumption[1]

Daniel Miller

INTRODUCTION: AN ANTHROPOLOGY OF SOAP OPERA?

This chapter has a substantive problem and a theoretical proposition. The substantive problem is the popularity of soap opera in non-metropolitan regions. In the early 1970s there was already a perennial anecdote among undergraduates in anthropology departments about a much-studied Middle Eastern society famed for its arduous annual migrations which had altered their date of departure that year in order to watch the end of the current series of *Dallas*. Even then, there seemed something in this that was shockingly subversive to the core of anthropology as discipline and as ideology which kept this anecdote fresh. Leaving aside the implications over concepts of authenticity, it is clear that soap opera is symptomatic of a shift by which myriad local cultures are increasingly reconstructing themselves in articulation with what has been termed 'global forms'. This is hardly a new discovery and there is a large body of anthropological writings which examine this issue in terms of imperialism (e.g. Wolf 1982), absorption (Sahlins 1985), resistance (Kahn 1985) and syncretism (e.g. Bastide 1978). While most such work on global trends has emphasized shifts in production relations, soap opera helps focus attention on the parallel process in mass consumption (see also King 1984). My own entry into this problem came during fieldwork in Trinidad when, for an hour a day, fieldwork proved impossible since no one would speak with me, and I was reduced to watching people watching a soap opera. It is likely that this anecdote could be cloned by many other contemporary anthropologists faced with Hum Log in India or a Brazilian telenovela. Consideration needs to be given not only to the sheer proportion of time spent watching, for example, the five hours of daily telenovela in Venezuela, but also individual programmes watched in over 100 countries (Lull 1988).

Much of the relevant research has been devoted to what might be called the pioneer colonizer of this type of television programme, *Dallas* (see Ang 1985; Silj 1988). Studies emphasize the value of comparative analysis, both cross-cultural (e.g. Silj 1988) and within a single area, as in the study of the reception of *Dallas* by four different ethnic communities in Israel (Katz and Liebes 1986). As Ang (1985) notes, the fascination with *Dallas* is at least partly due to its niche within a general discourse on Americanization, but at the risk of over-generalizing this diverse research, audiences are rarely portrayed as focusing on the dramatically exotic or on the potential for emulation in *Dallas*. On the contrary, the sense is of an extended patriarchal family drama with two dominant messages: first, that wealth does not bring happiness and, second, that, however hard one struggles to escape the constraints imposed by family membership, such efforts are doomed to failure. In general these are messages which, it could be argued, find a not uncomfortable niche within the classic moral tales of many parts of the world. Particularly poignant is the description of the response by Soviet immigrants to Israel who acknowledge the supposed critique of wealth but assume this is merely the kind of propaganda familiar from Soviet television (Katz and Liebes 1986).

Similar analytical approaches are applied to the still more important spread of local equivalents of soap opera which usually dominate in each individual country (Silj 1988: chapter 3). Britain, in particular, has a firmly established tradition of realist if nostalgic working-class serials which are seen as particularly characteristic and have been much studied. There is also the phenomenal success of telenovela in Latin America marketed mainly from Mexico and Brazil. All of this should be sufficient to establish the substantive basis for a proposed anthropological investigation of what clearly represents a major shift in the daily routines of most of the peoples of the world.

This substantive issue may now be set alongside a theoretical problematic, which is concerned to establish whether an approach to the nature of contemporary mass consumption can be applied to the articulation between global and local phenomena. It is increasingly the case that we do not make the products and images with which we live, but these come to us from other sources, so that our relationship is intrinsically one of consumption not production. This process was accelerated by the industrial revolution and is globalized as more countries are involved in wider commodity exchange. I have argued, however (Miller 1987), that consumption, as much as production, can be seen as a relation within which we create or objectify ourselves, in the expressivist tradition. Consumption is usually considered in terms of individuals but in this paper I am concerned with the manner by which a 'local', that is Trinidad, constructs itself in the consumption of the 'global', that is the foreign media. Within Trinidad itself there is a powerful discourse which argues that, given the forces of cultural imperialism, the air bases stationed there during the last war and similar factors, the country has been the passive victim of Americanization, a theme picked up by the Trinidadian novelist V. S. Naipaul (1967) in his book *The Mimic Men*. This, however, may be countered by many instances of more positive forms of appropriation. Trinidad is the home for one of the most eloquent instances of appropriation as transformation through the development of the steel band, using discarded products of the oil industry to create an original sound which has become familiar throughout the world. This example suggests that Trinidad does not merely accept, reject or transform foreign, i.e. global influences, but it is also a contributor to the construction of global forms, as in the increasing popularity of 'World Music'.

From this perspective, we no longer see the domestic sphere as merely the context for the reception of a foreign import. Rather my concern is with the manner by which a global media form is reconstituted in the same process by which it helps to transform Trinidadian domesticity. It will be argued that, paradoxically, an imported soap opera has become a key instrument for forging a highly specific sense of Trinidadian culture.

THEORIZING THE DOMESTIC

It has become something of a truism today to state that the domestic is culturally constructed, but the implications of this statement may be examined by comparing two diametrically opposed approaches to it. The first is derived from that relativism which has always been a core tradition of classic anthropology. We try and have as few preconceptions as possible as to what a term such as 'domestic' might mean, possibly preferring to assume that there will be no local concept into which it would easily translate. However, in the process of fieldwork we might find that there is a strong sense of a spatial nexus associated with the inside of some architectural form which is in turn associated with some kin-based unit such as a unit of reproduction, and an ideology of gender asymmetry. At a certain point we might feel justified in translating the local term which represents these cultural attributes as the 'domestic' discussed in the academic literature, while remaining constantly alert to the problems of projecting onto this term our expectations and categories (cf. Strathern 1988).

The other position in this debate is derived from an article by Bourdieu which examines the genesis of groups in social space (1985). The subject of Bourdieu's discussion is class rather than the domestic but it is not hard to transpose the argument. In the concluding section entitled 'Class as representation and will', Bourdieu argues that in many respects class is as much the product as it is the subject of writings on class, especially those of Marx and the interests which have maintained the discourse of class.

Though Bourdieu does not focus on the global nature of this discourse, this term seems increasingly appropriate. What proportion of the world's population today has not been exposed to the concept of class and the reorientation of their cultural perception in the light of this exposure? The implication of this approach is that we can no longer detach the prior existence of some social form based on, for example, the relations of production, from more than a century of explicit discourse on the nature and identity of class as a perspective from which to view the world and oneself.

The same point would apply to a global discourse about the nature of the domestic, which is evident in France or Australia or Trinidad where one of the most popular television programmes, *The Cosby Show*, is typical of those sit-coms that seem to use the experience of the domestic as the very core for their ethical and emotional appeal. In Trinidad also we can talk of the domestic as both representation and will. There is the ubiquitous presence of the church, the extreme domesticity historically represented by the colonial wife, or 'agony aunt'-style radio programme which continually affirm the fiction of the nuclear family against the actualities of Trinidad's varied domestic groups.

Given this history, some reconciliation of the two points of view is required. Although the ethnographic could never be seen as naive with respect to the long influence and didactic weight of a global discourse on the domestic, it does not necessarily follow that this model provides either the sole vision or the general experience of actual cultural life. From the perspective of consumption as objectification the 'local' is not a leftover prior form, studied in so far as it is unaltered by exposure, nor is it some kind of pure resistance. Rather it is that which arises ethnographically through consumption of the global discourse. Relativism comes now a posteriori rather than a priori.

THE YOUNG AND THE RESTLESS

The Young and the Restless may be introduced through a particularly Trinidadian perspective. Below is an edited transcript of one of the two calypsos launched in 1988 called 'The Young and the Restless'. This one was rapturously received by audiences from the moment it started with a copy of the soap's theme tune, and the laughter, provoked by what is largely a summary of plot, usually continued to the end.

Hear how it go,

> Philip and Cricket did love bad.
> For some reason Jack Abbott dohn like Brad.
> Nina, the old lady dohn like she,
> Nina stick Philip with a baby.
> Jack Abbott, he went crazy
> over Cricket' mummy,
> so though the woman got Aids
> he still went and marry she.
> You talk of commess
> check the young and restless,
> commess at its best
> check the young and restless.
> Everyday at noon precisely
> old and young in front their TV.
> Well believe me this ain no joke
> some people carry TV to work,
> to watch the bacchanal
> to watch the confusion,
> I tell you the picture
> is a sensation.
> It was *Dallas* and *Dynasty*
> that had TV fans going crazy,
> then came *Falcon Crest*
> but they can't touch *Young and Restless*,
> when it comes to bacchanal
>> (Extract from 'The Young and the
>> Restless' by calypsonian 'The
>> Contender')

The Young and the Restless fits the narrow category of true soap opera as given by Cantor and Pingree (1983) of afternoon serials as opposed to the prime-time series such as *Dallas*. It has been produced since 1973, though by Columbia pictures for CBS rather than the original 'soap' group produced by Proctor and Gamble. The targeted audience is the housewife, reflected in the emphasis on dialogue rather than visual content, so that it is compatible with domestic work. According to these same authors, *The Young and the Restless* is one of a group which tends to a greater orientation towards sex and social breakdown than the prime-time series. Within the field of soap opera *The Young and the Restless* is situated in the 'liberal' group, which is particularly so inclined (ibid.: 94).

The Young and the Restless was introduced to Trinidad following other lunch-hour soaps and was not therefore expected to have the same weight as serials such as *Dynasty* and *Dallas*. Advertising space was consequently cheaper at that period, which is seen as the housewives' slot, although by the end of fieldwork retailers were insisting that the producers target this time slot. Evidence that the effect of this soap opera emanates from the salience of its content and is not merely the product of well-targeted television comes from the manner in which it has completely overthrown the power of the prime-time slot and that Trinidadians have refused the logistical constraints and insisted on watching the series even when conditions should have constrained them. The case reveals something of the flexible potential of television as technology. Many of the favourite stories surrounding the aura of *The Young and the Restless* are about the extremes people go to in order to see what is generally termed the 'show' on a daily basis, although it is repeated in full at weekends. Particularly important are battery-operated miniature televisions, which are vital for those wishing to see the show at work. These are particularly conspicuous in retailing, where shop assistants have one eye to the screen, even as they serve, but many also find their way into office lunching areas. The miniature televisions are generally purchased abroad on shopping trips to places such as Caracas or Miami, or brought in by relatives resident in Canada or the USA. The disruptive impact of the show on work was heightened by the desire of those without access to a television to use the subsequent hour to pick up the details they had missed.

Much less common because of their relative scarcity, was the use of videos to reschedule watching to a more convenient time after work. Those with low income, for example, a large squatting community amongst whom I worked, were amongst the most resourceful in gaining access. The bulk of these homes have neither water nor electricity, but given the imperative to watch the 'show' many homes have televisions connected to car batteries which are recharged at a small fee per week by those who have electricity supplies.

A local marketing survey carried out early in 1988, I suspect before *The Young and the Restless* had peaked, suggested 70 per cent of those with TV watched the show regularly, slightly more than those who watched the news, both of these being well ahead of the third highest rating, which was less than 30 per cent. In my own survey of 160 households,[2] out of the 146 who had access to a television all but 20 watched *The Young and the Restless* regularly. There was no evident association with ethnicity, but only 5 out of 71 in the lower income bracket did not watch this show while 15 out of 75 in the higher income bracket did not watch it. In a separate question, where 44 households mentioned their favourite programmes, 37 gave *The Young and the Restless* as one of them.

The viewing of the soap opera is often both a social and a participatory affair. Few televisions fail to attract a neighbour or two on a regular basis. Individuals may shout deprecations or advice to the characters during the course of the programme. Afterwards there is often collective commentary and discussion. There is a considerable concern to spread news of important events quickly. I was slightly 'shocked' in my vicarious sense of propriety, when an important Muslim festival I was viewing was interrupted by three ladies who collectively announced to the assembled group some new development which we had missed by taking part in the ceremony. Typically also, people telephone each other to confirm that they knew all along that some event was going to occur.

For most of this century and particularly since the stationing of American troops there during the Second World War, Trinidad has been the recipient of sustained influences from the United States, reinforced by the number of families with relatives who have emigrated to North America, by macro-economic pressures and by the American dominance of the media. The nature of American society and the implications of its current influence upon Trinidad are certainly contentious issues, and one might have expected that the soap opera would be viewed in relation to these issues, but a review of the conversations in which the soap opera is discussed or used for illustrative purposes shows that this is not the case. Indeed, one of the most common comments about the show was its relevance to contemporary conditions in Trinidad. Typical would be:

'The same thing you see on the show will happen here, you see the wife blackmailing the husband or the other way around, I was telling my sister-in-law, Lianna in the picture, just like some bacchanal woman.'

'It really happening this flirtatious attitude, this one they living together that partner working this partner, and have a date with the next one or in bed with another.'

'People look at it because it is everyday experience for some people. I think they pattern their lives on it.'

From this sense of relevance comes also the idea that there are direct lessons to be learnt from the narrative content for moral issues in Trinidad, e.g.

'It teach you how husbands could lie and cheat and how a wife could expect certain things and never get it, the women always get the short end of the stick.'

'I believe marriage should be 50–50 not 30–70 the woman have to be strong she have to believe in her vows no matter what . . . that make me remember *The Young and the Restless*, Nicky want her marriage to work but Victor is in love with somebody else, but she still holding on.'

Or (as in a current story)

'You always to go back to the first person you loved, in my own family my elder sister went with a Moslem boy, and so was married off by parents to a Hindu man, but she left her husband, gone back to the first man and had a child by him.'

As evidenced in the study of *Dallas* in Israel this moral use of the show will depend upon the perspective it is being viewed from. The Trinidad evidence supports Buckingham in arguing that the audience feels quite able to retain both a sense of critical distance which breaks the frame of realism and yet have intense involvement in the 'as if scenario' which results (Buckingham 1988: 200; see also Vink 1988: 232–40). This may emerge in the desire to intervene in or comment on the construction, as in the following two comments on AIDS:

'We find that Jessica so nice they shouldn't have given her Aids they should have given Jill, somebody nice shouldn't have been given Aids.'

'I like the idea of Aids, since there was an episode which explain to Cricket how you get it, that you can't get it through swimming pools, so I find that was good, it's educational especially to housewives. It also show two sides to each person like Victor who would be warm and loving but cruel and nasty. In *Dallas* you hate JR and I don't think you would be able to like him again, but it is not like that on *The Young and the Restless*. I like the way they do their make-up, the Australian soap operas seem very dull make-up, but this one outstanding shades of lipstick, eye make-up, earring and kinds of jewellery, the way they dress and everything goes with everything else.'

There can also be criticism of over identification, as in

'With my mother in the USA she so involved you would actually think it is some of she children she is talking about.'

BACCHANAL

From both the calypso and the above quotations it is clear that Trinidadians have themselves developed a set of ideas which accounts for the attraction and success of this particular soap opera. This is encapsulated in the phrase 'they like the bacchanal'. Outside Trinidad this term would connote some kind of orgiastic or frenzied celebration, and so it is not surprising that the term is also frequently applied to the annual Carnival. But within Trinidad bacchanal has far more complex connotations. If one looks at the use of the term in calypso the first synonym is clearly 'scandal'. In 1988 David Rudder sang 'Bacchanal Woman, sweet scandal where she walks', while Carl and Carol Jacobs sang, 'We people like scandal. We people like bacchanal.' In the 1988 Carnival queen competition there was an entry with the title of 'Bacchanal Woman', the costume consisting of a voluminous pink/scarlet dress with exaggerated breast and buttocks, but above this was a spreading fan of layers like a peacock's tail emblazoned with a series of open eyes.

The second clear connotation of the term 'bacchanal' is confusion or disorder. The two major connotations are linked by the other unfamiliar term in the calypso, that is 'commess'. In dictionaries commess is translated as extreme confusion, but it will normally carry the connotation of confusion which results from scandal. Indeed, it seems that Trinidadian language has retained a set of terms from earlier French patois for constructing a network of concepts which are not well covered by English. My work as an anthropologist in uncovering or listening in to gossip rendered me a Maco, or Macotious, potentially instrumental in spreading news or Movay-Lang (*mauvaise-langue*) which again leads to commess and to bacchanal.

A final semantic linkage is the connotation of the term 'bacchanal' as truth, as in the notion of bringing to light. It is not just that scandal reveals the hidden, but for many Trinidadians there is a moral value in this exposure. Scandal and confusion have highly ambiguous moral overtones, at once undermining patiently constructed systems of order and stability but also bringing us closer to the true nature of social being. The benign element of bacchanal is most evident in the affection for Carnival, which is the moment of the year given to the exploration of bacchanal as an ideal. Indeed the central motif for many in Carnival is the ritual of Jouvert, where groups dressed in mud and ashes organized into bands such as 'Barbarians' or 'Kids in Hell', full of ironic commentary parodying topical items such as advertisements, TV evangelists or *The Young and the Restless*, throng the streets before dawn. The event is dominated by dawn itself, the bringing into light of that which is normally hidden.

Having established this semantic network for the term 'bacchanal', we may now reintroduce it into two contexts as the instrument which relates them: that is the concept of the domestic, and the reception of *The Young and the Restless*.

In one of the most influential anthropological accounts of Caribbean society, Wilson (1973) divides Caribbean societies into two opposing cultural projects, which he terms 'respectability' and 'reputation'. Respectability is seen as the abiding influence of colonial pressures towards the kind of domesticity which is enshrined by the colonial female. This includes the drive to social stratification, religiosity, familial forms sanctioned by the church, and its major enshrinement is through women's involvement in the construction of a domestic domain. This becomes, however, in the Caribbean context an even more gendered distinction, since most men are entirely uninvolved in this arena. Rather they embody an oppositional tendency termed 'reputation', in which they are mainly engaged in male-only activities with transient peer rivalry but longer term egalitarian pressures, involving drinking, gambling and above all verbal play, resistant to the hierarchizing and constraining pressures of the domestic. Working from the perspective of Trinidad, I would wish to modify elements of Wilson's portrayal of the origins and implications of these projects, and a dualism he associates most closely with gender I see as being projected equally onto ethnicity in Trinidad and class in Jamaica. However, I would confirm a framework based on two opposed cultural projects, which in the Trinidadian case I have termed 'transient' and 'transcendent', emphasizing an orientation either to the event, or to descent or continuity respectively.[3] It is fair, then, to attempt to derive some sense of the domestic from within the transcendent end of this polarity and associate this with a commonly gendered division. Furthermore, these projects refer back to the global discourse of the domestic, incorporating images from television sit-coms or feminism respectively.

To provide a sense of the domestic we have to incorporate the articulation between spatial, familial and even aesthetic orientations. In Trinidad the domestic is probably best represented as a continual process of interiorization, a kind of centripetal force which operates towards containment and protection. In a larger study of living-room decoration (Miller 1990) I have shown the way this project is found in the aesthetic of coverings and layering that is also to be located in forms of dressing, attitudes to educational qualifications, to money, to the family, to property, to religion and other areas. The striving is always to the maintenance of boundaries, which protect the homogeneity and clarity of transcendent values and, in particular, render them as constant and stable, untouched by that vicissitude of events which is the characteristic of transience. In general this is a project associated with women, who in turn act to construct the home as its spatial loci. The apotheosis of this domestic project is the festival of Christmas, where a rise in mass consumption is based not on gift-giving but on home decoration and associated familial visiting.

The relationship between the values and ideals here termed transcendent and oriented to the longer term and the exteriorizing project of transience which places its emphasis upon style and is oriented to the event is a complex one. Some people manage to live almost entirely within one or the other, a greater number have elements of both but lean to the transcendent at Christmas and embrace the transient at Carnival. It is also common to spend one's youth in transience and move rather suddenly into religion, a home and marriage, reversing one's previous values. This structural opposition, manifesting the intrinsic contradiction of modernity as it is expressed through Trinidadian culture, is the point of departure for the formation of the concept of bacchanal, which may be a key concept in relating the two modes to each other.

As already noted, the term 'bacchanal' is deeply ambivalent, but certain groups do manage to transform it either into an almost entirely derisory or a benign assertion. From the perspective of transcendence it was commonly asserted that the current government, which is called the National Alliance for Reconstruction, but which was in practice falling apart into warring factions, was a clear case of bacchanal. The previous government's insistence, through fairly heavy-handed control, on keeping its internal divisions from public view was seen as a much more 'serious' form of rule. In my interviews with people within the very private and protected houses of the middle class, I found that women, in particular, were extremely fearful, sometimes literally terrified, that their husbands would get to know that they had been talking to me (but equally to my female research assistant) about their domestic circumstances. Women are understood as being responsible for the domestic world. They not only build it but equally they are seen as the weak link whose revelations or wrong behaviour would lead to its collapse. It is here that the centripetal aesthetic is clearest, in the strategies for enclosure, layering and covering up to protect themselves from revelation and exposure. When, as often happens within the realm of the transcendent, an apparently stable and close family is broken asunder into disordered fragments following a dispute over inheritance, the appellation of 'bacchanal' has nothing good about it.

Equally common, however, is the use of the term 'bacchanal' from the perspective of the transient. Here the term was most frequently used in relation to domestic scandal and exposure. The quintessential case is the woman or family that has gradually built up an aura of respectability, has entered fully into the spirit of transcendence, when suddenly some behaviour is revealed which indicates the false or hollow nature of the claims to respectability. In the context of the domestic, this may also be seen as the collapse of culture into nature, of chastity into lust, of façades of domestic calm into revelations of domestic violence and strife. One of the clearest expressions of bacchanal is what are called 'cuss-outs', in which two people stand before their houses and exchange insults, often for hours, while an audience gathers to appreciate the quality of the verbal invective.

The background to this is the centrality of gossip to social relations and the control of access to potentially revelatory information. Gossip is both highly stylized and frequently leads to confusion. For the transient of the squatting community there may be a positive identification with this culture of gossip, as they see themselves as the true objectification of bacchanal. This was the area where you would hear the most elaborate cussing-out, where gossip flowed free and far, where the walls of houses built from the boxes in which car parts are imported could scarcely hope to conceal the activities of the domestic arena. From their perspective it is the connotations of truth and nature which are particularly important. It is they who can condemn as façade the 'social' (meaning anti-social) ways of the suburb, and who insist that eventually all such attempts to respectability will fail, as all will succumb to the natural drives which lead them into scandalous situations. One of the strongest instruments of bacchanal is clearly the sexual imperative, and the term 'nature' is as equally connotative of sex itself as it is of the male's world in nature outside the domestic.

From the transient view the domestic depends on a very different sense of 'being' than at least the colloquial sense of that term in metropolitan societies. The latter tends to a kind of depth ontology where 'being' is associated with inwardness but also of realness, firmness, solidity, something deep down that changes slowly if at all. Façade is by definition on the outside facing outwards, and always implies superficiality. For the transient the aesthetic of being works in a very different manner. Interiorization is more like hoarding, trying to keep private, keeping away from proper public scrutiny in whose gaze being is constantly reconstituted. From this perspective there should be no interior space. Rather, to know who one is depends upon the public response to a constructed exterior, locally to one's sense of 'style'. For these Trinidadians bacchanal is largely benign. It may lead to confusion, fighting, etc., but still it is a welcome return to a kind of natural state. Friendship in bacchanal is spontaneous, relationships are dyadic and transient, without the constraints on freedom imposed by social convention and structure.

As in other accounts of soap opera it is clear that the 'realism' with which it is identified has little to do with the environmental context of domestic presentation; the scenes cannot look like Trinidad. Realism rather is based on the truth of the serial in relation to key structural problematics of Trinidadian culture. It is the realism of myth. The soap opera is a meta-commentary on the nature of truth itself. It explores through its stories the processes by which natural forces such as lust and gossip break open the global discourse of the domestic into the confusion and disorder of true life.

A major preoccupation in the soap opera is the manner in which individuals are thrown off course or driven to extreme actions by sexual desire. So a person writing a critical biography, almost against her will, starts an affair with the object of her work. A female working hard to be integrated within the respectable family of her child's father is seduced from these efforts by a good-looking male recruited for the purpose. Here, as in the Trinidadian ideology of the domestic, it is often the females who assert one morality but find themselves inexorably drawn through sexual attraction into overturning these same principles. The viewer notes, 'look how she is a commess maker, just so some women come to some people house and do the same thing'.

For some of the squatters there is not enough bacchanal:

'People in *The Young and the Restless* can't have fun like people in Trinidad, their sort of fun is boring. There's more bacchanal here than in *The Young and the Restless*, in each soap you can tell what's going to happen but around here you can't tell.'

Almost all the literature on soap opera emphasizes the forms of identification between the audience and the characters portrayed as central to the attraction of the genre. When I reviewed the occasions upon which informants noted personal identifications, it became evident that these almost always take a particular form that I had not encountered in the comparative literature (though see Vink 1988: 227–8, 236, on the work of Milanesi). It is rarely the character or personality of the individual which is seen as the point of identification. In the first instance it is almost always the clothing which mediates the act of identification as in the following quotes:

'I love Lauren, how she dresses and I identify with her.'

'I like Nicky the way she dresses, my name is Nicky too, she is a loving person.'

'I look mainly at *Dynasty* I like the way Alexis dresses, she is so sophisticated and I like the way Crystal dresses.'

'I like Nicky's and Lianna's dress I always look at Nicky's hair, her braids and bows and stuff, Mrs Chancellor does dress nice.'

'Even if you don't like what is happening you could admire their earrings or their pearl necklaces. I would copy Brad wife though I wouldn't like a husband like Brad.'

This identification may often translate into direct copying of clothes, so that seamstresses may conceive of watching the soap operas as part of their job. Although this quotation was about a different programme, it illustrates the point:

'Nah, when you see that show is about to start, the phone does ring. Gloria yuh watching it . . . like every dress she see she say "Oh God I want one like that", and how many yards to buy and I think she was writing on the other end.'

Another seamstress waits for someone to request a copy from the show and then watches the repeat at the weekend in order to note the style, in this case, a low cut-across with a frill and mini worn by Ashly but the colours dictated by the fact that they were watching on a black-and-white TV. At another level it is fashion which dictates the identification with the particular show as opposed to the particular individual:

'It is so modernized with Aids, up to date music-wise, clothes-wise, when you look at the shoes you say this is nice this is really up to date, it's modern it's now, that why you appreciate it more, I admire the earrings, necklaces.'

'The first thing I like about *The Young and the Restless* is the way they dress, I find it look right up to date fashion, all the women are so beautiful.'

The point was summarized in a retailer's laconic comment: 'What is fashion in Trinidad today – *The Young and the Restless* is fashion in Trinidad today.'

The important point about this use of clothing is not that it shows the superficial level at which the programme is absorbed, but quite the opposite. Given the principal exteriorizing, centrifugal aesthetic of bacchanal, it shows the centrality of the programme to that aspect of Trinidadian culture. In the approach to ontology espoused by transience it is precisely in the response to stylistic display that one finds out who one really is. This being is based on the event and is not accretative or institutionalized in social structures. It is reconstructed with each performance, which ideally requires a new set of clothing. During the oil boom, when families who had been brought up in poverty obtained wealth, they outdid the hegemonic classes in the transience of their fashions, not out of some 'crass' materialism, but rather as an appropriation of goods which opposed their incorporation into longer standing accretative structures (see Miller 1990). The identification through fashion is therefore evidence for the profundity of the experience of this programme rather than its inverse.

TV IN TRINIDAD

So far the discussion has implied that bacchanal is of much greater importance to the transient aesthetic than the interiorized domestic of the transcendent. This is the case, but the term also acts beyond this dualism as central to the construction of national identity. When Trinidadians were asked to describe their country in one word, by far the most common response was the term 'bacchanal', said with a smile which seemed to indicate affectionate pride triumphing over potential shame. It seems quite common in media research, for example Marchand's (1985) study of American advertising, to argue that a genre represents collusion between media creators and consumers to construct a set of images which comment on and possibly help resolve contradictions in contemporary culture: in that case between aspirations of modernity and nostalgia for tradition. In Trinidad, a small country quite self-conscious about the degree of wealth, education and sophistication enhanced by the experience of the oil boom, there is considerable participation in debates over the proper nature of Trinidadian television and, as noted by Wilk (1990), the implications of such images for cultural development. The audience may well attempt some intervention in programme scheduling of imports as in the 'protest' calypso by David Rudder whose chorus goes 'dey take *Kojak* off de TV, but what about *Dallas* and *Dynasty*?'. More commonly, however, the core concern is with television programmes which are made within Trinidad.

In general, political and official culture is associated with respectability and transcendence; politics should be a 'serious' (in the sense used by

Abrahams 1983) matter. The flagship of local television is the news, which may be complemented by an hour of extremely dull discussion of, for example, problems involved in ministerial planning. There is considerable concern with the quality and significance of locally made television and a ready tendency to contrast it unfavourably with imports. There have been several locally made drama serials. The current series has the open-ended structure of a soap opera focused on ethnic distinctions, which is recognized as the 'proper' problematic of Trinidadian society, with a considerable political impact. The stereotypes are exaggerated, with the East Indian involved in an arranged marriage, something virtually extinct in contemporary Trinidad.

In the world of bacchanal, however, ethnicity is becoming dissolved, as all ethnic groups are represented on both sides of its boundaries. It is, however, hard for local television to construct images this close to the ground. One large female comedian does succeed in portraying a fairly anarchic sense of bacchanal in advertisements and with her own programme, with few pretensions to quality props or realism; and based on local dialect humour, but this is exceptional. The newspapers, by contrast, with more localized control, have developed a bacchanal tradition associated with the weeklies.

In contrast to Wilson (1973), I do not want to suggest that transience is more authentic for Trinidad or less founded in colonialism than its opposite. The seriousness of the transcendent has arisen at the same time in the same structural tension, and both are the products of a continual dialogue with global discourses. The point here is a slightly narrower one, that there are strong constraints upon an institution as serious as Trinidadian television in producing clear expressions of bacchanal. There is a sense, then, in which the imported programme has the potential to articulate that aspect of the 'local' which the locally produced cannot incorporate, given its continuous eye on the external judgemental gaze. A point of particular concern to anthropology is that it is *The Young and the Restless* (more than, for example, Shango religion) which in daily conversation is associated with the wise adages and saws of folk knowledge. The two most popular television programmes are those devoted towards the two kinds of truth, *Panorama*, the news programme which reveals the serious truth, and *The Young and the Restless*, which reveals the truth of bacchanal.

TRANSFORMING THE DOMESTIC

A question remains as to the impact of these images upon the nature of the domestic in Trinidad. Clearly the serial represents a displaced form of gossip. Bacchanal is generally associated with innuendo and is not entirely provenanced. This is not a new phenomena, however. 'Town talk', as it used to operate, was also often based on the circulation of generalized genre suspicions before they could be pinned onto any particular person or place. Nevertheless, *The Young and the Restless* is still more displaced, which means that a considerable amount of gossip can take place in which people's actual interests are not involved, as in

> 'I prefer that, you see it is safer to talk about the celebrities' business than to talk about people's business. You won't get into trouble, nobody will cuss you if you say Chancellor was with this one husband . . . but it is just bacchanal . . . all them soaps is bacchanal.'

This comment helps account for the particular significance of *The Young and the Restless* at this point of time. Trinidad is an extraordinarily dynamic society. With the oil boom post-1973 it was catapulted into the world of mass consumption, but with the decline of the oil price, especially in 1986, it has suffered an almost equally precipitous recession. I would argue that bacchanal is more important than wealth *per se* in determining the local equivalent of class. The disdain felt by the suburban for the squatters is based on the uncontrolled commess of the latter. Wealth, however, is of considerable importance in allowing groups to struggle towards the respectability of transcendence and its instruments of interiorization and enclosure.

The oil boom gave a tremendous impetus to the growth of the middle class, to the extent that they emerged at its peak as dominant both numerically and culturally. With the recession, however, many of the more fragile pretensions of the *nouveau* element within this class are becoming exposed. There is a continual discourse about the financial plight that exists behind the closed doors of the domestic, which is only brought to light by events such as cutting off the phone because of unpaid bills. Even in the suburbs there were frequent rumours about how many properties were back in the hands of the banks or deserted by migrants to Canada. The crisis was largely financial but it is very possible that this was instrumental in the displaced crescendo of activity around the concept of exposure based on the more familiar theme of sexuality. Therefore this unprecedented orientation towards an imported soap opera may well have its roots in the near-exquisite tension that had built up between transcendence and transience and which is highlighted by the focus upon bacchanal.

Many of the writings on soap opera and serials tend to assume that these lend some reassurance, stability and so forth as part of their power. Much of this may stem from the legacy of the mass culture critique which treated soap operas as a kind of visual Valium that stupefies its audience in the interest of some dominant will. In certain cases this may well be the impact, but not in Trinidad. Here, so far from patching up a wound, or 'functioning' in the interests of social cohesion, the attraction of the programme is that it forces its point into the key fissure which manifests the basic contradiction of Trinidadian culture, at a time when this is especially sensitive. This is precisely why Trinidadian television cannot produce a programme of this kind. *The Young and the Restless* reinforces bacchanal as the lesson of recession which insists that the domestic and the façade of stability is a flimsy construction which will be blown over in the first storm created by true nature.

As such, the soap opera is merely a new transformation of a concept of bacchanal which has already a number of alternative forms of objectification, for example in Carnival. It is, nevertheless, innovatory in certain respects. The soap opera is closer to the everyday activities of those for whom bacchanal is a more constant experience, the world of gossip, scandal and confusion that generates the constant narrative structure of community life. It may thereby comment more directly on the current dynamics of the domestic while Carnival reflects more on a slower moving structural dualism within which the domestic is implicated. *The Young and the Restless*, in particular, colludes with the local sense of truth as exposure and scandal. The soap opera is not just Trinidadian but, as in a popular local expression, 'True True Trini'.

CONCLUSION: THE LOCAL AND THE GLOBAL

The terms 'global' and 'local' as used here are dialectical categories, which are proposed only to be productively dissolved in analysis. Indeed, the impossibility of a simple dualist approach to the local and the global is given by the juxtaposition of two points. On the one hand, bacchanal is the term many people gave as their one-word description of the essential character of Trinidadian society, and at the same time the principal form used to exemplify bacchanal in 1988 was not an indigenous production but an imported American soap opera. The mistake made by some studies is to assume that we are dealing with an 'American' product which others may not have the cultural knowledge to interpret 'properly', or that it simply slips into some local context (e.g. Katz and Liebes 1986; Schroder 1988). Although, in terms of production, we are dealing with what might be called the unintended consequence of international media marketing for profit, this chapter has argued that at the level of consumption we can observe both the recreation of the soap opera as Trinidadian and also its role in the refinement of the concept of Trinidad as the culture of bacchanal.

The term 'global' is useful because it does not exclude Trinidad, which is by definition as much a part of the world as, say, France. It accepts, then, that the work of writers such as V. S. Naipaul and C. L. R. James or music such as the steel band may be found today in shops in virtually any country in the world. At the same time we should not assume that the term 'global' connotes the massive homogenization presupposed by the debate on consumer culture. The influence of America includes everything from full gospel black churches and Miami brand names to youth music, to the creation of all of which the Caribbean contributed, and which represent the United States as an extremely heterodox society. Trinidadians are very keen on dissecting the stylistic distinctions between, say, New York and California, not to mention Puerto Rico.

Trinidadians sense their disadvantage in being small scale compared to larger national or multi-national forces. In particular, they are well aware of the highly authoritarian and ideologically charged pressures represented by the IMF, which presently dictates Trinidadian politics to what is regarded as a quite unacceptable degree. At the same time many see their fellow Trinidadians as often highly successful entrepreneurially and otherwise within the United States, which, while it is held in a kind of awe as the centre of metropolitan style, is simultaneously derided as often less sophisticated, less highly educated and a bit of a pushover by comparison with their own social milieu. The soap opera might have been used to comment upon the relationship between America and Trinidad or the nature of American 'bacchanal' but, as is often the case with melodrama, the setting is taken as a fantasy, under the cover of which viewers can consider intensely personal and local relations.

An individual case study tends to stress certain conclusions which need to be qualified in a comparative context. The example described here suggests that, in the production of one's own culture, indigenously created forms may provide for easier cultural appropriation, but imported forms may also have transformative potential as vehicles for objectification. A broader understanding of mass consumption within the global and the local, however, requires appreciation of the many constraints on possible appropriation. It also requires acknowledgement that in other cases the effects of an import may be detrimental, and what is produced is merely that sense of alienation which comes from an inability to appropriate that which is given by larger corporations as the means of cultural identity. To achieve a balance, a case study such as this one needs to be seen in conjunction with the findings of Mattelart (1983) on the deleterious effects of international media imperialism.

Trinidad was never, and will never be, the primary producer of the images and goods from which it constructs its own culture. To that extent an analysis of Trinidadian culture has at least in part to incorporate a theory of consumption. As with most nation-states today, Trinidad is largely the recipient of global discourses for which the concept of spatial origin is becoming increasingly inappropriate. This applies both to finance capital and to media ownership, which are becoming increasingly stateless (Harvey 1989: 163). If Trinidad wishes to participate in the wealth of images created through mass production, then it cannot hope to manufacture them all locally. This is merely the original lesson of the industrial revolution writ large. Trinidadians themselves are perfectly well aware of the advantages of global products made to higher specifications than they can manage, while being alert to inequalities in the terms of trade and potential insensitivity of global marketing to the needs of small markets. The fact that Carnival is derived from French colonial culture, Anansi stories from Africa, Divali from India, *Sesame Street* from the United States, Rasta from Jamaica does not dictate the process of local consumption with its considerable transformative properties. The mistake is to assume this means the end of specificity for Trinidadian culture. As noted at the beginning of this chapter, authenticity has increasingly to be judged a posteriori not a priori, according to local consequences not local origins.

ACKNOWLEDGEMENTS

Thanks are due to many friends and helpers in Trinidad who provided assistance during fieldwork and particularly my research assistant Shanaz Mohammad. Financial assistance towards various aspects of this project have been given by the British Academy, the Nuffield Foundation, the University of London Central Research Fund, the Wenner-Gren Foundation for Anthropological Research. Thanks also to Rickie Burman and Mike Rowlands, who commented upon a draft of this chapter.

NOTES

1 The fieldwork on the topic of mass consumption took place in 1988–9. The major component consisted of work in four communities in and around the town of Chaguanas in central Trinidad. Although often viewed as a centre for East Indians, the communities studied – which comprised a middle-class suburban residential area, a government housing project, an incorporated village and a settlement of squatters – reflected the ethnic make-up of the national census with approximately 40 per cent ex-East Indian, 40 per cent ex-African and 20 per cent Mixed and others. As one part of the fieldwork, a survey of forty households from each of the communities was carried out.

2 Although I conducted no interviews directly on the topic of *The Young and the Restless*, which was not an intended object of study, I frequently tape-recorded general conversations between informants, once it became evident that this did not seem to detract from their spontaneity. The quotations given in this and subsequent sections come from the transcriptions of these conversations. It may be noted that the bulk of these quotations are from women, partly because most of my fieldwork was conducted with women, but also because it was they who were more ready to acknowledge or refer to the soap opera in casual conversation.

3 These two terms, 'transient' and 'transcendent', are used here as analytical categories. I do not want to overextend their literal meaning, but they are intended to express polarized sets of values which are fundamental to Trinidadian culture, the former associated with individualism, the outside, and a refusal of institutionalization, the latter expressive of a concern for the longer term (e.g. roots or planning) and often conventional religion. There are some groups of people whose lifestyles and values seem clearly to embody such values, so that the text may speak of the transient from

the squatting area, i.e. those in that neighbourhood who consistently embody transient ideals. Most Trinidadians, however, will affirm both sets of values, depending on circumstances or season. The terms may also refer to these values as expressed in some cultural form, as with the transcendence found in living-room decorations.

REFERENCES

Abrahams, R. (1983) *The Man of Words in the West Indies: Performance and the Emergence of Creole Culture*, Baltimore: Johns Hopkins University Press.

Ang, I. (1985) *Watching* Dallas, London: Methuen.

Bastide, R. (1978) *The African Religions of Brazil*, Baltimore: Johns Hopkins University Press.

Bourdieu, P. (1985) 'The social space and the genesis of groups', *Theory and Society* 14: 723–44.

Buckingham, D. (1988) *Public Secrets*: East Enders *and its Audience*, London: British Film Institute.

Cantor, M. and Pingree, S. (1983) *The Soap Opera*, Beverly Hills: Sage.

Harvey, D. (1989) *The Condition of Postmodernity*, Oxford: Blackwell.

Kahn J, (1985) 'Peasant ideologies in the third world', *Annual Review of Anthropology* 14: 49–75.

Katz, E. and Liebes, T. (1986) 'Mutual aid in the decoding of *Dallas*: preliminary notes from a cross-cultural study', in P. Drummond and R. Patterson (eds) *Television in Transition*, London: British Film Institute, 197–8.

King, A. (1984) *The Bungalow*, London: Routledge & Kegan Paul.

Lull, J. (1988) *World Families Watch Television*, Beverly Hills: Sage.

Marchand, R. (1985) *Advertising the American Dream*, Berkeley: University of California Press.

Mattelart, A. (1983) *Transnationals and the Third World*, Massachusetts: Bergin & Garvey.

Miller, D. (1987) *Material Culture and Mass Consumption*, Oxford: Blackwell.

——(1990) 'Fashion and ontology in Trinidad', *Culture and History* 7: 49–77.

Naipaul, V. S. (1967) *The Mimic Men*, Harmondsworth: Penguin.

Sahlins, M. (1985) *Islands of History*, Chicago: University of Chicago Press.

Schroder, K. (1988) 'The pleasure of *Dynasty*: the weekly reconstruction of self-confidence', in P. Drummond and R. Paterson (eds) *Television and its Audience*, London: British Film Institute, 61–82.

Silj, A. (ed.) (1988) *East of* Dallas, London: British Film Institute.

Strathern, M. (1988) *The Gender of the Gift*, Berkeley: University of California Press.

Vink, N. (1988) *The Telenovela and Emancipation*, Amsterdam: Royal Tropical Institute.

Wilk, R. (1990) 'Consumer goods as dialogue about development', *Culture and History* 7: 79–100.

Wilson, P. (1973) *Crab Antics*, New Haven: Yale University Press.

Wolf, E. (1982) *Europe and the People without History*, Berkeley: University of California Press.

Chapter 11

The Amish and the telephone
Resistance and reconstruction

Diane Zimmerman Umble

Since 1909, the Amish in Pennsylvania, USA, have banned the telephone
from their homes. Through the description of the meaning of the telephone
as perceived through Amish eyes, this chapter attempts to bring a cultural
and historical perspective to our ongoing enquiry into the adoption of the
telephone and to the adoption of communication technologies in general.
The Amish response to the telephone highlights two perspectives that,
while obvious, are not always explicitly accounted for in research. First,
historical and cultural orientations shape the meaning of the telephone for
particular social groups. The telephone has little universal meaning apart
from that which is constructed or negotiated by those social groups who
make use of it. Its meaning is transformed as social and cultural boundaries
are crossed. Second, the telephone is not universally welcomed. The history
of those who reject, or in time reconfigure, telephone use for certain social
objectives can provide insight into our working assumptions about the
social meaning of the telephone. In the case of the Amish, rejection of
communications technologies such as the telephone seems to articulate
distinct social boundaries and in turn facilitates maintenance of those
boundaries and the community as a whole.

Telephone history in the United States has tended to focus on inventors
and institutions.[1] What is missing from instrument-centred accounts is
an examination of the ways in which the telephone began to challenge
existing social arrangements, an appreciation of the variety of responses
it engendered, and an understanding of the debates and negotiations that
illustrated the meaning it had for various subcultures. I address some of
these dimensions using a framework borrowed from Carolyn Marvin that
views new technologies less as 'transformative agents than as opportunities
or threats to be weighed and figured into the pursuit of ongoing social
objectives' (Marvin 1988: 232). She asks how habitual social intercourse
is restructured and renegotiated with the appearance of a new medium.

The debates within the Amish community over the meaning of the
telephone demonstrate how social, religious and cultural contexts set
the terms by which the meaning of a new communications technology is

constructed, and suggest that negotiated constructions serve specific social purposes. The decision by Amish leaders to ban the telephone from the home in 1909 figures prominently in accounts of a church split that resulted in the loss of one-fifth of their membership in 1910. This chapter describes Amish perceptions of the telephone and discusses how and why decisions to protect the Amish home from the telephone served to preserve social order.[2] First, allow me to set the contemporary context.

If you visited Lancaster County, Pennsylvania, today, you could arrive in Philadelphia by air, drive an hour and a half west by freeway to Lancaster, and find there all the marks of modern life: fast food restaurants, radio and television stations, shopping malls, manufacturing of products ranging from breakfast cereal and frozen chicken to floor coverings, colour television picture tubes and triggers for neutron bombs. You could observe any number of contemporary problems: traffic jams, air pollution, urban decay, drug abuse, homelessness. Then you could drive east of the city, and within ten minutes be in the heart of the oldest Amish settlement in North America. Here a community of 14,000 German-speaking men, women and children dress in plain black, blue, green and purple home-made clothing without zippers. In the fields, horses are used for ploughing, cultivation and harvesting. Horse-drawn carriages are used by the Amish for transportation. You would see windmills that pump water, one-room school houses where Amish children are educated, and tidy Amish farms with large vegetable gardens. The Amish home has no electricity, no radio or television, and no telephone.

Though banned from the home, the telephone has not been banished completely from the community. Throughout the Amish community, you would see, here and there, little buildings that look much like outdoor lavatories. These 'shanties' are what the Amish call 'community telephones'. Located at the end of lanes, beside barns, or in the garage of a non-Amish neighbour, these telephones have unlisted numbers, are used primarily for outgoing calls, and are shared by six or seven Amish families in a particular neighbourhood.

Community telephones are carefully managed by church leaders. Loud call bells to announce incoming calls are discouraged or prohibited. The telephone must be separate from the house. One Amish man describes it this way: 'If you have a place of business and need a phone it must be separate from the building, and if it's on the farm it must be separate from the house. It should be shared with the public so others can use it. It's just not allowed in the house, where would it stop? We stress keeping things small and keeping the family together' (Kraybill 1989: 149).

Community telephones represent an Amish compromise – access to the telephone without its intrusion. In order to understand the telephone ban, and the contemporary compromise, I will briefly sketch Amish history and culture. Since their origin, the Amish have practised nonconformity and maintained separation from 'the world'. Amish identity was (and is today) forged in the martyr tradition of the European Reformation. The Amish are descendants of Swiss Anabaptists (or rebaptizers), whose core beliefs threatened the authorities of their day. Anabaptist tenets included: adult baptism, unwillingness to take up arms, prohibition against swearing of oaths, separation of church and state, separation from the evils of the world, and an emphasis on simplicity and nonconformity. Persecution scattered the Swiss Anabaptists across Europe into remote areas in Moravia, Alsace, the Palatinate and the Netherlands, where they retreated to the hills and became skilful farmers.

The Amish take their name from Jacob Ammann, a young Alsatian church leader who wanted to reform the Swiss Anabaptist congregations. In 1693, Ammann advocated changes in the observance of communion and insisted that excommunicated members be avoided socially, or 'shunned'. When his reforms were resisted, Ammann and his followers left the main body of Swiss Anabaptists (known today as Mennonites).

On trips through Europe seeking immigrants to North America in the early 1700s, William Penn promised religious freedom and promoted fertile Pennsylvania soil. On the basis of Penn's promises, Amish migrations to Pennsylvania began. The first settlements were established in 1737.[3] The Amish carried their emphases on nonconformity and separation, along with considerable farming skills, to Pennsylvania, where they organized distinctive and prosperous farming communities, maintained through face-to-face communication and a strong oral tradition. Their distinctive plain dress, their German dialect, and the traditional patterns of life and worship served and still serve to mark and emphasize their distinctiveness.

Communications patterns within the Amish community are structured through the rituals of community life and anchored in the home. Communication is local, informal and highly contextualized. Amish faith is not separated from other spheres of life. Faith permeates every aspect of social practice and provides the context in which social relationships are managed.

The church is not a set of doctrines. Neither is faith expressed in words. Rather, for the Amish, faith is expressed in the 'way of life'. The community is an expression of faith in a hostile world. Eternal life is attained through the maintenance of a redemptive community – small, rooted in the land, mindful of its traditions, nonconforming and separate from the world.

A good Amish man or woman lives by his/her faith instead of talking about it. The ordering principle for that life is captured in the concept of *Gelassenheit* – a German word the Anabaptists used to convey the ideal which each member is to strive for. Roughly translated, *Gelassenheit* means submission – yielding to higher authority: God, the church, elders, parents, community or tradition. In practice, *Gelassenheit* demands obedience, humility, submission, thrift and simplicity.

One 'gives up' or 'gives in' in deference to another or for the sake of community.

The spirit of *Gelassenheit* is expressed in community rituals and social practices. One ritual that demonstrates both *Gelassenheit* and the centralization of communication is worship. The Amish do not have meeting houses; they worship in members' homes, rotating from one house to the next in a particular church district (or parish). Worship services are held every other Sunday. On the 'off Sunday', Amish families stay at home, visit family and friends, or attend services in a nearby church district. The Amish home is designed to accommodate the worship service. The typical house has two large rooms on the main floor: a large kitchen and a sitting room or parlour.

The typical Amish kitchen is a large room that serves as the family's primary living space. Since the Amish do not have electricity, lighting, cooking and refrigeration are often provided by propane or kerosene appliances. The main heat source for the home is usually in the kitchen. Heat is often provided by a kerosene, propane, wood or coal stove or space heater. In addition to appliances, most Amish kitchens include a large table with chairs or benches, a sofa and rocking chair near the stove, and a china cupboard. The second room on the main floor is a large parlour. This room adjoins the kitchen and is often separated by folding doors or removable partitions. The parlour is used on Sundays for visitors and for worship services when it is the family's turn to serve as host. On 'church Sundays', the partitions between rooms are opened, and benches and chairs are arranged facing the area where the preacher stands. Approximately 125 adults and children are in attendance. No district is larger than the number of persons who can be accommodated in an Amish home. When the congregation outgrows a home, it is divided.

Sunday gatherings are an all-day affair. People begin arriving around 7.30 in the morning. The three-and-a-half hour worship service includes slow singing, silent prayers, scripture readings and two sermons. The service is conducted in German. The service is long, sober and unhurried. The morning culminates in a simple, shared noon meal, followed by visiting throughout the afternoon.[4] At this fortnightly gathering, the problems and troubles of the members are addressed, both formally (in members' meetings following the worship service) and informally. The community comes together to exchange news, information, advice and to extend discipline.

The Amish home is the centre of social experience. Births, funerals and marriages occur in the home. Eating, leisure and work all revolve around the home. It is the centre of faith and life, the scene of face-to-face, often non-verbal, highly contextualized communication. The home is a refuge from the complexities and temptations of the outside world.

While Amish language, dress and social practices reinforce their separateness, the Amish are not isolated from the communities in which they live. They provide agricultural products and other goods and services for the local economy. They use public transportation, medical services and frequent local businesses. They are the object of a tourist industry that earns the county millions of dollars annually. Though not isolated from the wider community, they still strive to maintain their separateness.

Separation, but not isolation, was practised at the turn of the century as well. By 1900, Lancaster City was a thriving centre of commerce and industry, and a strong marketplace for agricultural products produced in the county. The village of Intercourse, at the centre of the Amish community, had connections to the city by train service, trolley service and rural mail delivery several times daily. Amish farmers made regular trips to the village (daily trips to the milk station) and patronized local stores and businesses. They joined their non-Amish neighbours to build barns, bring in the harvest and organize country schools (Fisher 1978). Here, too, contacts among neighbours – Amish and non-Amish alike – were built on face-to-face communication, common understandings, the rhythms of farm life and personal acquaintance. Relationships were personal and grounded in shared life experiences.

The coming of the telephone introduced new linkages both with and beyond the plain community, rearranging existing patterns and forms of communication. Bell Telephone service in Lancaster City began in 1879 and a competing Independent Telephone Company was founded in 1898 Both companies quickly extended their lines to surrounding towns and villages. In addition to the development of various independent companies, farmers organized their own private lines, stringing wire from fence post to fence post, linking four to six neighbours on a single party line. Oral sources suggest that hundreds of 'farmers' lines' existed in the county before 1910.

To the various residents of Lancaster County at the turn of the century, the telephone had multiple meanings. To proponents, telephone owner-ship served as a mark of the progressive farmer or the efficient rural businessman, doctor or lawyer. The telephone was hailed for providing efficient access to current information: market reports, weather reports, transportation schedules. The telephone facilitated doing business by preventing unnecessary trips to town. Emergencies could be handled quickly by telephone.[5]

While Old Order Amish were not blind to the benefits that proponents claimed, the telephone had another set of meanings for them. In the mind of the Old Order Amish today, the telephone stands as a principal issue behind the 1910 division of the Amish church that resulted in the loss of one-fifth of its membership (Kraybill 1989).[6] Prior to 1910, Amish leaders had taken no firm position on the telephone. Certain Amish families had telephones in their homes. They were connected by farmers' lines that linked families in the immediate neighbourhood on party lines. Oral sources suggest that most were not connected to organized telephone companies at the time.[7] This is how one Amish man describes what happened: 'our ministers have conference every year and what they think should be or what they think shouldn't be, they counsel over it and then the church people are supposed to listen.' Around 1910, he explains, some members had acquired telephones:

> The preachers had a meeting about it, a convention, and these people that had the phone, one said to the other, 'What are you going to do? Are you going to put yours away?' One said, 'I'm going to wait to see what the ministers come up with.' And the other one said, 'I'm not going to put mine away.' So it caused a division in the church . . . . He refused and the other one accepted what the ministers [said] before the congregation.'

Most Amish accounts of the events of 1909 and 1910 are oral. One of the few published accounts written by an Old Order Amish man born in 1897 reflects the common themes of the Amish story:

> About 1910 the phone lines were put up thru [sic] the country and our Amish people at least some got them in and it did not seem to make any trouble, then a couple women got to talking about another woman over the phone and this woman also had the phone in and had the receiver down and heard what they said, this made quite a stink and at last came into the gma [Gemeinde] to get it straightened out, then the Bishops and ministers made out if that is the way they are going to be used we would better not have them. Some were willing to put them away and others were not so that is when the King gma [the splinter group] started, the telephone was one of the issues but I suppose there were some more.
> (John K. Lapp 1986: 7)

Whether the catalyst was the stubbornness of the men, or the gossip of the women, there was dissension within the community over the telephone. An Old Order Amish historian writes that the 1910 split was caused by 'indifferent views in church discipline, most concerning newly invented contraptions that our conservative church leaders could not tolerate' (Beiler 1986: 14). So telephone ownership became one of the issues for discussion at the fall ministers' meetings. Each fall and spring, the bishops and ministers meet to discuss issues facing the community. Their purpose is to reach consensus and restore harmony within the community before communion is observed. Communion is not observed as long as disharmony persists.

After joint consultations with ministers from another county, the Lancaster leaders announced their intentions to hold to the 'old order' followed by their forefathers. In their statement, they reiterated support for the practice of shunning (social avoidance) of those who were unfaithful. Furthermore, they made it clear that the telephone had no place in the Amish home.

Through Amish eyes, the telephone in the home manifested traits contrary to the spirit of *Gelassenheit*. They explain that the telephone was not a necessity. The telephone was of 'the world', that is, it came from outside the Amish community and led to association with outsiders. The telephone contributed to individualism and pride rather than humility. Women were prone to use it for gossip which disrupted social harmony. In general, the use of the telephone did not conform to the time-honoured principles of nonconformity and separation from the world. By their decision, Amish leaders reaffirmed and reapplied the tradition of the past to a challenge of the present. Reaffirming the 'old order' excluded the telephone and, in the process, reiterated the cost of unfaithfulness – the prospect of being shunned.

While Old Order Amish accounts are primarily oral, some accounts have been written by descendants of those who left the Amish church in 1910 (Glick 1987). Known today as the Beachy Amish, they attribute the split to disagreements over strict applications of shunning. In written histories, the Beachys argue that those who left the Amish church to join Mennonite churches should not be banned. The Amish, however, upheld the ban for those individuals who joined the Amish church and then left to join Mennonite churches. Despite the Beachy version of the event, the Old Order Amish today continue to maintain that the telephone was a prominent issue in the split. The Beachys later built meeting houses and allowed telephones, cars and electricity (all choices rejected by the Amish). To the Amish, the contemporary Beachys represent what happens when 'worldliness' is allowed to creep in.

Neither side accounts for telephone company developments in the community at the time. A company was founded in the heart of the settlement in the summer of 1909, and it connected with Bell Telephone trunk lines for long-distance service several months later. By the fall of 1909, it was possible for interested persons to be connected with 'the outside world'.

For those desiring to hold on to the old ways, the telephone presented a formidable challenge. Telephone service created new business affiliations through the formation of farmers' mutual lines and later telephone companies. Telephone ownership indicated where one belonged. Telephony required some to use English when they preferred to communicate in German with German speakers. It also required plain people to enter businesses they would otherwise not frequent (e.g. hotels) to gain access to the telephone. Rules about the telephone marked the edges of appropriate association – who could be connected to whom, in what context and under what circumstances. Rules about telephone ownership highlight the struggle over who had authority over what realms of knowledge or information. The telephone debates tested the authority of the bishops to regulate social practices. The debate also tested the principle of *Gelassenheit*, as 'unwillingness to submit' was perceived to be part of the problem. Telephone use also highlighted the borders of language communities.

Furthermore, the telephone had the potential to invade the Amish home – the very centre of Amish faith and life – in a sense, Amish sacred space. Note that telephone use itself was not banned, but rather the installation and private ownership of the telephone in the home. The telephone was both a symbolic and a physical connection to the outside world. It opened the home to outside influence and intrusion. It removed communication from the context of community and made possible private and individual links with sources of information from outside – unmediated by the style, rhythms and rituals of community life. It demanded verbal expression and often necessitated English speaking – challenging in practice the cherished expressions of Amish nonconformity and separation. Telephone use decontextualized communication from the Amish community and decontextualized the Amish communicator.

This challenge to *Gelassenheit* could not be encouraged. The linking of the two issues – the telephone ban and social avoidance of wayward members (shunning) – stood as a decisive corrective for any who were tempted to set their sights too far beyond the context of community. The order of community had to be preserved, even if the cost was the loss of some of its members.

For the next twenty years, the Amish upheld the telephone ban. If access to a telephone was necessary, they travelled to a public telephone or used a neighbour's telephone. In the mid-1930s, several Amish families made an appeal to church leaders for a shared telephone. They argued that access to a telephone was important in times of emergency – calling a doctor or the fire company. 'It was tolerated', according to an Amish leader, 'and that was the beginning of the "community phone". They had a phone in someone's building but it had to be taken out and put into a phone shanty like the ones we have today' (Kraybill 1989: 146).

In the intervening years, community phone shanties have gradually appeared throughout the community, the bulk appearing since the 1960s. Some Amish explain that community phones were necessary because non-Amish neighbours did not appreciate the 'barn and tobacco smells' that were left behind when an Amish neighbour came to use the telephone. Others cite economic reasons. Amish farmers became involved in dairy farming and, along with that, artificial breeding.[8] To maintain their herds, they needed faster access to the veterinary surgeon than the postal service provided. Community telephones made quick access possible. The Amish also explain that doctors stopped holding open office hours. Now appointments are necessary, and so is access to a telephone.

Community telephones represent the Amish attempt to protect their homes from interruptions. They say that home phones would 'spoil' the natural rhythm of family life.[9] Furthermore, community phones protect the home from unwanted intrusions by outsiders and outside influences. They feel that it helps maintain the family unit by eliminating the temptation to participate in activities outside the home. Limited access to the telephone promotes reliance on face-to-face contacts within the context of community. And the arrangement discourages 'visiting' or the temptation to gossip over the telephone.[10] The community telephone stands as a mark of separation. Since the numbers are unlisted, the Amish are not identified with the others of 'the world' in a directory. Using the community telephone separate from the home reminds Amish users where they belong and keeps community contacts primary.

An Old Order Amish historian estimates that at least 200 such telephones exist throughout the community today. Community telephones are managed by rules articulated by local bishops. They carefully monitor and limit the number of telephones in a given area. The telephones are shared, usually by six or seven families. The telephone is to be used primarily for outgoing calls. Loud call bells to announce incoming calls are discouraged or prohibited. And the telephones are separate from the house.

Economic pressures today have fostered a new round of debate about telephones. In Lancaster County, developers consume 21 acres of agricultural land each day. In response to a growing population and a dwindling supply of farm land, Amish families have developed small businesses in carpentry, light manufacturing, foods and the like – businesses that often serve both the needs of the Amish community and the general public. Amish entrepreneurs argue that access to the telephone is now a necessity for running a business. Permission to have telephones in the shop varies from district to district, depending on the position of the local bishop. In one case, an Amish businessman argued that he needed a telephone exclusively for business purposes. The bishop's reply was 'It's either a community telephone or no phone at all.' This bishop's position reflects an insistence that community needs take priority over individual needs, community service over personal convenience.

Amish reconfiguration of telephone access represents a negotiated solution – community telephones maintain the traditional ban on the home telephone. The compromise maintains separation from the world, while making an accommodation to economic pressures and social change. But that accommodation is shaped to value community over individual needs. It allows access at a distance. The contemporary compromise upholds tradition, while at the same time preserving community in the face of change.

Within Lancaster County at the turn of the century, the telephone had multiple meanings, serving as a medium through which subcultural codes about roles, beliefs, practices and boundaries were articulated. The terms and patterns of the 1909 telephone debate among the Amish were later elaborated and applied to other agricultural, electrical and communications technologies in the following years. Each new technology called for a reinterpretation and restatement of what it meant to maintain the tradition of nonconformity and separation from the world. The course the Old Order Amish followed for the telephone served as a guide for their negotiations over future innovations – tractors, automobiles, electricity, radios and television. Today's renegotiation of telephone rules is again in the service of community needs.

The Amish case stands as a useful contrast for those who study communications technologies. First, we are reminded that the meanings of technologies, old and new, are culturally constructed and negotiated in the service of particular values or needs. Second, social groups can and do exercise a measure of control over communications technologies. Technologies and the industries that promote them are not the sole agents of influence or control. And third, understanding the dynamic grounds for rejection of the telephone or other communications technologies can be as useful as understanding those who accept them. For the Amish, the community telephone manages the intrusions and interruptions from the outside, while providing access when necessary. The Amish reshape telephone use in the service of community maintenance. Community telephones remind the Amish communicator that his or her point of reference is within the community, not the outside world, even in the act of using the telephone.

In terms of other writers in this collection, Amish telephone practices are expressive of a distinct moral economy. These communicative practices foster the negotiation of particular meanings within their community. Their telephone practices serve both to elaborate and maintain the boundaries that articulate a specific social identity.

For the Amish, identification is not limited to the individual household. The crucial identification is with the community. The work of social reproduction enlists communicative practice to articulate and maintain the community as distinct and separate from the world.

NOTES

1 Conventional histories include Danielian (1939), Brooks (1976) and Garnet (1985). Sociological studies of the telephone are represented by Pool's collection, Aronson, Ball and Singer. Rural telephone history in the US has been studied by Fischer and Atwood. Marvin provides the model I adapt here.
2 The limited scope of this chapter precludes description of the telephone debates within other communities. The Amish, along with the Old Order Mennonites across the United States and Canada, experienced tension and some church splits over telephone issues (Umble 1991).
3 Dyck provides historical background on the Anabaptist movement. The classic anthropological study of the Amish was done by Hostetler; sociological analysis by Kraybill.

4 Hoestetler (1993: 208–19) and Kraybill (1989: 101–7) provide extended descriptions of Amish worship rituals. Kraybill describes the expression of *Gelassenheit* in social practices (ibid.: 25–33).
5 Proponents' perspectives are developed in Umble 1991 and Marvin 1988.
6 I am indebted to Kraybill for sharing data he collected on Amish attitudes towards technology. His insight informs my understanding of Amish attitudes towards the telephone.
7 I will not identify Old Order Amish informants here in order to protect their privacy and my ongoing relationships with them. I have interviewed elderly Amish men and women who are considered to be historians by their peers. Published Amish accounts are cited.
8 The Amish permit artificial breeding because it allows dairy farmers to remain competitive with farmers in the dominant society, thereby ensuring the economic survival of the family farm. They use hybrid seed, veterinary medicine and fertilizer for the same reason. Adoption of modern techniques is selective and based on choices that maintain the community as small, self-sufficient and separate.
9 Amish life is slower paced than that of their modern neighbours. It is patterned by the rhythms of the seasons, travel by horse and carriage, and fortnightly worship. *Gelassenheit*, with its emphasis on waiting, submission and simplicity, also infuses the temporal dimensions of Amish practice. The Amish resist the telephone, in part, because outside involvements could potentially quicken the pace of daily life.
10 Rules about telephone use are designed, in part, to manage the behaviour of women and youth. Accounts from the turn of the century suggest that fathers or older children were sent to the neighbours' or to town to use the telephone for business or in emergencies. Contemporary practice is more complex. I am currently investigating the gender and age dimensions of practices associated with community telephones: public telephones and shop telephones. Farm families retain traditional divisions of labour: the barn and fields are male domains; the house, yard and gardens are female. On the other hand, Amish businesses are family affairs and many wives and daughters participate. The variation in division of labour fosters variation in communicative practices and in the gendered use of the technology.

REFERENCES

Aronson, Sidney H. (1971) 'The sociology of the telephone', *International Journal of Comparative Sociology* 11: 153–67.
Atwood, Roy Alden (1984) 'Telephony and its cultural meanings in southeastern Iowa, 1900–1917', Ph.D. dissertation, University of Iowa.
Ball, D. W. (1968) 'Toward a sociology of telephones and telephoners', in M. Truzzi (ed.) *Sociology and Everyday Life*, Englewood Cliffs, N.J.: Prentice Hall.
Beiler, Joseph F. (1986) 'Foreword', in Hugh F. Gingerich and Rachel W. Kreider, *Amish and Amish Mennonite Genealogies*, Gordonville, Pa.: Pequea Publishers.
Brooks, John (1976) *Telephone: The First Hundred Years*, New York: Harper & Row.
Danielian, N. R. (1939) *AT & T: The Story of Industrial Conquest*, New York: Vanguard.
Dyck, Cornelius J. (1967) *An Introduction to Mennonite History*, Scottdale, Pa.: Herald Press.

Fischer, Claude S. (1987) 'The revolution in rural telephone, 1900–1920', *Journal of Social History* 21(1): 5–26.

Fischer, Claude S. and Caroll, Glenn R. (1988) 'Telephone and automobile diffusion in the United States, 1902–1937', *American Journal of Sociology* 93(5): 1153–78.

Fischer, Gideon L. (1978) *Farm Life and its Changes*, Gordonville, Pa.: Pequea Publishers.

Garnet, R. (1985) *The Telephone Enterprise*, Baltimore: Johns Hopkins University Press.

Glick, Aaron S. (1987) 'Pequea Amish Mennonite church twenty-fifth anniversary', unpublished manuscript.

Hoestetler, John A. (1993) *Amish Society*, 4th edn, Baltimore: Johns Hopkins University Press.

Kraybill, Donald B. (1989) *The Riddle of Amish Culture*, Baltimore: Johns Hopkins University Press.

Lapp, John K. (1986) 'Remarks of by-gone days: a few remarks of old times', pamphlet, Gordonville, Pa.: Gordonville Print Shop.

Marvin, Carolyn (1988) *When Old Technologies Were New*, New York: Oxford University Press.

Pool, Ithiel de Sola (ed.) (1977) *The Social Impact of the Telephone*, Cambridge, Mass.: MIT Press.

Singer, Benjamin D. (1981) *Social Functions of the Telephone*, Palo Alto, Calif.: R. & E. Research Associates.

Umble, Diane Zimmerman (1991) 'The coming of the telephone to plain country: a study of Amish and Mennonite resistance in Lancaster County, Pennsylvania at the turn of the century', Ph.D. dissertation, University of Pennsylvania.

Chapter 12

Regimes of closure
The representation of cultural process in domestic consumption

Tim Putnam

DOMESTIC CONSUMPTION AS A PROBLEM IN CONTEMPORARY CULTURE

Domestic consumption, in the sense of the purchase by the household of commodities for a home-making process with complex social and cultural objectives, has a history as long as the participation of households in the exchange economy. However, recent important changes have taken place in the home – in the distribution of space, in technology, in the array of goods and in the basis upon which they are offered. The elaboration of the material culture of the home has also involved a redefinition of standards, qualities and hierarchies of value (Duncan 1981; Forrest and Murie 1987; Miller 1987; Putnam and Newton 1990). These changes have been conveyed by advertising as well as artefacts. The advertising and advice surrounding the home has become not only more elaborate and extensive but it has shifted its address towards a problematic of pleasure, choice and self-fulfilment (Goodall 1983; Partington 1989; Morley 1990b). Labour-saving has become leisure, and hygiene has been sublimated into pleasure.

Sociocultural investigation suggests that these shifts have their parallels in domestic practices: they testify to the incorporation of much technological innovation into the standard of living, to increasing involvement and investment in DIY, often as a conjugal project (Saunders and Williams 1988; Allen and Crow 1989; Almquist 1989; Miller 1990; Putnam 1991). Studies of consumers' discourse suggest a convergence across region, occupation and gender, as younger respondents adopt forms of expression employed in merchandising goods for the home (Swales 1990). Together with design elaboration, this may be taken as evidence of a process of acculturation as profound as that embodied in the eighteenth-century encomiums of taste or the domestic manuals of the early Victorian middle class (cf. Trumbach 1977; Davidoff and Hall 1987; Campbell 1988). It has been characterized by a veteran interior designer as 'popular design education beyond the wildest dreams of the post-war design reformers' (James 1989). However, from another point of view the extensive new promotions of domestic design and their reception are more problematic. Concurrent with a greater commonality of commodity evaluation is the increasingly rapid depreciation of established values among those making discriminations. This re-establishes the distance between those who have the economic and cultural resources to play and those unable or unwilling to do so (Bourdieu 1984; cf. Marshall *et al.* 1988) One effect, as Spooner has shown in a study of carpet cognoscenti, may be to encourage the pursuit of an 'authenticity' as evanescent as the actuality of fashion (Appadurai 1986). Contrasting efforts to acquire lifestyles, whole, involve the pursuit of a goal which is equally chimerical. While satisfaction may be gained from self-conscious 'critical consumerism', which may be pleasurable in itself, establish a range of personal possessions and communicate chosen identity (Silverstone and Morley 1990, and chapter 1) one can question the depth of satisfaction thus obtained. One can also raise the problem of the status of judgement in living practices.

So the contemporary culture of domestic creation has become problematized as a self-defining and fulfilling activity oriented towards consumer choice. The notion of a self-determining, consuming subject may be considered either as self-evident or as a seduction (cf. Goodall 1983; Saunders 1984; Tomlinson 1990). Beyond this dichotomy one may envisage consumption as a necessary reappropriation of the impersonally produced, where the subjective moment in consumption is entailed by the increasing autonomy of the domestic sphere from the centres of planning and control (Miller 1987; Lofgren 1990). Certainly, capital concentration has removed large areas of work from the home, and the character of much remaining household work has been progressively, if unevenly, transformed by purchased goods (Pahl 1984; Cowan 1989). Knowledge has become progressively elaborated outside the domestic sphere. The prevalent and dominant form of direction in economic and political life is bureaucratic, not familial, and the dominant experience of work is time spent exercising or executing that direction for monetary reward (but see Pahl 1984). Thus the redefinition of the home as a sphere of consumption necessarily poses questions about cultural process and structure.

One set of such questions has to do with the definition of social meaning, and the 'meaning of things' in particular. Life in the advanced countries has moved away from the society of tradition, in which common meanings are established through manifestly related practices in a shared environment. To the extent that we live in a world which permits diverse interaction and self-definition, which recirculates goods and reattaches signifiers, contexts of production and of consumption become autonomous. The meaning of artefacts, never inherent, becomes less transitive between contexts (Baudrillard 1981; Barthes 1983).

To draw attention to domestic consumption as a problematic point of cultural creation, the Victoria and Albert Museum and Middlesex Polytechnic set up the Household Choices project in 1987. It aimed to examine the intransitivity of meaning between contexts by building a documentary record of use. It probed the relationship between fashionableness and established ideals, 'standards' and self-expression, principally through photography and interview. It attempted to discover the essential points which people take into consideration when setting up home, or re-establishing it at a major turning point. It sought to know what happens when two objectives or values clash, and how people feel about the legacy of past decisions which survives about the house. Results of some forty studies from different perspectives were brought together in the exhibition 'Household Choices – Design in Domestic Consumption' at the Victoria and Albert Museum in 1990 and the project is currently being extended nationally with the support of the Arts Council of Great Britain. The exhibition strategy of juxtaposing interview excerpts with photography has had the effect of validating many little narratives of consumption against an overarching cultural critique or encomiums of taste. This is an exercise in 'new museology', which aims to learn from several disciplines, but particularly the 'new ethnography' (de Certeau 1984; Clifford and Marcus 1986; Geertz 1988).

HOUSEHOLD CHOICES AND THE CONCEPTUALIZATION OF CONSUMPTION

The diversity of recent academic interest in the home reflects the complexity of the home as a cultural nexus (Putnam and Newton 1990). It is doubtful whether the problematic of consumption can provide an adequate account of this complexity. Consumption is, after all, hardly an innocent category in relation to the home. Consumption's legacy from political economy precludes an iterative description of domestic activities, internal or external relations. Rather, 'consumption' constitutes the home as a dependent entity in a hierarchy of social and economic space. It privileges externally derived income over household productive activity. The ends of the household are read through commodity derivations. Externally, talk of consumption abstracts commodity relations from the nexus of socializing mediations. It postulates the agent outside material culture, provoking a dichotomy about agency, between consumer sovereignty and manipulation. Contamination extends to other concepts which have been shaped by or become situated within a problematic of consumption, such as 'leisure' (Deem 1989).

In political economy, the impetus or finality offered by consumption is a necessary postulate, but the character of that finality remains to be considered. Neither the postulating of 'needs' nor the acceptance of given demand patterns is of much use in understanding the formation of the complex ends of home-making attested to by the diversity of meanings ascribed to the home in recent studies (Miller 1987; Lofgren 1990; cf. Heller 1984 and Haug 1986). One cluster of meanings has to do with security and control, and includes the often-used term 'privacy', which may equally indicate control of space and boundary, or freedom of action and personal security. A second group has to do with the extension or representation of the self, for the self or for the other, and may include both the collection and preservation of memorabilia and the alteration of decorative order or structure. A third group has to do with the relations and activities in the household: the continuities of domestic routine, the associations of family life (see Despres 1989 and Sixsmith and Sixsmith 1990).

This pattern of meanings indicates a differentiated finality which recognizes relations and constraints both within and beyond the household.

On one level the household may be regarded as a unit. Purchases and time are inputs in a practice of home-making defined by the interaction of personal and family strategy (e.g., see Wallman 1984). A perception of the home as a conjugal project has been recorded in several countries and appears significant in patterns of arrangement and alteration (Miller 1987; Segalen 1990). It is clear, however, that this is an ideal or life project which exists in tension, more or less creative, with the gender inequalities which show up readily in inventories of space and time allocation. To the extent that external social and economic change feeds the possibility and expectation of individual fulfilment, this can have complex and even contradictory implications in the domestic sphere (Allen and Crow 1989; Roberts 1991; Putnam 1991).

Home-making continues to depend not only on family structure and process but on the social networks into which household members may be inserted. Although the importance of face-to-face groups has been cut across to some extent by media representations of a common commodity culture, and it has become usual to note an attenuation of previously established class differences between domestic interiors, patterns of contact at work and leisure continue to be important in defining the use and meaning of the home, particularly in relation to gender (Franklin 1990). When such networks become more complex and extensive with the aid of communication and transport technologies, the boundaries of home and neighbourhood appear more diffuse; but the cultural importance of the ordering of space is not thereby reduced (Hillier 1984; Feldman 1989).

However, while strong group affiliations can exert an influence on household arrangements, these do not necessarily imply conformity in material culture (Duncan 1981). It is necessary to recognize that the significance accorded material culture can vary considerably and the sense of belonging to place which makes a 'home' need not be related to any particular attribution of value to things. Parallels drawn between modes of attachment to things and sociability indicate important patterns in the way both objects and words are deployed in producing accounts of the self (Csikszentmihalyi and Rochberg-Halton 1981; Swales 1990). But as Feldman (1989), among others, has shown, the particular prominence given to objects as carriers of value is variable between and within context. For mobile Middle America, settlement-type and portable collections of artefacts appear to be more important than attachment to features of domestic architecture.

If household choices establish historically specific relationships between personal subjectivity, social processes and material culture, then these must be addressed in accounts of domestic consumption. Accounts of consumption have drawn attention to the importance of discrete strategies of marketing and the role that advertising plays in linking these marketing strategies with the commodities themselves (Williamson 1977). But we know much less about the other and less manifest side of the contemporary 'social life of things'. Appadurai (1986) has pointed out that the inflection and lack of direction permitted by the commodity form, and its separation of production and consumption, depends not only on economic organization but also on the way in which social life is organized. The nature of the home as a socially constituted space makes it necessary to distinguish between three things: the kind of communication which takes place in buying and selling the various forms of communication which take place between occupants of different households in the construction of identity; the interplay between subjects sharing the same domestic space; and the place of the actual and imagined home in life histories and projects. It is necessary to to articulate these relations in successive life stages without subsuming one under another (Altman and Werner 1985; Giuliani 1991).

The problem of the non-transitivity of meaning of objects can be refocused as a search for ways in which definite relationships are established between those orders of events within which meaning is situated; a search for 'regimes' of consumption which closes alternatives within each field by providing links between them. In a traditional society the stylistic and typological characteristics of the object systems that are produced are related in determinable, if constantly modified, ways to their arrangements and circumstances of use; the design of houses or pots as produced and consumed are culturally linked in a vernacular process (Glassie 1975; Devillers and Huet 1981; Miller 1984).

This validation of design becomes less certain when we are talking about professional design produced speculatively for indeterminate markets, or when an object moves into new contexts. The meaning of an old house has not only to be rediscovered by investigators, but reinvented by inhabitants themselves; and the patterns of use, decoration, furnishing and alteration become the principal site from which the house is to be understood (Boudon 1972). Yet this separation of what archaeologists would call the 'formal' and 'informal' contexts (cf. Miller 1984) is never complete. Both type forms and stylistic variation are still a condition for commercial success. The study of the emergence of type forms shows that the convergence of competitive experiments by producers is shaped by a received design vocabulary and method, production contingencies, market transparency and the categorization of the new object by users (Flatman 1988).

From the profile of output it appears that both type, form and stylistic variation are ultimately determined by the requirement that product identity and its potential use and significance must clearly be intelligible and assimilable in terms of current cultural categories. But without knowledge of the actual placing of objects in social life, the interpretation of their produced qualities is incomplete.

Of the accounts of contemporary consumption, Bourdieu's sociology of taste makes the most systematic attempt to relate the qualities of objects produced with those of objects consumed. The research methodology set out in *Distinction* (1984) obtains loose correlations between categories, things, activities and socioeconomic identifiers. These 'homologies' are placed on a two-dimensional grid of 'cultural' and economic capital. At the micro-scale, cultural process is envisaged through a concept of second nature ('habitus') which interacts with objective conditions in a dialectic of acceptance and refusal. On a macro-scale, orientation in the changing cultural map is ultimately provided by the objective difficulties and apparent rewards of being able to appropriate unfamiliar entities. Perhaps the greatest interest of Bourdieu's scheme is that the axis of cultural capital offers more than additive knowledge: it presents formal abstraction as a relation of social power. The positive valuation given to the local and concrete by the powerless is set against identification with an analytic system deployed in domination.

However, this apparatus, and the elegant and suggestive essays on judgement which accompany it, leave unanswered questions for any account of domestic creation. The concept of 'habitus' is used in such a way as to elide the individual and the household. How its ensemble of objects, practices and values is articulated cannot be traced from their loose statistical correlation but requires an examination of second nature in process. The relationship between such ensembles and the cultural process on a macro-scale can be articulated through identifying the many intermediate circuits whose closure constrains, and thus structures, the general circulation of commodities and values.

CLOSURE AND CULTURAL COMPETENCE IN DOMESTIC CREATION

Creating a home evidently requires a many-faceted competence, integrating several different kinds of reference, contingency, objective and effect. Such competence is acquired in diverse ways from several sources, and may be exercised in different modes with varying degrees of deliberateness, ranging from 'second nature' to explicit rationale. Discourses which establish the home as a site of consumption have difficulty in recognizing this aspect of competence in home-making activity; nevertheless, focusing on its elaboration provides a point of orientation from which to examine the possibilities of closure between personal, domestic and social worlds.

I make no assumption as to the coherence of such competence, with respect to the unity of its fields of reference, its modes of reasoning or its purposive orientations (cf. de Certeau 1984; Geertz 1988). There are multiple paths by which the psychology of home-making competence and its place in a sociology of culture may be explored. Several contributors to this volume offer perspectives on the performances and constructs which surround the selective appropriation of technologies, and this approach may be complemented by considering those choices which householders make in the ordering of the home environment. The competence exercised in this ordering has normally been discussed in relation to aesthetic rather than technological discourses.

When the consumption of technologies in the home is being considered, it is conventional to presume that the elements of skill and competence required for the mastery of domestic technology have been elaborated outside the home, and are learnt selectively within it. Behind the apparatus which is offered for consumption in the home is a hierarchical and systematic knowledge. Only when the appropriation of technology into domestic life is examined closely does it emerge that there is also an extensive competence within the home, which comprises a technical culture, and uses representations of it as part of its self-representation. Thus the acquisition of new technologies can been shown to depend on their anticipated or discovered inflexion of this pre-existing order.

The relationship of domestic competence to that of dominant aesthetic discourse at the social level is more open. The design of the home can be seen to involve the decoration of surfaces, the articulation of space, the choice and arrangement of objects, as well as the choice and modification of the dwelling itself. Interview and observation reveal that design is understood both instrumentally and as an autonomous value, and that it can function as both a means and a message. The organization of the discourse of domestic design reflects its contingency and consequences, but design differences among households involve more than the acquisition of cultural forms which are elaborated outside the domestic sphere. Instead, the selective appropriation exercised in domestic design may equally be considered as an autonomous pole of cultural creation which has ends and performances which cannot be wholly measured or subsumed in terms of the dominant discourse.

Nevertheless, the arrangement of the home falls into culturally specific patterns. Bonnes *et al.*'s (1987) major comparative studies of the organization of principal living rooms in Europe has thrown up many national differences. Whereas in Italy the type and quality of furniture is the principal signifying variable, in France the organization of elements and in Sweden the decoration of surfaces offer greater possibilities for discrimination. However, all three axes of discrimination were found to be significant in each country, suggesting common registers of significance in certain aspects of contemporary European domestic design competence.

At a deeper level of abstraction Bernard *et al.* (1989) found that complexity and profusion in the repertoire of objects or decorative features deployed was associated with a simple and regular order of arrangement, while complex and ambiguous arrangements were associated with simpler repertoires. The contrasting treatment of range and repertoire effects across differences in locale and type of design problem point to a common deep structure in visual rhetoric and suggest that in the matter of room arrangement domestic design competence deploys complex cultural-cognitive features which may be compared with those of language. The interdependence of visual schemata and linguistic coding in environmental recognition is a subject of continuing psychological research (Mainardi Peron *et al.* 1985).

However, as our focus moves away from the decor and arrangement of the principal living room to the interstices of the dwelling and the order of everyday practices, householders' design competence presents a different aspect. As Kaufmann (1990) suggests, one has only to follow the tortuous path of laundry within the home to see how different cultural categories (dirty/clean, private/public, leisure/work, male/female), each with their own implications for spatial and temporal order, become entangled in domestic routines. Conflict between cultural values and the resulting improvisation is a recurrent feature of home-making. What is more, improvised results are particularly vulnerable to external effects; so any movement towards functional purity or higher standards of presentation in the kitchen or bathroom has repercussions along the laundry chain.

The specificity of such improvisation provides one reason why, as we noted at the outset of this discussion, domestic design does not offer a closed semantic field, but one characterized by significant non-correspondence between usages current in different sociocultural locations and both local and aggregate slippages over time between signifier and referent. Patterns of closure and correspondence may be taken as evidence of confirmed and continuing relationships, whereas incommensurability suggests separation or opposition, and slippage indicates induced alteration.

Thus Bernard's group found that the national vocabularies of domestic design in Europe were incommensurable, and other studies have noted differential design practice and terminology on class, gender and generational lines (Segalen 1990; Swales 1990; Roberts 1991). Such discontinuities are most often explained by a combination of differences in life situation and non-communication, which may occur within a household as well as between nations. The south London working-class respondents of Morley's (1990b) enquiry into values guiding furniture choice were quite unaware of the design debates raging over their heads in post-war Britain, but deployed a vocabulary which reflected their own experience. Their usage of the term 'modern', as against that likely to be offered by a design professional, reflected the prestige of being able to purchase 'their own' furniture, so long as it was 'proper', i.e. conformed to type and exhibited established marks of quality of materials and workmanship.

Such usage was reinforced by family and peers and supported by a substantial section of the furniture trade, against the uncomprehending critique of design reformers. The circuit of circumstances and values remained closed until, and sometimes beyond, a major change in life situation. However, the circuit between values and goods was disrupted by post-war upheaval in the British furniture trade. Post-war foreign exchange penury and labour shortages eroded established marks of quality to such an extent that veneered chipboard rectangles could pass as 'proper'. Acceptance of such slippage was part of the realistic tenor of this aesthetic, but it also confirmed the dominance within it of satisfaction in being able to buy new.

Semantic realignment within domestic design discourse is a reflection of the contingency of domestic arrangements. In addition to the functional conflicts and changes in availability instanced above, life stages unfold inexorably. Households which accommodate inherited furniture, like the teachers of Evreux studied in Segalen (1990), redefine the meaning of both piece and place. The encounter with contingency gives domestic design discourse a somewhat disjunctive character. Terms are embedded in figures of judgement or 'considerations' which offer explanatory power or practical implications, but may be combined in varying ways to produce or justify differing results. Such figures of judgement may be compared with the 'interpretative repertoires' of Potter and Wetherell (1987). The closure which they effect is partial: their reference is adjustable and their respective status shifting.

The inventory of 'favourite things' carried out for Household Choices by the Tom Harrisson–Mass Observation Archive showed how such figures of judgement may be incorporated into personal histories. Many respondents, especially older men, refused to place themselves in a relation to things which was either affective or appetitive, a position often belied in subsequent accounts of substantial collections or fine points of discrimination. On the other hand, we have the woman whose motley collection of chosen things was revealed, through close analysis of the text, to have all been created or repaired by her own efforts, and thus stood as a very positive account of her reappropriation of her material surroundings (Swales 1990).

Both positive and negative accounts of consumption employ similar figures of judgement; they differ in the way they consider the mode of production of the self. It is valuable to explore how the different modes of producing the self in the world may be compared and connected. Although the occasion of reflective accounts is quite different from that of practical reason, the resulting judgements are not as dissimilar as might be expected. This may be because everyday household choices often involve compromises which also produce a distanced reading of the self: aspiration, deprivation and interpersonal dynamics mean that competence – in execution as well as statement – may be voiced with hope, irony or despondency.

By itself, the looseness of householders' design discourse might be taken as an indication of the ineffability of material culture. But viewed over time, against changes in domestic routines and patterns of object choice and arrangement, it is possible to detect the terms both of compromise and the boundaries of autonomy. In Morley's (1990a) furnishing study the accommodation of an uncalled-for change of availability subtly redefined the meaning of things, but if the new stylistic repertoire was validated by consumption, it did not mean that it was a result of the adoption of new sets of value priorities. This offers an important caution against inferring consumption values from the artefactual record in contemporary society.

Despite such discrepancies, it is nevertheless possible for a closure in the nature of tradition to exist between certain home-makers' design values and design as produced. The three-piece suite found in many British living rooms may be considered as such a vernacular type. The underlying continuity of architectural qualities in the suite as a composition can be shown to be firmly related to representations of the family and to values of security, respectability, luxury and comfort which play a large part in the domestic culture of user groups, while the variety of covering detail not only accommodates co-ordination with differing room decors but offers the possibility of displaying newness as a mark of achievement. The pertinence of design qualities to these values is also shown to be appreciated and often shared by furniture store salesmen, if not always by designers and managers (Morley 1990a).

This analysis of past and present evaluations of three-piece suites, set against patterns of use, object availability and choice, suggests that the ability of the suite to 'see off' alternatives preferred by the design profession evidently rests on the way in which its defining qualities approximate to norms of interaction in the 'living room', as well as the representation of 'proper' family structure and the cultural definition of social location. It may be no accident that the strength of tradition in this case is related to the suite's central place in the 'architecture' of the living room: the most definitive zone for home arrangement.

This discussion has indicated some of the ways in which competence in domestic consumption is situated by conjunctural closure between values, terms, practices and artefacts; its object – and unintended consequence – is to modify that situation. At a time when the quality of personal fulfilment in domestic creation is much in question, these relations need to be viewed through the imaginative spatiality and temporality of life projects. The woman in a Cumbrian house eight years into renovation who said, 'We learned not to say "when the house is finished"' but also said 'When the house is finished, I can get on with the rest of my life', stands in very different relations of consumption from the woman in Birmingham who was profoundly disappointed when her fitted kitchen failed to transform her life. The wives of socially mobile husbands interviewed by Swales who continued the practice of recycling male underwear as cleaning cloths are keeping a grip on their place in the world (and their husbands) with a subtlety and effectiveness beyond the reach of many more ostensibly sophisticated.

REFERENCES

Allen, G. and Crow, G. (1989) *Home and Family*, London: Macmillan.
Almquist, A. (1989) 'Who wants to live in collective housing?', unpublished paper, Gavle: Swedish Institute for Building Research.
Altman, I. and Werner, C. (eds) (1985) *Home Environments*, New York: Plenum.
Appadurai, A. (ed.) (1986) *The Social Life of Things*, Cambridge: Cambridge University Press.
Barthes, R. (1983) *Barthes: Selected Writings*, London: Cape.
Baudrillard, J. (1981) *For a Critique of the Political Economy of the Sign*, London: Telos.
Bernard, Y., Giuliani, V. and Bonnes, M. (1989) 'Social determinants and aesthetic choices in everyday life', unpublished paper, Paris: Laboratoire Psychologie de l'Environnement.
Bernstein, B. (1971) *Class, Codes and Control*, London: Routledge.
Bonnes, M., Giuliani, V., Amoni, F. and Bernard, Y. (1987) 'Cross cultural rules for the optimisation of the living room', *Environment and Behaviour* 5: 331–7.
Boudon, P. (1972) *Lived-in Architecture*, London: Lund Humphries.
Bourdieu, P. (1984) *Distinction*, London: Routledge & Kegan Paul.
Campbell, C. (1988) *The Romantic Ethic and the Spirit of Consumerism*, Oxford: Blackwell.
Certeau, M. de (1984) *The Practices of Everyday Life*, Berkeley: University of California Press.
Clifford, J. and Marcus, G. (eds) (1986) *Writing Cultures*, Berkeley: University of California Press.
Cowan, R. S. (1989) *More Work for Mother*, London: Free Associations.
Csikszentmihalyi, M. and Rochberg-Halton, E. (1981) *The Meaning of Things: Domestic Symbols and the Self*, Cambridge: Cambridge University Press.
Davidoff, L. and Hall, C. (1987) *Family Fortunes*, London: Hutchinson.
Deem, R. (1989) *All Work and No Play?*, Milton Keynes: Open University Press.

Despres, C. (1989) 'The meaning of home', unpublished paper, Milwaukee: University of Wisconsin.

Devillers, C. and Huet, B. (1981) *Le Creusot*, Paris: Seyssel.

Douglas, M. and Isherwood, B. (1982) *The World of Goods*, Harmondsworth: Penguin.

Duncan, J. (ed.) (1981) *Housing and Identity*, London: Croom Helm.

Feldman, R. (1989) 'Psychological bonds with home places in a mobile society', unpublished paper, Chicago: University of Illinois.

Flatman, D. (1988) 'The origin of the handset telephone', M.A. dissertation, Middlesex Polytechnic, London.

Forrest, R. and Murie, A. (1987) 'The affluent homeowner', in *Sociological Review* 35: 370–403.

Franklin, A. (1989) 'Working class privatism: an historical case study of Bedminster, Bristol', *Society and Space* 7(1): 93–115.

——(1990) 'Variations in marital relations and the implications for women's experience of the home', in T. Putnam and C. Newton (eds) *Household Choices*, London: Futures.

Geertz, C. (1988) *Local Knowledge*, New York: Basic Books.

Giuliani, V. (ed.) (1991) *Home Environment: Physical Space and Psychological Processes*, Rome: CNR – Istituto di Psicologia.

Glassie, H. (1975) *Folk Housing in Middle Virginia*, Knoxville: University of Kentucky Press.

Goodall, P. (1983) 'Gender, design and the home', *Block* 8: 37–43.

Harris, C. (ed.) (1979) *The Sociology of the Family*, Keele: British Sociological Association.

Haug, F. (1986) *Critique of Commodity Aesthetics*, Cambridge: Cambridge University Press.

Hebdige, D. (1990) *Hiding in the Light*, London: Comedia.

Heller, A. (1984) *Everyday Life*, London: Routledge.

Hillier, B. (1984) *The Social Logic of Space*, London: Routledge.

James, H. (1989) 'The packaging of design for the domestic interior 1950–90', M.A. dissertation, Middlesex Polytechnic, London.

Kaufmann, J.-C. (1990) *La vie ordinaire*, Paris: Editions Greco.

Lofgren, O. (1990) 'Consuming interests', *Culture and History* 7: 7–36.

Mainardi Peron, E., Baroni, M., Job, R. and Salmaso, P. (1985) 'Cognitive factors and communicative strategies in recalling unfamiliar places', *Journal of Environmental Psychology* 5: 325–33.

Marshall, G., Newby, H., Rose, D. and Vogler, C. (1988) *Social Class in Modern Britain*, London: Hutchinson.

Mass Observation (1944) *People's Homes*, London: Mass Observation.

Meyerowitz, S. (1985) *No Sense of Place*, New York: Viking.

Miller, D. (1984) *Artefacts as Categories*, Cambridge: Cambridge University Press.

——(1987) *Material Culture and Mass Consumption*, Oxford: Blackwell.

——(1990) 'Appropriating the state on the council estate', in T. Putnam and C. Newton (eds) *Household Choices*, London: Futures.

Morley, C. (1990a) 'The three piece suite', M.A. dissertation, Middlesex Polytechnic, London.

——(1990b) 'Homemakers and design advice in the postwar period', in T. Putnam and C. Newton (eds) *Household Choices*, London: Futures.

Pahl, R. (1984) *Divisions of Labour*, Oxford: Blackwell.

Partington, A. (1989) 'The designer housewife in the 1950s', in J. Attfield and P. Kirkham, *A View From the Interior*, London: Women's Press.

Potter, J. and Wetherell, M. (1987) *Discourse and Social Psychology*, London: Sage.

Putnam, T. (1991) 'Gender and generation in today's household choices', in V. Giuliani (ed.) *Home Environment: Physical Space and Psychological Processes*, Rome: CNR – Istituto di Psicologia.

Putnam, T. and Newton, C. (eds) (1990) *Household Choices*, London: Futures.

Roberts, M. (1991) *Living in a Man Made World*, London: Routledge.

Rybczynski, W. (1986) *Home*, New York: Viking.

Saunders, P. (1984) 'Beyond housing classes: the sociological significance of property rights and means of consumption', *International Journal of Urban and Regional Research* 8: 202–27.

Saunders, P. and Williams, P. (1988) 'The constitution of the home: towards a research agenda', *Housing Studies* 3(2): 81–93.

Segalen, M. (ed.) (1990) *Etre bien dans ses meubles*, Paris: Institut d'Ethnologie Française.

Silverstone, R. and Morley, D. (1990) 'Families and their technologies', in T. Putnam and C. Newton (eds) *Household Choices*, London: Futures.

Tomlinson, A. (1990) *Consumption, Identity and Style*, London: Routledge.

Sixsmith, A. and J. Sixsmith (1990) 'Places in transition: the impact of life events on the experience of home', in T. Putnam and C. Newton (eds) *Household Choices*, London: Futures.

Swales, V. (1990) 'Reading other people's letters', in T. Putnam and C. Newton (eds) *Household Choices*, London: Futures.

Trumbach, R. (1977) *The Rise of the Egalitarian Family*, London: Academic Press.

Upton, D. and Vlach, J. (1986) *Common Places*, Athens: University of Georgia Press.

Wallman, S. (1984) *Eight London Households*, London: Tavistock.

Williamson, J. (1977) *Decoding Advertisements*, London: Boyars.

Chapter 13

The long term and the short term of domestic consumption

An ethnographic case study

Eric Hirsch

INTRODUCTION

Ever since Mauss's classic essay, *The Gift* (1990), anthropologists have debated the issue of how to understand the way persons relate socially through the mediation of things. Much of this debate has centred on processes of exchange. There is a vast literature on this topic, much of it associated with the ideas of Lévi-Strauss. It was Lévi-Strauss who developed a specific interpretation of Mauss's insights based on objective or structural models of exchange relations. An important shift in theoretical perspective resulted from Bourdieu's critique of Lévi-Strauss's 'objectivism': what Bourdieu summed up as a move 'from the mechanics of the model to the dialectic of strategies' (Lévi-Strauss 1969; cf. Bourdieu 1977: 3–9; Sahlins 1974, chapter 4).

A central element of Bourdieu's alternative formulation was the factor of time and the way in which the social relationships between persons, as mediated through things, work themselves out through different, culturally specific temporalities. More recently, Bourdieu has extensively investigated these person–thing relationships in another context: around the class-based, consumption practices of contemporary French society (Bourdieu 1984). And yet, as I shall argue below, the centrality of the temporal dimension has significantly disappeared in the work focused on contemporary consumption. Is this because exchange and consumption are fundamentally different processes?

The seeming shift from a critique of exchange theory in Bourdieu's work to a focus on consumption belies an important continuity between the perpectives. As Gell has pointed out in a related discussion of exchange and consumption practices: 'What distinguishes consumption from exchange is not that consumption has a physiological dimension that exchange lacks [as in food consumption], but that consumption involves the incorporation of the consumed item into the personal and social identity of the consumer' (Gell 1986: 112). As Gell indicates, there is much ethnographic evidence to support the view that social relations are produced and sustained through events that are structured around commensality, periods of drinking or smoking together, and so on (cf. Douglas and Isherwood 1979). So although consumption in many cases appears to be about the destruction of things, it is really about a process of reincorporation into the social setting in which things were either produced or acquired through exchange. All things – such as food – are from this perspective as indestructible as pieces of technology, works of art, or kula valuables from the Trobriand Islands of Papua New Guinea: '[they] live on in the form of the social relations they produce' and which are in turn responsible for reproducing these things. Thus, '[t]he incorporation of consumer goods into the definition of the social self arises out of a framework of social obligations and also perpetuates this framework' (ibid.; cf. Carrier 1990).

What Gell's comments on consumption as incorporation point towards – with its emphasis on a framework of social obligations – is the specific moral dimensions of such processes. It is significant in this light, then, that in Bourdieu's analysis of consumption the moral dimension which shapes the interrelatedness of persons and things receives little attention. This is especially the case given the fact that a large percentage of the consumption practices that Bourdieu's analysis focuses on are within domestic contexts of family and kinship where issues of obligation and morality come very much to the fore (Bourdieu 1984: chapters 2–3; cf. Csikszentmihalyi and Rochberg-Halton 1981).

The argument I am making here relates to the point indicated above, where the importance of temporality, as demonstrated in Bourdieu's critique of 'objectivist' exchange theory, has virtually disappeared in his large-scale study of consumption practices. Consumption, according to Bourdieu, as a struggle for distinction between the objectified forces of economic and symbolic capital, seemingly occurs outside the moral and temporal dimensions which are intrinsic to domestic life. The material and symbolic appropriations of domestic consumption are not all of the same temporal dimensions.

The variety of temporality present can be correlated with the differing moral content of particular social relationships. There are aspects of the moral content of social relationships that have a short-term time span associated with a relative intolerance of imbalance in the reciprocal aspects of relationships; other aspects are predicated on a long-term time frame where there is a greater tolerance of imbalance: '[I]t is this variety of term existing concurrently which . . . [can be seen as] . . . the basis of social and economic life' (Bloch 1973: 76).[1]

The appropriation of 'things' makes explicit the potentially contradictory relations between distinct moralities valorized within the family: it is the family relationships as realized through the factors of age, gender, siblingship, race, etc. which constrain the possibilities inherent within the appropriated thing. *It is these constraints and possibilities which work themselves out over time given the 'moral economy' in which the relationships exist.* Each household strikes its balance between relatively individualistic behaviour and a locally constructed cosmological order. The point I am making here is that there is a 'moral economy'[2] to the household, predicated on specific relations between persons and things, and which cannot be reduced to the more general struggles that occur around the accumulation of economic and symbolic capital as described by Bourdieu.

The acts of appropriation that constitute consumption and the social relationships thereby sustained and constructed are two sides of the same coin. But both are shaped by the particular moral character of the relationships involved. These in turn are based on different time frames expressive of the reciprocal aspects of the relationships themselves.[3]

One of the objectives of this chapter is to highlight the significance of the domestic setting and family structure for understanding the way in which 'things' are consumed and how this relates to the family's particular moral-temporal structure. Information and communication technologies (ICT) provide particular insights into this process. They are generally perceived to be those things which are at the forefront of socioeconomic change although a large percentage is consumed within the domestic settings of household and family. At the same time ICTs become part of the moral economy of the household – as material objects – but they also bring into this setting the public culture from which they originated. A question is raised, then, whether, given this dual nature, their consumption is significantly different from that of other material objects and whether they make explicit aspects of family moral and temporal structure which are not evident with other things consumed within the home. It is on the theme of incorporation[4] associated with distinct personal and social identities formed through consumption that I want to focus in this chapter. Particular attention will be given to one household and the processes of incorporating items of ICT into their family life.[5]

THE BACKGROUND RESEARCH CONTEXT OF THE STUDY

The intellectual and methodological origins of this study emerged out of a number of related research agendas that converged around the study of domestic consumption: these included that of family studies; the audience as formulated by media studies; and technology, particularly that of information and communication technology (ICT).

The relationship seen to exist between these research traditions also highlights some of their limitations. For example, family studies (as in Bott (1957) and Wallman (1984)) have generally taken very little account of technological and media relations as part of the domestic environment. The study of media audiences, in turn, had foundered precisely at the point at which it was to be confronted in its social and cultural complexity, i.e. within the household, among family members. Studies of technology had opened the question of its status as culture, but had not yet approached, other than in broad terms in contemporary society, the issue of its construction in consumption. Finally, studies of consumption had just begun to examine the social and social-psychological processes[6] of the appropriation and use of objects in general, of information and communication technologies in particular, and specifically in the context of the domestic spaces of families.

A key site, then, where these processes unfold in all their complexity is the domestic domain of kinship, family and household. I want to highlight further three related factors that can be identified as crucial to an analysis of this domain and which are illustrated in the ethnographic case study below.

First, not only is the housing in which most British people live of a mass-produced nature – a problem of appropriation Daniel Miller addressed with specific reference to kitchens in his study of a council estate (1988) – but a significant percentage of consumer goods that are produced (either within Britain or abroad) find their way into this same domestic environment. Hence, the work of appropriation that needs to be undertaken on a potentially large-scale artefactual environment is of substantial scope and variety.

Second, the social relationships – of kinship and family – in which this consumption takes place have, in the English case at least, been shown to be remarkably stable in their form over a period of several centuries. In fact, in a recent review of literature on the sense of kinship obligations in Britain, Janet Finch has remarked:

> [I]f there has been any discernible change in a single direction over time, it has been an increase rather than a decrease in the significance of the feelings which people have for their relatives [the particular blend of instrumentality and expressiveness for given individuals is a matter for empirical investigation] . . . . All of this makes sense in relation to the historical context of England in particular where, on MacFarlane's (1978) evidence, social and economic structures have been based upon a strong sense of individualism, and not upon traditional ties of kinship, for at least 600 years.
>
> (Finch 1989: 84)

The 'strong' view of this historical evidence suggests that English family form, with its emphasis on the individual and a nuclear type of family arrangement is in itself a prime source of many of the transformations which led to capitalist industrialization. Whether or not this strong view can be shown to be empirically correct (cf. Gellner 1988: 162–4) is open to question. What did emerge as a consequence of industrialization – around the mid-nineteenth century (cf. Davidoff and Hall 1987) – was a new middle-class culture with an emphasis on the separation of public and private domains. In this industrialized setting, kinship and family were made to appear less evident in the public domain, as both were construed as part of domestic relations, and domesticity became only a relatively invisible part of social life.[7]

Third, the separation between public and private parallels the separation between home and work which Raymond Williams has documented for this same period. In tandem with these social separations came new forms of public technology – railways and city lighting – which were then later supplemented by those for private accommodations: 'that which served an at once mobile and home-centred way of living' (1975: 26); what Williams has called 'mobile privatisation' (ibid.). Most of our information and communication technologies, and broadcasting in particular, are a product of this tendency towards a separation between public/private and home/work.[8]

It is around this last factor, ICT and broadcasting, that what is perceived to be most modern in modern culture is to be found: what many theorists and social forecasters see as the cutting edge of social and even revolutionary change (Bell 1973; Kumar 1978; Thompson 1990: 15). And yet, these very developments are largely experienced via the consumption practices of individual households (e.g. the purchase and use of telephones, radios, televisions, VCRs, computers, etc.), where, as I have indicated, a marked stability in family form and relationships has been in evidence over a considerable time period. This is the case even amongst those who would claim that the English family is vanishing. In fact, it has always been 'vanishing' in the same way as Williams has shown in his book, *The Country and City* (Williams 1973; cf. Strathern 1981), that the English village has been vanishing for numerous centuries.[9]

We thus have a paradoxical picture emerging. From one perspective – that of ICT and its associated consumer culture – the most radical changes are occurring in modern culture. But from a second, complementary perspective, that of family relations and their associated consumption practices, a picture of continuity with the past is in evidence.[10]

The aim of the case study that follows, then, is to engage with the site where three key factors shaping our contemporary culture seem to converge and around which this particular paradox emerges: these are the factors of consumption in an increasingly mass-produced, commodity world; the domestic domain of family relations; and the ever-increasing presence of ICT and broadcasting as part and parcel of these two other factors.

It is one of the claims of this chapter that in the contemporary domestic context – as in social contexts more generally – a balance needs to be struck between the short-term morality associated with acquisitive individualistic behaviour, and long-term moral actions associated with forces of collective and cosmological reproduction. Each household strikes its own balance between the calls of the individual and its own locally constructed cosmology. In the case study that follows I will be largely concerned with the way appropriations are transformed to correspond with the balance between the short-term and long-term time frame associated with these particular family relationships.

CASE STUDY

The family presented here has been chosen because it exemplifies, in perhaps an extreme form, processes of domestic consumption in general, and of ICT in particular, that are evident in the other families studied; but in these other cases the processes are evident in either transformed or less accentuated ways. What is particularly highlighted by the following example is the manner in which issues surrounding the formation of boundaries and a controlled moral environment are connected with various types of conventional and locally innovatory ICT uses.

The family to be considered is one which has the cultural and economic resources to extend its domestic life beyond the city, into the country, and through this extension has been able to radically transform the boundaries conventionally associated with a single domestic environment.

The family will be referred to as the Simon family. They live in north London and occupy two adjoining terraced houses, both of which they own. They have lived in one terraced house for twenty years and bought the second, which had a shop on the ground floor, a few years ago. The family comprises a mother, father, three boys and two girls. The two girls are adopted and each has a black parentage origin. The Simon parents are both in their early forties and the age range of the children is 8–16: a son is the eldest, followed by the two daughters and then two sons. The father, Charles,[11] describes himself as a technologist or inventor and his current work is in the development of new forms of microchip technology. He was originally trained in medical engineering and has a Ph.D. in this field. The mother, Natalie,[12] is a teacher in a primary school and works with children aged 4–7. She has only recently returned to full-time teaching four days per week, having left when her first son was a year old. The Simon children all attend state schools and the two youngest boys are currently at the school where their mother teaches.

In terms of our sample of families, the Simon family has the greatest amount of disposable income and personal assets. Their combined income is roughly £60,000 per year, of which roughly three-quarters is Charles's income. Charles and Natalie have separate bank accounts; her salary is mostly devoted to the recreational and material needs of the children. Natalie is given a monthly food cheque by her husband and his income is used primarily to service their various capital assets. In addition to their London residence the family also possesses a cottage and sailing-boat in Cornwall. During the early 1980s Charles sold his computer and medical instrument company. This was prompted by, as he put it, seeing 'the writing on the wall', with the projected introduction of IBM's own PC. The assets from this sale allowed the Simons to buy the second terraced house and cottage. The cottage is inaccessible by road and the family, in addition, spend six weeks every summer on their boat sailing around the south coast. Last summer they sailed to Guernsey. During the rest of the year the family visit their cottage about every six weeks and/or during half-term holidays. Depending on his work schedule, the father will spend shorter periods during these visits. During all their married life they have had a sailing-boat in Cornwall. The details of the cottage and sailing-boat in Cornwall are not of incidental interest but form part of the more general processes intrinsic to the ethnography of this family. In brief, these processes can be characterized as an open, public form of sociability associated with life in London and a closed, private sociability associated with life in Cornwall. Charles and Natalie assert that each of these life-worlds forms a kind of sustenance or support for the continuity of the other.

The openness of the Simon home and its family life is explicitly emphasized by Charles and Natalie. On one occasion when talking about their various family activities, Charles remarked on how the bustle of London spilled over into their house. And on another occasion, when discussing the possession and use of their telephone-answering machine, it was suggested that such a device could be used to monitor calls entering their home, thus ensuring them a greater degree of privacy. Both Charles and Natalie seemed rather surprised by this suggestion and remarked that 'When we are in London we are available . . . twenty-four hours per day'. Their intense and busy existence was reflected – particularly in the case of Natalie – in the content of the time-use diaries completed by each family member over a one-week period. Both emphasized, however, that the intensity of activity they sustained in London was only possible because of the periodic and secluded times in Cornwall.

The openness of their London home and its clear separation from that in the country was evident in the network of kin and non-kin relationships recognized as 'significant' by family members. For example, of the approximately 130 individuals and/or families we discussed with them as comprising their major social universe, a half-dozen of this total lived in the Simon household at one time or another. This was for periods varying from several months to several years. These were people the Simons considered as either colleagues or friends and there was no indication given that they had the status of lodgers. The Simon home is often the scene of meetings and the gathering of persons associated with some organization or another (e.g. school governers, campaigns against the abolition of ILEA, adoption causes, etc.).

Their London home is large and some sections of it are in a greater state of physical completion than others. For example, the kitchen was designed and built by Charles. This contains fully fitted cabinets, counter space and built-in washing machine, dishwasher and gas hob with electric grill. At the other end of this space is a large table where all meals are eaten and a radio is strategically placed. Radio 4 is listened to every weekday morning and the Archers at 7 o'clock in the evening. There is a telephone near the radio as well. The Simons have two lines, one for incoming and one for outgoing telephone calls. A second line became necessary some years ago when Charles's business was located at home. The kitchen has the appearance and feeling of a completed and fully lived-in space.

The preparation, purchasing and eating of food is highly marked in the culture of this family. The Simons are vegetarians and Natalie buys all her fruit and vegetables from a local market and grains and other health foods from a shop in north London. She has a complicated and time-consuming shopping pattern. She shops not only for her own family but for the several other children that come to the Simon home on different days after school. On any given weekday she will have between six and nine children at home after school for varying periods of time. This involvement with food and persons within the home resembles the parents' and children's involvement in a number of locally based institutions. For example, the parents are governors at different schools. Charles says he likes problem-solving and he can do this in his capacity as a school governor.

Adjoining the kitchen is a large sitting room, which has a different character. The sitting room is connected to the kitchen/eating area where the wall has been partially removed between the two terraced houses. This room is not completely furnished and looks rather incomplete. It contains a colour television and a recently purchased compact disc player (and most recently a video, see p. 219). Apart from three large, two-seater settees, two of which are at one end of the room and the third at the other by the television, and an antique sewing-machine next to the television, the room has little in the way of furnishings. It does, however, have a newly laid, stripped pine floor which they put down. They explained this contrast with the kitchen quickly and easily. They both agreed that each had different taste and could not decide how the room should be completed: she prefers an antique style and he likes modern. The settees and flooring were a compromise solution. A complete solution is difficult, whereas for the kitchen Natalie just let her husband get on and design it as he saw fit. She did not see it as her space, although she spent the most time in the kitchen. Her ambivalence towards the kitchen was most explicitly revealed in relation to its technology.[13] Although the technologies in the kitchen, as she indicated, make her life easier and more 'efficient', she does not identify with them (in contrast to a number of other families) and feels they are there to get a job done and then move on. Her ambivalence about the kitchen and the lack of personalized relations with its technology indicate her lack of interest in transforming this space and its objects into a form associated with her person.[14]

The first floor of both houses is for the parents and this contains their bedroom and individual offices. Natalie's office is not used a great deal for her own work. For example, at the moment the stereo record player is in there and she is in the process of transferring their records to tapes so they can be listened to in the car. Charles's office is used much more and has two IBM computers, an AT and XT, two printers and two oscillascopes. The children use the computers with a recently purchased graphics software called Dr Halo plus. The eldest son uses the computers for word-processing purposes. Charles's office has a telephone and there is one in the parents' bedroom. There is also a small room on this floor known as the 'music room', which contains an electric synthesizer and amplifier, cello, violin, bassoon, clarinet, saxophone, E-flat clarinet and flute. All the children have been encouraged to play instruments and most of those listed here have been played by the eldest son at one time or another. He is now learning the piano and practises on the synthesizer, while the youngest is learning the violin. Charles and Natalie told us that the eldest son had performed with his school at the Royal Festival Hall.

The second floor has also been connected together and this area is devoted to the children. Each child has his/her own room. All the children, with the exception of the second-youngest, have a radio in their room; three have tape/cassette recorders and Walkmen. Above this floor is a small attic which has a spare bedroom, where an old black-and-white TV has been placed. Natalie said this is used occasionally if there are great disputes over programmes on the downstairs television. The room is frequently used by friends and relatives for short periods of time.

Unlike the upper floors of the house, the basements have not been connected. The basement in their original house used to contain Charles's business office when he worked from home. This is now a clutter of old computer components and spare parts. The second-youngest son also has his chemistry lab. set up in this space. The other basement is cluttered with various odds and ends. The plan expressed by both of them is to convert these basements into a children's area so that they can have a large space, in addition to their rooms, that is separate from the parents/adults. This will be particularly used for entertaining their friends.

Having roughly sketched the spaces and boundaries intrinsic to this house, I now want briefly to turn to some of the forms of control that they embody and aspects of the moral environment which they express.

Charles and Natalie described to us the three forms of technological control which they (but particularly Charles) have instituted over the labyrinth of spaces in their home. The first is a computer for the central heating. This has been in operation for three years and is zoned throughout the house. It is not just timed but timed for different areas of the house at different times of the day. A series of heat sensors regulates the operation of the computer programme.

Second, there is a light controller to prevent lights from being left on. This has been recently installed and was prompted by the problem of there being two separate staircases to the upper floor of the house. It works by daylight sensors and automatically goes off at night.

Finally, this entire system of rooms and floors is interconnected by an intercom system that was again installed by Charles. The main terminal of this system is in the kitchen. The intercom is like an internal telephone and rooms can only be contracted when signalled from a particular phone. It does not have surveillance-like capabilities. The entire system was put in four years ago. Prior to this, a smaller version connected the kitchen and basement office. This was first installed about twelve years ago, but the intercom to the office has since been disconnected. The expanded system was prompted by the distances that needed to be traversed if one wanted to get in communication with someone else in the house. This was particularly the case for Natalie when she was calling the children down for meals and to go to school. What the intercom is perhaps best known for is its use in waking up and/or calling down the children for breakfast on school days. Breakfast starts at 7 a.m. and the intercom is used at 6.50. This is what has come to be known as the '10-minute call'. It is an idiom which was first picked up by the second-youngest when he recently acted for the RSC, although the idea of a pre-breakfast call was already in existence. But its reformulation in this theatrical idiom is not fortuitous. It is indicative in a more general way of the processes at work in the dichotomy of the Simons' domestic life between city and country and of its relationship to their domestic consumption of ICT.

I have identified some of the key elements and processes intrinsic to the material, social and moral environment of the Simon home, such as those to do with forms of technology, boundaries and control. I now want to turn to two examples which illustrate how the work of appropriating objects of ICT consumption involves their transformation into objects which correspond with what has been referred to as the 'moral economy' of the household. In each case the introduction of an ICT into the home made visible aspects of the reciprocal relationships between family members that were incompatible with their long-term moral character, as defined by the nature of the family structure. What is of interest is the manner in which these incompatibilities were made visible, particularly to the Simon family, and how they were resolved through a distinctive appropriation of the ICTs concerned.

Charles and Natalie and each of the children indicated that television viewing was not valued as a key individual or family activity. This was also borne out by discussion of their time-use diaries and participant observation. The family as a whole will watch nature and science programmes and some comedies such as *The Two Ronnies* and *Fawlty Towers*. The younger children enjoy the after-school programmes and the cartoons at the weekend. The eldest watches a variety of sports programmes. The viewing pattern of the two girls is less easy to define.

Charles and Natalie both enjoy television plays, but only Charles watches films on television. They both watch what they call 'mindless things' like *Inspector Morse*. The television viewing of their children is carefully regulated and only the eldest is allowed to watch television after supper. The doing of homework has a high priority among the children and is clearly separated from any TV viewing. Homework is often done by several children in a group around the kitchen table. Again and again in our discussions about television, it was downgraded as a passive and inappropriate form of activity to spend much time on. Charles and Natalie place a high value on active doing rather than passivity. The word 'activity' was frequently used by the Simons during our period of fieldwork with them. Their relationships with objects and others, and those of their children, are informed by this and related values. This sentiment was exemplified early on in our visits. When talking about whether or not they had a video, Charles said they made a conscious decision not to get a video, that they would watch more television if they had one:

> I thought on some occasions it is too late for them to watch, I would love to have recorded it. It was probably my decision not to get one.

But Natalie said there was heavy pressure from her not to get one:

> I knew we would watch a lot more television and I thought that the children would be tempted to. They do an awful lot of other things other than television which I think is very valuable to them. I think . . . television is always going to be there but perhaps the opportunities to do these other things might not be.

When we asked whether the children expressed a desire for a video, the discussion swiftly moved on to the idea of a video camera.

> *Charles*. A video camera, that would be the thing for the children . . . they would be 'making' . . . not just sitting there watching *Neighbours*!

> *Natalie*. I would encourage them . . . if they came up with that bright idea I would seriously consider getting a video camera for them . . . if one of them really wanted to.

> *Charles*. So anytime they make their own video they can watch them; if they make their own videos they can watch them anytime.

> *Natalie*. They will be getting pleasure from it and learning at the same time.

Through our discussion we revealed a set of values in the Simons' thinking which was inconsistent with the use of a video in the home. The most significant way in which they imagine this item could be appropriated is if an active relation could be constructed with it, i.e. the watching of videos made by the children themselves.

It is interesting, then, that in the six months that separated the start of our fieldwork from its completion a video made its way into the Simon home. Prior to our last visit, Charles purchased a video at Natalie's insistence. He showed us the video as he was in the process of programming it to record *Inspector Morse* later that evening:

> *Charles*. It invalidates everything we said to you . . . . Too many people in the family on the television so we thought we had to get one to record ourselves.[15]

> And later in the evening Natalie says: It was my idea, always been against getting a video. Occurred to me that whole family is on television and I said to [Charles] this is ridiculous I don't suppose ever in the future that it may occur that one of us ever is on television ever again. We have two children on television in separate things and the whole family on television. I said . . . I think this is a good idea to have a video so that we could record it because we may never see any of our children on TV again, or us.

Charles said on several occasions throughout the evening that the problem with the video remained: they would watch more television now than in the past. What seemed to trouble him, and to a lesser extent Natalie, was their potentially more passive relation to the television than in the pre-video time. It was not the technology as such which was the problem but the capacity to construct an active relation with it.

It is of interest to note here that three of the Simon children attend a local theatre company. The second-youngest boy and the youngest girl have both attended for several years and, as a result of their participation, they both secured parts in the theatre and/or television; the eldest girl has just started attending. The children were encouraged to attend the theatre company initially by their parents. Charles and Natalie said this was to help them build up their confidence and be able to present themselves in public. The fact that this has led to theatre and television parts was, according to them, incidental. In addition, both of the parents have been on television in the past: Charles every few years in relation to some aspect of his work; Natalie, about twelve years ago, in connection with a political affair to do with childbirth at home. More recently, as mentioned above, the whole family was on television.

This first example illustrates a particular axis of values which are intrinsic to the moral economy of the Simon family and which form a continuum from what they have called that of the fully active to the 'mindless' (*Inspector Morse*) and passive. In contrast, the next example focuses on the tensions revealed by another dimension of their family experience which they seemed to value highly, that of individual autonomy in relation to a form of communal, collective cohesiveness.

Until about a year before the research with the Simons began they possessed a second-hand Spectrum computer for playing arcade games. This was purchased at very low cost from a family friend. As Charles and Natalie expressed it during one of our discussions:

> *Charles.* The children have a Spectrum . . . technically they don't because it is broken. I have made no effort at all to repair it. It was a disappointment, not a reflection of the types of games. . . . It was not the types of games that I disapproved of. It is because of their behaviour.
>
> *Natalie.* This is the three boys.
>
> *Charles.* And their relationship to the girls. They behaved differently than we expected them to.
>
> *Natalie.* It is true . . . . caused a lot of trouble and ill feeling. They'd get really angry with each other . . . . Someone hadn't the same amount of time as another one, it was somebody's turn and they went out of turn and then someone had come in and interrupted them and someone was playing a game and they got shouted and screamed at. They were pretty nasty to each other.
>
> *Charles.* The girls were not allowed near it.
>
> *Natalie.* They did not get any practice so they did not get any quicker.
>
> Anne (the eldest daughter) adds from the kitchen: I got sick of it.[16]

The Simons' relationship[17] with the Spectrum was transformed over time, given the moral economy of this family. The possibilities inherent within the technology were constrained by the factors of age, gender, siblingship, etc. and were made visible and explicit through the structure of relationships intrinsic to this family. Once an acquisitive and individualistic, short-term morality emerged around the Spectrum, its incompatibility with the long-term moral order of the family structure was revealed and resolved in a particular manner.

Natalie's relation to this series of events is also of interest. When a 'computer culture' around the Spectrum (and later the IBMs) began to emerge, Natalie felt excluded and out of touch with a key activity taking place inside her home. Her appropriation of this technology, like that of video described above, occurred in relation to the moral and temporal dimensions intrinsic to this domestic setting.[18] What her interest represents is a particular inflection of gender around this emerging computer culture.

Natalie's exclusion from this computer culture continued until about one and a half months before my visit, when she decided to do a computer course.

> *Natalie.* I got fed up with everybody knowing about computers and I didn't. There comes a time when I will no longer tolerate the situation.

> Charles then added jokingly from his position of supreme competence: You can bring computers into the house but you can't force people to the keys.

The presence of the Spectrum revealed an incompatibility in another set of values emphasized in the Simon family culture: that of individual autonomy in conjunction with a sense of communality. The resolution of this problem was achieved once the Spectrum 'died', by replacing it by a 'non-competitive' form of software programme (e.g. the Dr Halo Plus which they currently use). Initially, Natalie was keen for her children to gain experience in using keyboards and in programming, and this was the intention behind the purchase of the second-hand Spectrum. However, its presence created a situation in which individual abilities were being valued more greatly than long-term 'communal cohesiveness and spirituality'. The resolution of this problem was achieved through another type of software; not by getting rid of computers altogether. The children play with Dr Halo Plus in a way analogous to that of their theatrical activities: one or more children perform on the computer while there is occasionally an audience around to watch.

CONCLUSION

The Simon household oscillates between an urban life of intensely hard work and wide-ranging social relationships and a rural, private and cut-off life (when sailing on the boat) where social relationships are at a minimum and where the long-term ideals of the nuclear family are perhaps realized in all their intensity. As I have suggested, they exemplify, in perhaps extreme form, processes of domestic consumption that are at work in the other households of the study but not in such explicit and accentuated form.

In conclusion I would like to comment on several issues raised by this case study. The first has to do with the representativeness of the Simon family. It might be suggested that the Simon family are a middle-class family and are not typical of the range of families in contemporary Britain. This is partially correct, but also wrong in an important respect. As a middle-class family the Simons are individual, but they are no more individual than other middle-class families, who create differences in order not to be perceived by themselves, or by others, as typical. Anyone familiar with middle-class life in north London or other urban centres of Britain will clearly recognize the Simons as exemplifying elements and processes found in this wider context.

Do the Simons' middle-class credentials have a relevance to a wider range of families than the middle class? A number of the symbolic and material practices that the Simons are able to realize (such as the cottage and boat in Cornwall, or their educational competence) are ideals that some of the working-class families in the study expressed an interest in aspiring towards. In this way, the middle class make explicit certain values, cultural agendas and aspirations which impinge on the thinking and evaluations of non-middle-class families and kinship. This is not to suggest that working-class or lower-class families are just incomplete shadows of their middle-class contemporaries. Rather, as Strathern, paraphrasing Firth's 1960s study of middle-class family and kinship in London, suggests:

> Lower class [family and] kinship did not comprise a separate subculture, but promoted values and attitudes specifically in reference to middle class ones, which thus held hegemonic status . . . middle class values were symbolically deferred to as ideal and generalisable, while lower class values were taken to represent a particular kind of struggle with 'the real world' of limited resources.
>
> (Strathern 1992: 25)

The crucial issue, then, is not whether the Simons are representative but whether they are recognizable within the more general category of English/British family relations. By all accounts they are, in fact, recognizable (cf. Finch 1989: 190).

Second, my description and characterization of the Simon household has emphasized its coherence and the complementarity of its various dimensions. This may give the appearance of evaluating in highly positive terms their family life and lifestyle. Such an evaluation is not intended. What I want to convey through my description is a set of symbolic and material conditions within the Simon household that coexist with distinct values of family structure and relationships. There are numerous day-to-day tensions and conflicts in the Simon household engendered by the incompatibility and contradictions of these values which I did not highlight because this was not my intention. Instead, I have sought to portray what we might call the 'ideal' which the structure of the Simon household aspires towards and how, through the introduction of various ICT objects of consumption, the moral tensions become explicit and visible: *What is resisted, then, is not the technology per se but a particular appropriation of it which transgresses the long-term moral environment of the household.*[19]

Finally, the analysis which I have presented, focusing on the relations between family structure and the appropriation and incorporation of ICT, raises the question of whether the revealed tensions and conflicts engendered by its entry into the home are specific to this type of technology.[20] I broached this question in the opening pages of this chapter but do not have a conclusive answer at this point. What the case study and literature discussed in this chapter suggest is that this is an area where more in-depth, ethnographic research is required before an answer to this problem can be adequately discerned.

What I have hoped to show in this chapter, then, is that domestic consumption, even that which is associated with objects supposedly at the cutting edge of social and cultural change, is still appropriated within moral environments given shape by the long-term and short-term characteristics of social relationships; of which the temporal dimensions associated with family relationships and structure are central.

ACKNOWLEDGEMENTS

For their helpful comments on various drafts of this chapter I want to thank Allen Abramson, James Carrier, Adam Kuper, Daniel Miller, Roger Silverstone and Marilyn Strathern. A version of this chapter was presented to the Department of Sociology, Lancaster University and to the Institute of Anthropology, University of Copenhagen. My thanks for the helpful comments from members of the seminar audiences on both those occasions. Finally, any errors in either fact or form rest solely with the author.

NOTES

1 The first is associated with what has come to be known in anthropology as the morality of commodity exchange, while the latter is associated with the morality of the gift. One is related to short-term, individualistic, market-like behaviour, while the second is related to a long-term morality of collective and cosmological reproduction (cf. Gregory 1982; Hart 1986; Parry 1986; Parry and Bloch 1989).
2 See chapter 1.
3 This can be viewed from a related perspective. What has been called the cultural biography of things – how the 'social life' of an appropriated object can be seen to change over time – is part and parcel of the social and moral relationships in which it is entangled (Kopytoff 1986); and it is these social and moral relationships which have their own temporal dimensions.
4 Compare the section on 'Incorporation' in chapter 1.
5 The material reported in this chapter is part of an ethnographic study of households conducted in southeast England together with Roger Silverstone, Sonia Livingstone and David Morley. The study focuses on a small number of households – sixteen in total – in central London and Slough in Berkshire. The locations for the selection of households were chosen for the following

reasons. The central London location links with an established body of literature on family and household, most notably Elizabeth Bott's study of twenty households reported in *Family and Social Network* from the 1950s (Bott 1957) and Sandra Wallman's in-depth study of eight households in Battersea during the early 1980s (Wallman 1984). Slough was chosen, on the one hand because of its relative proximity to Brunel University, but more importantly because it represented a 'suburban' location outside Greater London and also because it is the entry point to Britain's 'Silicon Valley' or 'high-tech' corridor. It was felt that the two locations represented significant contrasts (within a narrowly defined range of 'high-tech' families) in the types and locations of work and the centre of activities that family members might be engaged in. Further details of the content of the research and the methodology developed for this purpose can be found in Silverstone *et al.* 1991.

6 See chapter 7.

7 These transformations have recently been reinterpreted by Marilyn Strathern (1992) and are at the core of what has come to be seen as the pluralistic form of English society.

8 Many of the contradictory developments in ICT and broadcasting have been traced by Williams in his book on television as 'technology and cultural form' (1975).

9 A point which is made with much anthropological originality in M. Strathern's Lewis Henry Morgan Lectures (Strathern 1992).

10 In R. Williams's insightful words, commenting on developments in a related context: 'A main characteristic of our society is a willed coexistence of very new technology and very old social forms' (Williams 1990: 191). I want to thank Roger Silverstone for pointing out to me this quote from Williams and its relevance to my argument.

11 The father's family history is associated with Cornwall, which is also where the family cottage is located.

12 The mother's family history is associated with the north and in particular the area around Manchester.

13 Through discussions with Sonia Livingstone.

14 This example recalls Miller's discussion of the processes intrinsic to transforming commodities into 'inalienable culture' (Miller 1987); see Putnam's comments relevant to this example (chapter 12).

15 He was referring to the second-youngest son's part in a recently produced series, the youngest daughter's non-speaking part on an afternoon series, and their own recent appearance as a family relating to a topic of current political interest.

16 Natalie went on to remark how her ability to perform a task on the computer at school which her two younger boys did not know evoked in them a feeling of competitiveness similar to that displayed at home on the old Spectrum. She said they acted aggressively because she knew how to do something on the computer that they did not know how to do. And yet both Natalie and Charles went on to say that the boys' behaviour on the computer (even the old Spectrum) when they used it on their own was markedly different and more in line with that which the parents found acceptable for the children's other home-based and outside activities.

17 As expressed through the processes of appropriation and incorporation (see introductory section).

18 In this light, compare the critique of Bourdieu's position in the introductory section of this chapter. It will be recalled that, unlike his earlier critique

of 'objectivist' exchange relations, where the element of time is of central importance, in his work on consumption (particularly domestic consumption) the moral and temporal dimensions are significantly ignored.

19 In a personal communication D. Miller suggests an alternative formulation to the one presented here, which focuses on his use of the concept of objectification:

> [W]hat is clear with the Simons is that it is not some prior moral culture into which technology is placed, but that technology and life-style are the form through which the ideal of morality is itself constructed. If it is ever abstracted as morality this is done on the basis of these lived relationships, where people discover what their morality is: it is the interaction with the technology which makes the morality as much as the other way around.

20 Or, whether ICT is part of a more general phenomenon to do with the nature of novelty in modern society and intrinsic to modern consumerism, as argued by Campbell (1987). In other words, are goods particularly associated with novelty, and hence with individuality in Campbell's theory, often drawn into contexts where their appropriation must contend with distinctly non-individualistic, collective patterns? What I am suggesting is that in modern, industrialized societies, at least, a full understanding of the relations between persons and things (especially 'novel' things) must take into full account the final destination of much of our consumption.

REFERENCES

Bell, D. (1973) *The Coming of Post-industrial Society*, New York: Basic Books.
Bloch, M. (1973) 'The long-term and the short-term: the economic and political significance of the morality of kinship', in J. Goody (ed.) *The Character of Kinship*, Cambridge: Cambridge University Press, 75–87.
Bott, E. (1957) *Family and Social Network*, London: Tavistock.
Bourdieu, P. (1977) *Outline of a Theory of Practice*, Cambridge: Cambridge University Press.
——(1984) *Distinction*, London: Routledge.
Campbell, C. (1987) *The Romantic Ethic and the Spirit of Modern Consumerism*, Oxford: Blackwell.
Carrier, J. (1990) 'Reconciling commodities and personal relations in industrial society', *Theory and Society* 19: 579–98.
Csikszentmihalyi, M. and Rochberg-Halton, E. (1981) *The Meaning of Things: Domestic Symbols and the Self*, Cambridge: Cambridge University Press.
Davidoff, L. and Hall, C. (1987) *Family Fortunes*, London: Hutchinson.
Douglas, M. and Isherwood, B. (1979) *The World of Goods*, New York: Norton.
Finch, J. (1989) *Family Obligations and Social Change*, Cambridge: Polity Press.
Firth, R., Hubert, J. and Forge, A. (1970) *Families and their Relatives*, London: Routledge & Kegan Paul.
Gell, in A. (1986) 'Newcomers to the world of goods: consumption among the Muria Gonds', in A. Appadurai (ed.) *The Social Life of Things*, Cambridge: Cambridge University Press, 110–40.
Gellner, E. (1988) *Plough, Sword, Book*, London: Collins Harvill.
Gregory, C. (1982) *Gifts and Commodities*, London: Academic Press.
Hart, K. (1986) 'Heads or tails? Two sides of the coin', *Man* 21 (4): 637–56.

Kopytoff, I. (1986) 'The cultural biography of things: commodization as process', in A. Appadurai (ed.) *The Social Life of Things*, Cambridge: Cambridge University Press, 64–91.

Kumar, K. (1978) *Prophecy and Progress*, Harmondsworth: Penguin.

Lévi-Strauss, C. (1969) *The Elementary Structures of Kinship*, Boston: Beacon Press.

MacFarlane, A. (1978) *The Origins of English Individualism*, Oxford: Blackwell.

Mauss, M. (1990) *The Gift*, London: Routledge.

Miller, D. (1987) *Material Culture and Mass Consumption*, Oxford: Blackwell.

——(1988)'Appropriating the state on the council estate', *Man* 23: 353–72.

Parry, J. (1986) 'The gift, the Indian gift and the "Indian gift"', *Man* 21 (3): 453–73.

Parry, J. and Bloch, M. (eds) (1989) *Money and the Morality of Exchange*, Cambridge: Cambridge University Press.

Sahlins, M. (1974) *Stone Age Economics*, London: Tavistock.

Silverstone, R., Hirsch, E. and Morley, D. (1991) 'Listening to a long conversation: an ethnographic approach to the study of information and communication technologies in the home', *Cultural Studies* 5 (2): 204–27.

Strathern, M. (1981) *Kinship at the Core*, Cambridge: Cambridge University Press.

——(1992) *After Nature. English Kinship in the Late Twentieth Century*, Cambridge University Press.

Thompson, J. (1990) *Ideology and Modern Culture*, Cambridge: Polity Press.

Wallman, S. (1984) *Eight London Households*, London: Tavistock.

Williams, R. (1973) *The Country and the City*, London: Hogarth Press.

——(1975) *Television: Technology and Cultural Form*, London: Routledge.

——(1990) *Problems in Materialism and Culture*, London: Verso.

Postscript
Revolutionary technologies and technological revolutions

Jonathan Gershuny

THE PROBLEM

One new technology alters the structure of economies, and changes in fundamental ways the day-to-day life of whole societies. The name of this new technology is sufficient to evoke the spirit of the historical era it has helped to create. Another new technology, no less technically exciting, has little or no effect, finds narrow and specific applications, if any, and remains invisible to all except professional engineers and the mechanically minded. What is the difference between them?

In retrospect, of course, we know which was which. The steam engine had, in the nineteenth century, social and economic effects which might be classified as revolutionary. The scientific and technical principles which underlay the development were distinctly prosaic – the application of a lathe designed for boring cannons to grind more accurate cylinders, the capture of exhausted steam in a condenser – and as such are quite appropriately symbolized by the nonsensical myth of Watt's invention of the steam engine while watching the kettle at his mother's hearth. But, prosaic technically, the steam engine still provoked revolutionary economic consequences; 'the Steam Age' accurately describes a historical period made what it was by the steam engine.

In the 1950s, some wrote speculatively of an analogous 'Atomic Age': a century to be made prosperous by the cheap energy from nuclear power stations. The science and the technology were in this case anything but prosaic. On the contrary, they reflected a sublime progress from the establishment of the most abstract scientific principles to the most complex of engineering practice (contrast the first publication of Carnot's 'steam-cycle' physics nearly half a century after Watt's practical application of the principle in his condenser). This must be considered revolutionary science, revolutionary technology. But it is a revolutionary technology without revolutionary economic consequences. There are certainly profound (though very indirect) economic and social consequences of the military applications of this technology (e.g. the freezing of the Cold War). But no one would now refer to the 'Atomic Age' except in ironical recognition of the lack of substantial impact of the civil nuclear technology on the way we conduct our daily affairs.

Steam had revolutionary effects on social and economic conditions. Atomics has not (or at least not yet).

We might note here two quite distinct meanings of the term 'revolution'. One is the revolutionary change in knowledge or techniques, the change in the system of ideas which underpin our understanding of how some aspect of the universe works, or of how we might control some part of our environment. The other is a revolutionary consequence: some advance in our knowledge or techniques, leading to a transformation of social or economic organization. We may have revolutionary advances in our science or technology, without experiencing revolutionary consequences for our economy or society. And conversely, technological revolutions may occur without revolutionary technologies.

What distinguishes the technologies which have revolutionary social impacts from those which do not? We can recognize revolutionary scientific ideas, technological advances, as they emerge, simply because they are new and different; technological advances with revolutionary consequences, by contrast, are very much more difficult to identify at the time that they first emerge – their consequences have not happened yet! We can identify technological revolutions, in this second sense, retrospectively, but it is much more difficult to know when they are in prospect. Perhaps one central question, for the members of the conference at which the preceding chapters were first presented, was whether Information Technology was to be considered as revolutionary in this 'consequential' sense.

AN ILLUSTRATION

Let us start with an illustration of the problem. To make my point, I must ask readers to imagine themselves living in the London of the 1890s, in the midst of the previously mentioned 'Steam Age'. This is a rich society; many of its riches are to be explained by the exploitation of mechanical power. Power for manufacturing and transport purposes is derived directly and instantaneously from the steam engine, transmitted by belts or levers or rotating shafts. But new applications are emerging which require power to be delivered in ways to which such systems are not well suited. Large amounts of power may be needed intermittently, but for short periods (as in a passenger lift, or a dockside crane). Or relatively small amounts of power may need to be delivered in conditions where a steam 'prime mover' would be inappropriate (for light industry, or for domestic applications such as vacuum cleaning). What is needed is a system for storage of power, and its subsequent transmission and distribution to remote locations, for delivery where and when it is needed.

This is, remember, 1894. There is only DC electricity generation; distribution is at low voltages (and hence subject to substantial transmission losses); electric motors are large, clumsy, expensive and inefficient. The only really large commercial application for electric power is electric lighting. And there is an alternative technology for the distribution of power: hydraulic power distribution.

This is not the 'water power' which uses the kinetic energy in flowing water (as in the waterwheels providing the motive power for early factories). Distributed hydraulic power derives, not from the kinetic energy of water in motion, but from the potential energy of water under pressure. At various points in London (Wapping, Tower Bridge), we find hydraulic power accumulators. These look a little like gasometers; they are in fact water tanks, closed and sealed at the top with heavily weighted floating lids. Steam engines continuously pump water into the towers, so that the water level rises, and the heavy lids are slowly raised within the tank. Raising the weighted lids stores the energy produced by the steam engines.

Beneath the city streets is a vast hydrostatic energy transmission system. Pipes, containing water under great pressure, lie under every main road and many of the minor roads in London. Every house, shop, factory, warehouse, office in London either is (in 1894), or soon will be, within a few feet of the hydraulic water main. At its peak, the London Hydraulic Power Company has nearly 200 miles of water main covering the whole of the central area of London. The map of the system, is in effect, a street plan of the city.

The pressurized water in the hydraulic main can be converted into rotary motion, (using a motor manufactured by the Brotherhood Company of Northampton) and used to turn lathes or milling machines – or alternatively, to drive domestic machinery, such as vacuum pumps for house cleaning, or even, in principle, to drive generators for electric lighting. Or it may drive hydraulic rams, used to power passenger lifts or cargo cranes. The roadway of Tower Bridge is raised by a hydraulic ram, and the safety curtain of the Savoy Theatre is lowered by one.

Does the electric light company pose a threat to the future expansion of this system? The London Society of Civil Engineers has just published in its Proceedings a careful comparison of the costs of hydrostatic and electric power transmission. For equivalent calorific levels delivered to consumers, hydrostatic power costs 30 per cent less to produce than electricity, is sold more cheaply, and makes more profits for the company's shareholders.

Such is scientific progress in the greatest city of the world's richest nation in the 47th year of the reign of the Queen-Empress. Instant, flexible, silent power, at the turn of a tap. At present only a few thousands of establishments in London may be connected to the hydrostatic power mains, and the average Londoner might only encounter it when travelling to the basement of Harrods department store in a product of the Hydraulic Lift Company. But, as we consider the prospects for the first decades of the twentieth century, might not every respectable house have its almost noiseless Brotherhood engine in the basement, driving the cook's spit and the butler's lift and a domestic washing machine and a vacuum pump (with vacuum outlets in each room) for domestic cleaning, and perhaps an electricity generator to replace the smelly and dangerous town gas as a source of light and heat? Such are the domestic comforts to be expected from engineering advance.

This is not a science fiction 'alternative history'. There really was a London Hydraulic Power Company. It eventually grew to serve 4,500 establishments, and, astonishingly, survived as a functioning commercial enterprise until the mid-1970s. Its subsequent fate forms another part of our story. But we must first consider why this promising new technology of the 1890s turned out to have such a small impact on the twentieth century.

IMPLICATIONS

We might, in the 1890s, have been tempted to see hydrostatic power transmission, rather than electricity, as the basis of a future technological revolution. The two technologies were, in 1894, rather similar. They both used steam engines as the means of extracting energy from coal. They both transmitted power to remote locations, for intermittent use. The hydrostatic system had, in 1894, lower costs per unit of work delivered – but electricity had the revolutionary consequences.

We can easily see why. In part it relates to the technical issues that underlie the relative costs of the two systems. Hydrostatic systems delivered relatively cheap energy because of low losses in power transmission: they used broad-bore pipes, and had low frictional losses, since water moved only very slowly within the pipes. But enlarging the system brought, if anything, increasing diseconomies (the larger the distribution system, the larger the probabilities of failures of pressure which would disable the whole system). Electricity, by contrast, had virtually endless potential economies of scale (the move to larger boilers gives geometric advances in efficiency; and as markets got larger, transmission at higher voltages, and the introduction of AC power, meant an increasingly efficient distribution system).

But the advantages of electricity are not just costs. AC generation meant that more power could be delivered, doing more jobs – the heavy lifting jobs, for instance, for which DC power had disadvantages when compared with hydrostatics, could be done efficiently by AC.

The range of potential applications of electricity eventually emerged as being very much greater. Water power was an appropriate means for the wide distribution of mechanical power in its most basic form, of linear or rotary motion. And this basic form of mechanical power has a number of obvious applications, both commercial and domestic. But we need power in our factories and homes to do other sorts of work than just spinning or pushing things. We need – we needed even in the 1890s – power for heating and cooling and lighting. And as the twentieth century advanced, we also needed power for the transmission and reception of broadcast entertainment and other sorts of information to and from distant sources. Water power could not provide space heating or lighting, nor could it directly drive a telephone or radio or television system. As the costs of electricity fell relative to water power, its range of effective application grew. Simply: you could do more different things with transmitted electricity than with hydraulic power.

In retrospect, this is all very obvious. But it was not at all obvious in prospect. In 1894 we did not know that electric power was going to get a lot cheaper. We did not know that people were, over the course of the next seventy-five years, going to become much more dependent on mechanical devices to provide their domestic services. We certainly did not know that people were to become largely dependent for their leisure on radio and television. We did not know that it would eventually seem convenient to draw all of our domestic comforts – space-heating, cooking, cleaning, lighting, and a range of entertainment services that did not even exist in 1894 – from a single source of power.

Given the pattern of daily life in 1894, and the states of development of the two technologies, hydrostatics would seem to have more to offer. We know now that electricity generation could find a range of applications vastly wider than was apparent in 1894; it could transform daily life and also (in so far as the developments in the conduct of daily life required a vast range of new consumer products and services) change fundamentally the structure of the economy. It appears to us now that hydrostatic power transmission could not have supported such transformations (though of course we cannot be certain of this). We know these things now. We did not know them in 1894. So, in 1894, we would not have been able to distinguish the technology with the revolutionary potential from the merely revolutionary technology.

A PROPOSITION

This boils down to a perfectly simple proposition. In order to understand the transforming potential of a particular line of technological development, it is necessary to know the range of its possible applications.

The applicability of a technology depends in part on the technical characteristics of the technology itself. Does it, for example, transform energy into work? If so, how safely, efficiently, flexibly, controllably? How much physical space does it occupy, how much does it weigh? Can it be used to transmit information, and at what speed, what reliability? We also need to know something about the costs of the technology. The most flexible and broadly applicable technology will never achieve mass applications if its costs are too high.

The costs and technical characteristics of the technology are not sufficient to tell us of its consequences. We also need to know *how it may be used in people's lives*. The declining cost of electricity and its increasing flexibility and rate of power delivery would have been for nothing if individuals in households had not wanted heating and lighting and domestic services and radio and television. It was precisely the applicability of electric power to the satisfaction of these particular human wants for particular sorts of services in the home that meant that this particular technology had its revolutionary impacts.

The 'applicability' of a technology is a peculiarly abstract notion. What determines whether a technology with given characteristics can be put to use is the social and physical circumstances of the people who may wish to use it – and the possible changes to these. If everyone goes to bed with the sun, the diffusion of the electric light requires the development of new after-dark activities. Technologies require concrete circumstances for their application. New equipment is used for particular purposes, to satisfy old wants more efficiently, or to meet newly emerging ones. The technology may itself stimulate these new wants, but such new wants must at least be capable of emerging. In 1894 we did not know how far electrical technology might develop. But quite as important, we did not know how many and varied were the practical uses that would be found for it.

And 'applicability' is not merely a matter of individuals' own daily practices; it is also in part determined by social structure. It is not just how many applications can be found for the new technology, but also, how many people can use these applications. In the 1930s, domestic equipment was bought by middle-class households for use by domestic servants. When the BBC opened its first television service in 1936, fewer than 500 households could receive its transmissions, and by the outbreak of the Second World War there were only a few thousand receivers in the London area which was the limit of all broadcasting. (So, of all the distinguished 1930s writers about the future, not one, to my knowledge, correctly identified the impact of TV; George Orwell remember, in the late 1940s, had the TV camera in every living room, as an instrument of mass surveillance.) The scale of application of the equipment that used the distributed electricity depended on the size of the class which could afford to buy the equipment. It was the emergence of a new 'mass class' with income sufficiently larger than was required for physical subsistence and basic housing, in the years following the Second World War, that eventually provided the markets that gave electricity its revolutionary transforming effect on the economy.

To understand whether the consequences of a new technology are revolutionary, we need to know its influence on styles and patterns of consumption. What options does the technology provide, to encourage us to do or not do particular things in our daily lives? What are the processes through which we choose to take up some of these options and not others? What are the differences in the response of different social groups to these options (and do new patterns of social differentiation emerge as a result of them)? We are accustomed to think of the impact of technologies in terms of their effects on production system: Which jobs come and which go? What happens to the rate of profit, or the requirement for particular skills? But the traditional production questions give us no purchase on the question of the applicability of the technology. To understand the revolutionary potentials of technologies, we need what economics and sociology have been rather slow to provide, an understanding of the processes through which patterns of consumption are determined, and which change through history.

POSTSCRIPT

This is really the end of my story. But there is (for me a rather eerie) postscript. I introduced the failed hydrostatics revolution in an attempt to illustrate the difficulty of predicting the potential applicability of a technology. While researching the technology, I looked in the modern newspaper indexes, and discovered (as I said previously) that the London Hydrostatic Power Company had survived into the 1970s. In 1976 it went into liquidation (for some reason the technology provokes great hilarity: a 'Times Diary' piece of that year suggested that the extensive system of hydrostatic pipework might be sold to the Dayville's Icecream Company for transporting their delicate product across the capital). The company disappears from the public record for several years; it was sold to a distinguished merchant bank; and then in 1982, its assets were purchased by Mercury Telecommunications. Its assets include, of course, wayleaves along all the major streets of London, and into every major building. So cabling the City of London for the information and communications technologies of the 1990s (which may or may not turn out to have revolutionary consequences) has proceeded by courtesy of engineering legacy of the failed technological revolution of the 1890s.

Index

Bourdieu, Pierre 19, 62, 116, 165–6,
   196, 200, 208–9, 224–5; criticized
   10; quoted 28–9
Breakwell, G.M. and C. Fife-Shaw
   115
British Telecom, chatline 74
Brooks, John 192
brown goods 127; purchase 102; as
   technology of leisure 107, 111
Brunel University 27
Buckingham, D. 170
Burns, S. 98
Byng-Hall, J. 113, 115

Callon, Michel 33, 43
Campbell, Colin 62, 63, 195, 225
Cantor, M. and S. Pingree 167
Carnot, N.L.S. 227
Carrier, James 15, 209
Cawson, A. *et al.* 75
Certeau, Michel de 17, 133, 139,
   142–3, 197, 201
Chaney, David 24
change, revolutionary 228
chase and flight model 50
Cheal, David 16
Chesterman, J. and A. Lipman 93
children, as computer users 103–4,
   106, 107, 108, 109–10
cinema 134; attendance 132; films as
   discrete media products 131
class 165–6
classification 116; principles 22
Clifford, J. and G. Marcus 197
Cockburn, Cynthia 36
cognitive construction 115
Collett, Peter 143
commercials, objections to showing
   131
commodity, culture 198; evaluation
   196; exchange 223
Commodore Dynamic Total Vision
   (CDTV) 69
communication technology 2–3, 4, 15;
   and biography of ideas 17–18; and
   social reproduction 19
competition 67
computers, addiction 83; and boys
   87–90; and children 151; culture
   220–1; dependency 83; domestic
   84–5; and the family 92–4;
   games 88, 91–2, 95; and girls

90–1; personal computing 70–1;
   problematic status 20; programme
   writing 88–9; related activities
   89–90; restricted activity 150; talk
   development 87–9; *see also* home
   computers, personal computers
constructs, common 117–18;
   functional 119; gender difference
   127; perception and attention
   124–5; possible conflict 125; and
   technologies 122
consumer/s 74; feedback 75; ideal
   142; real 142
consuming technologies 1–3
consumption 5, 9, 10, 113; central
   dynamic 48; concept 197–200;
   conspicuous 48–9; described
   196; domestic 195–7, 199, 200–5;
   essential function 115; and exchange
   208–9; images 80; as incorporation
   209; regimes 199; studies of 211;
   studies 85–6; subjective moment 196
'Control of Space Invaders (and Other
   Electronic Games) Bill' 157
conversion 21, 25–6
cooking 35; pattern 40–1
core technologies 68; development
   71–2; improvement 70
Cosby Show, The 166
Country and City, The (Williams) 212
Cowan, R.S. 36, 125, 196
Csikszentmihalyi, M. and E.
   Rochberg-Halton 15, 22, 114, 121,
   126, 199, 209
cultural lag 112
culture, local 3; material 198;
   peer-group 26
Curry, Chris 77
cuss-outs 173

Dahlberg, Andrea 27
Dallas 163, 164, 170, 176
Danielian, N.R. 192
Danko, William D. and James M.
   Maclachlan 146
Davidoff, L. and C. Hall 195, 212
Davidson, C. 114, 125
Davis, Bob 140
day-dreaming 60–1
Deem, R. 197
design, improvisation 202; paradigm
   79

UNIVERSITY OF
WOLVERHAMPTON
DUDLEY CAMPUS LIBRARY